This book belongs to

_____

Table Of Contents

Solutions at back of book!

Instructions for parents/teachers!

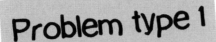

Problem type 1

$$6$$
$$+\ 5$$
$$\overline{}$$

In the problem shown to the left, the child should attempt to add up the two numbers and write the sum below!

Problem type 2

In the problem shown to the right, the child should attempt to fill in the missing number so that the equation is complete! The missing number will rotate position!

$$\begin{array}{r} 5 \\ +\ \square \\ \hline 14 \end{array} \qquad \begin{array}{r} \square \\ +\ 7 \\ \hline 8 \end{array}$$

This format will be followed progressively throughout the book, starting with addition, then moving towards subtraction!

Make sure to cut each page from the book and laminate so that the child can improve on their times & scores!

Adding numbers 0-5

Name:

Score: /60

time :

1) $\begin{array}{r} 5 \\ + 5 \\ \hline \end{array}$
2) $\begin{array}{r} 2 \\ + 3 \\ \hline \end{array}$
3) $\begin{array}{r} 5 \\ + 4 \\ \hline \end{array}$
4) $\begin{array}{r} 3 \\ + 4 \\ \hline \end{array}$
5) $\begin{array}{r} 1 \\ + 0 \\ \hline \end{array}$
6) $\begin{array}{r} 5 \\ + 1 \\ \hline \end{array}$

7) $\begin{array}{r} 2 \\ + 3 \\ \hline \end{array}$
8) $\begin{array}{r} 4 \\ + 1 \\ \hline \end{array}$
9) $\begin{array}{r} 0 \\ + 0 \\ \hline \end{array}$
10) $\begin{array}{r} 4 \\ + 3 \\ \hline \end{array}$
11) $\begin{array}{r} 5 \\ + 1 \\ \hline \end{array}$
12) $\begin{array}{r} 2 \\ + 4 \\ \hline \end{array}$

13) $\begin{array}{r} 5 \\ + 0 \\ \hline \end{array}$
14) $\begin{array}{r} 1 \\ + 0 \\ \hline \end{array}$
15) $\begin{array}{r} 1 \\ + 3 \\ \hline \end{array}$
16) $\begin{array}{r} 0 \\ + 2 \\ \hline \end{array}$
17) $\begin{array}{r} 4 \\ + 4 \\ \hline \end{array}$
18) $\begin{array}{r} 0 \\ + 2 \\ \hline \end{array}$

19) $\begin{array}{r} 0 \\ + 4 \\ \hline \end{array}$
20) $\begin{array}{r} 2 \\ + 5 \\ \hline \end{array}$
21) $\begin{array}{r} 0 \\ + 5 \\ \hline \end{array}$
22) $\begin{array}{r} 2 \\ + 0 \\ \hline \end{array}$
23) $\begin{array}{r} 3 \\ + 5 \\ \hline \end{array}$
24) $\begin{array}{r} 4 \\ + 0 \\ \hline \end{array}$

25) $\begin{array}{r} 1 \\ + 5 \\ \hline \end{array}$
26) $\begin{array}{r} 4 \\ + 1 \\ \hline \end{array}$
27) $\begin{array}{r} 2 \\ + 4 \\ \hline \end{array}$
28) $\begin{array}{r} 2 \\ + 4 \\ \hline \end{array}$
29) $\begin{array}{r} 3 \\ + 4 \\ \hline \end{array}$
30) $\begin{array}{r} 2 \\ + 5 \\ \hline \end{array}$

31) $\begin{array}{r} 5 \\ + 0 \\ \hline \end{array}$
32) $\begin{array}{r} 3 \\ + 0 \\ \hline \end{array}$
33) $\begin{array}{r} 1 \\ + 5 \\ \hline \end{array}$
34) $\begin{array}{r} 0 \\ + 5 \\ \hline \end{array}$
35) $\begin{array}{r} 5 \\ + 4 \\ \hline \end{array}$
36) $\begin{array}{r} 1 \\ + 4 \\ \hline \end{array}$

37) $\begin{array}{r} 4 \\ + 1 \\ \hline \end{array}$
38) $\begin{array}{r} 2 \\ + 3 \\ \hline \end{array}$
39) $\begin{array}{r} 3 \\ + 3 \\ \hline \end{array}$
40) $\begin{array}{r} 4 \\ + 4 \\ \hline \end{array}$
41) $\begin{array}{r} 0 \\ + 0 \\ \hline \end{array}$
42) $\begin{array}{r} 3 \\ + 0 \\ \hline \end{array}$

43) $\begin{array}{r} 4 \\ + 4 \\ \hline \end{array}$
44) $\begin{array}{r} 2 \\ + 2 \\ \hline \end{array}$
45) $\begin{array}{r} 2 \\ + 5 \\ \hline \end{array}$
46) $\begin{array}{r} 5 \\ + 4 \\ \hline \end{array}$
47) $\begin{array}{r} 3 \\ + 0 \\ \hline \end{array}$
48) $\begin{array}{r} 3 \\ + 4 \\ \hline \end{array}$

49) $\begin{array}{r} 5 \\ + 5 \\ \hline \end{array}$
50) $\begin{array}{r} 0 \\ + 5 \\ \hline \end{array}$
51) $\begin{array}{r} 2 \\ + 1 \\ \hline \end{array}$
52) $\begin{array}{r} 4 \\ + 3 \\ \hline \end{array}$
53) $\begin{array}{r} 4 \\ + 2 \\ \hline \end{array}$
54) $\begin{array}{r} 5 \\ + 0 \\ \hline \end{array}$

55) $\begin{array}{r} 4 \\ + 2 \\ \hline \end{array}$
56) $\begin{array}{r} 3 \\ + 5 \\ \hline \end{array}$
57) $\begin{array}{r} 4 \\ + 1 \\ \hline \end{array}$
58) $\begin{array}{r} 3 \\ + 0 \\ \hline \end{array}$
59) $\begin{array}{r} 5 \\ + 0 \\ \hline \end{array}$
60) $\begin{array}{r} 0 \\ + 3 \\ \hline \end{array}$

Name:

Score:

/60

time   :

1)   3
   + 0

2)   2
   + 4

3)   1
   + 3

4)   0
   + 3

5)   1
   + 3

6)   5
   + 2

7)   3
   + 4

8)   1
   + 0

9)   3
   + 1

10)   4
    + 4

11)   2
    + 3

12)   5
    + 0

13)   2
    + 4

14)   1
    + 4

15)   5
    + 0

16)   2
    + 2

17)   5
    + 0

18)   4
    + 0

19)   3
    + 2

20)   3
    + 0

21)   2
    + 0

22)   0
    + 5

23)   2
    + 3

24)   0
    + 1

25)   1
    + 5

26)   5
    + 3

27)   2
    + 4

28)   2
    + 3

29)   3
    + 5

30)   1
    + 2

31)   2
    + 2

32)   4
    + 3

33)   1
    + 2

34)   4
    + 2

35)   4
    + 3

36)   2
    + 4

37)   2
    + 2

38)   3
    + 2

39)   5
    + 0

40)   0
    + 1

41)   0
    + 1

42)   1
    + 1

43)   3
    + 5

44)   3
    + 4

45)   2
    + 2

46)   4
    + 5

47)   4
    + 5

48)   0
    + 1

49)   1
    + 2

50)   4
    + 5

51)   4
    + 5

52)   0
    + 4

53)   1
    + 0

54)   3
    + 5

55)   1
    + 3

56)   0
    + 1

57)   5
    + 0

58)   0
    + 5

59)   3
    + 3

60)   3
    + 4

Name:

Score:

/60

time   :

1)   2
   + 5

2)   5
   + 4

3)   4
   + 4

4)   3
   + 5

5)   1
   + 5

6)   3
   + 5

7)   4
   + 4

8)   5
   + 4

9)   5
   + 2

10)   3
    + 3

11)   2
    + 4

12)   2
    + 4

13)   3
    + 2

14)   2
    + 2

15)   4
    + 2

16)   1
    + 5

17)   3
    + 5

18)   0
    + 4

19)   3
    + 5

20)   1
    + 2

21)   4
    + 0

22)   5
    + 3

23)   2
    + 2

24)   1
    + 5

25)   0
    + 5

26)   0
    + 4

27)   0
    + 3

28)   2
    + 5

29)   2
    + 0

30)   4
    + 5

31)   1
    + 4

32)   1
    + 1

33)   0
    + 2

34)   3
    + 3

35)   2
    + 5

36)   1
    + 5

37)   2
    + 3

38)   4
    + 4

39)   1
    + 2

40)   0
    + 1

41)   1
    + 2

42)   2
    + 4

43)   1
    + 1

44)   1
    + 1

45)   1
    + 5

46)   3
    + 5

47)   2
    + 5

48)   1
    + 0

49)   3
    + 2

50)   4
    + 2

51)   2
    + 1

52)   4
    + 2

53)   4
    + 3

54)   2
    + 5

55)   5
    + 2

56)   1
    + 4

57)   4
    + 2

58)   3
    + 1

59)   0
    + 5

60)   2
    + 5

Name:

Score:

/60

time   :

1)   4
     + 3

2)   4
     + 5

3)   4
     + 3

4)   5
     + 0

5)   1
     + 4

6)   3
     + 2

7)   1
     + 2

8)   0
     + 2

9)   3
     + 0

10)   3
     + 3

11)   1
     + 2

12)   5
     + 5

13)   3
     + 5

14)   5
     + 1

15)   1
     + 2

16)   2
     + 4

17)   5
     + 0

18)   5
     + 5

19)   3
     + 2

20)   4
     + 0

21)   4
     + 5

22)   3
     + 4

23)   0
     + 0

24)   0
     + 5

25)   0
     + 5

26)   4
     + 2

27)   3
     + 1

28)   2
     + 4

29)   3
     + 5

30)   4
     + 4

31)   4
     + 4

32)   1
     + 4

33)   5
     + 1

34)   4
     + 1

35)   4
     + 2

36)   0
     + 3

37)   3
     + 5

38)   3
     + 1

39)   5
     + 1

40)   4
     + 4

41)   5
     + 1

42)   2
     + 2

43)   2
     + 1

44)   5
     + 1

45)   0
     + 1

46)   2
     + 2

47)   1
     + 0

48)   4
     + 5

49)   4
     + 5

50)   4
     + 5

51)   5
     + 5

52)   4
     + 5

53)   5
     + 3

54)   0
     + 1

55)   5
     + 5

56)   2
     + 4

57)   2
     + 1

58)   5
     + 1

59)   4
     + 4

60)   3
     + 4

Score:

/60

Name:

Time   :

1)   4
   + 3

2)   0
   + 5

3)   5
   + 2

4)   4
   + 4

5)   0
   + 4

6)   4
   + 1

7)   3
   + 3

8)   4
   + 0

9)   2
   + 5

10)   0
   + 3

11)   2
   + 0

12)   0
   + 2

13)   3
   + 3

14)   3
   + 5

15)   0
   + 0

16)   4
   + 4

17)   0
   + 1

18)   2
   + 1

19)   5
   + 5

20)   4
   + 4

21)   0
   + 3

22)   2
   + 5

23)   4
   + 1

24)   5
   + 3

25)   1
   + 5

26)   0
   + 0

27)   4
   + 3

28)   1
   + 3

29)   1
   + 4

30)   1
   + 0

31)   1
   + 5

32)   5
   + 0

33)   2
   + 3

34)   1
   + 0

35)   3
   + 5

36)   0
   + 1

37)   2
   + 0

38)   1
   + 4

39)   0
   + 3

40)   2
   + 0

41)   1
   + 0

42)   5
   + 3

43)   5
   + 2

44)   2
   + 1

45)   3
   + 0

46)   3
   + 2

47)   3
   + 4

48)   2
   + 4

49)   2
   + 1

50)   0
   + 4

51)   4
   + 0

52)   1
   + 2

53)   0
   + 4

54)   2
   + 0

55)   3
   + 2

56)   3
   + 2

57)   3
   + 0

58)   0
   + 0

59)   5
   + 4

60)   5
   + 2

Adding numbers 0-5

Name:

Score: /60

Time   :

1) 1
   + 3

2) 5
   + 4

3) 2
   + 1

4) 3
   + 4

5) 5
   + 2

6) 4
   + 2

7) 3
   + 1

8) 1
   + 4

9) 5
   + 1

10) 1
    + 0

11) 2
    + 0

12) 5
    + 1

13) 2
    + 5

14) 4
    + 1

15) 3
    + 0

16) 4
    + 2

17) 3
    + 2

18) 5
    + 5

19) 2
    + 4

20) 0
    + 0

21) 5
    + 5

22) 4
    + 1

23) 5
    + 1

24) 2
    + 5

25) 0
    + 2

26) 1
    + 1

27) 1
    + 5

28) 3
    + 4

29) 3
    + 4

30) 2
    + 4

31) 2
    + 0

32) 0
    + 4

33) 4
    + 0

34) 1
    + 4

35) 3
    + 0

36) 1
    + 1

37) 1
    + 4

38) 1
    + 4

39) 0
    + 2

40) 5
    + 1

41) 5
    + 4

42) 3
    + 1

43) 2
    + 0

44) 0
    + 0

45) 2
    + 0

46) 5
    + 1

47) 0
    + 3

48) 2
    + 5

49) 5
    + 3

50) 5
    + 3

51) 4
    + 4

52) 1
    + 4

53) 2
    + 5

54) 4
    + 5

55) 5
    + 5

56) 1
    + 4

57) 3
    + 5

58) 2
    + 0

59) 1
    + 3

60) 2
    + 2

Name:

Score:

/60

time   :

1)
$$\begin{array}{r} 4 \\ + 2 \\ \hline \end{array}$$

2)
$$\begin{array}{r} 4 \\ + 3 \\ \hline \end{array}$$

3)
$$\begin{array}{r} 3 \\ + 0 \\ \hline \end{array}$$

4)
$$\begin{array}{r} 0 \\ + 1 \\ \hline \end{array}$$

5)
$$\begin{array}{r} 1 \\ + 1 \\ \hline \end{array}$$

6)
$$\begin{array}{r} 1 \\ + 4 \\ \hline \end{array}$$

7)
$$\begin{array}{r} 4 \\ + 2 \\ \hline \end{array}$$

8)
$$\begin{array}{r} 5 \\ + 3 \\ \hline \end{array}$$

9)
$$\begin{array}{r} 1 \\ + 0 \\ \hline \end{array}$$

10)
$$\begin{array}{r} 0 \\ + 1 \\ \hline \end{array}$$

11)
$$\begin{array}{r} 4 \\ + 0 \\ \hline \end{array}$$

12)
$$\begin{array}{r} 2 \\ + 0 \\ \hline \end{array}$$

13)
$$\begin{array}{r} 5 \\ + 2 \\ \hline \end{array}$$

14)
$$\begin{array}{r} 2 \\ + 1 \\ \hline \end{array}$$

15)
$$\begin{array}{r} 4 \\ + 1 \\ \hline \end{array}$$

16)
$$\begin{array}{r} 3 \\ + 4 \\ \hline \end{array}$$

17)
$$\begin{array}{r} 2 \\ + 5 \\ \hline \end{array}$$

18)
$$\begin{array}{r} 4 \\ + 3 \\ \hline \end{array}$$

19)
$$\begin{array}{r} 3 \\ + 1 \\ \hline \end{array}$$

20)
$$\begin{array}{r} 2 \\ + 5 \\ \hline \end{array}$$

21)
$$\begin{array}{r} 2 \\ + 5 \\ \hline \end{array}$$

22)
$$\begin{array}{r} 1 \\ + 1 \\ \hline \end{array}$$

23)
$$\begin{array}{r} 3 \\ + 1 \\ \hline \end{array}$$

24)
$$\begin{array}{r} 5 \\ + 1 \\ \hline \end{array}$$

25)
$$\begin{array}{r} 3 \\ + 1 \\ \hline \end{array}$$

26)
$$\begin{array}{r} 0 \\ + 5 \\ \hline \end{array}$$

27)
$$\begin{array}{r} 3 \\ + 4 \\ \hline \end{array}$$

28)
$$\begin{array}{r} 5 \\ + 4 \\ \hline \end{array}$$

29)
$$\begin{array}{r} 0 \\ + 3 \\ \hline \end{array}$$

30)
$$\begin{array}{r} 5 \\ + 4 \\ \hline \end{array}$$

31)
$$\begin{array}{r} 0 \\ + 5 \\ \hline \end{array}$$

32)
$$\begin{array}{r} 0 \\ + 1 \\ \hline \end{array}$$

33)
$$\begin{array}{r} 3 \\ + 3 \\ \hline \end{array}$$

34)
$$\begin{array}{r} 2 \\ + 3 \\ \hline \end{array}$$

35)
$$\begin{array}{r} 3 \\ + 0 \\ \hline \end{array}$$

36)
$$\begin{array}{r} 3 \\ + 4 \\ \hline \end{array}$$

37)
$$\begin{array}{r} 5 \\ + 4 \\ \hline \end{array}$$

38)
$$\begin{array}{r} 3 \\ + 3 \\ \hline \end{array}$$

39)
$$\begin{array}{r} 2 \\ + 1 \\ \hline \end{array}$$

40)
$$\begin{array}{r} 3 \\ + 2 \\ \hline \end{array}$$

41)
$$\begin{array}{r} 0 \\ + 5 \\ \hline \end{array}$$

42)
$$\begin{array}{r} 0 \\ + 5 \\ \hline \end{array}$$

43)
$$\begin{array}{r} 3 \\ + 4 \\ \hline \end{array}$$

44)
$$\begin{array}{r} 4 \\ + 2 \\ \hline \end{array}$$

45)
$$\begin{array}{r} 2 \\ + 4 \\ \hline \end{array}$$

46)
$$\begin{array}{r} 5 \\ + 2 \\ \hline \end{array}$$

47)
$$\begin{array}{r} 2 \\ + 5 \\ \hline \end{array}$$

48)
$$\begin{array}{r} 2 \\ + 5 \\ \hline \end{array}$$

49)
$$\begin{array}{r} 4 \\ + 2 \\ \hline \end{array}$$

50)
$$\begin{array}{r} 3 \\ + 4 \\ \hline \end{array}$$

51)
$$\begin{array}{r} 1 \\ + 3 \\ \hline \end{array}$$

52)
$$\begin{array}{r} 4 \\ + 2 \\ \hline \end{array}$$

53)
$$\begin{array}{r} 1 \\ + 5 \\ \hline \end{array}$$

54)
$$\begin{array}{r} 3 \\ + 1 \\ \hline \end{array}$$

55)
$$\begin{array}{r} 0 \\ + 1 \\ \hline \end{array}$$

56)
$$\begin{array}{r} 0 \\ + 5 \\ \hline \end{array}$$

57)
$$\begin{array}{r} 5 \\ + 0 \\ \hline \end{array}$$

58)
$$\begin{array}{r} 2 \\ + 2 \\ \hline \end{array}$$

59)
$$\begin{array}{r} 5 \\ + 5 \\ \hline \end{array}$$

60)
$$\begin{array}{r} 3 \\ + 2 \\ \hline \end{array}$$

Name:

Score:

/60

Time   :

1)   3
   + 2

2)   0
   + 3

3)   1
   + 3

4)   4
   + 4

5)   4
   + 5

6)   0
   + 2

7)   3
   + 1

8)   2
   + 2

9)   4
   + 0

10)   0
    + 5

11)   5
    + 5

12)   2
    + 5

13)   3
    + 5

14)   4
    + 0

15)   4
    + 5

16)   1
    + 1

17)   3
    + 3

18)   5
    + 0

19)   5
    + 4

20)   5
    + 0

21)   3
    + 1

22)   1
    + 0

23)   5
    + 3

24)   4
    + 5

25)   3
    + 3

26)   3
    + 3

27)   0
    + 1

28)   0
    + 2

29)   1
    + 2

30)   1
    + 5

31)   2
    + 3

32)   3
    + 3

33)   5
    + 0

34)   2
    + 0

35)   0
    + 4

36)   2
    + 0

37)   0
    + 1

38)   5
    + 4

39)   2
    + 0

40)   2
    + 3

41)   0
    + 0

42)   5
    + 1

43)   2
    + 2

44)   4
    + 2

45)   1
    + 1

46)   2
    + 4

47)   2
    + 1

48)   0
    + 5

49)   3
    + 5

50)   1
    + 0

51)   2
    + 1

52)   3
    + 3

53)   5
    + 0

54)   4
    + 1

55)   0
    + 5

56)   2
    + 1

57)   5
    + 4

58)   2
    + 1

59)   1
    + 1

60)   1
    + 0

Name:

Score:

/60

time   :

1)   3
  + 3

2)   2
  + 2

3)   3
  + 0

4)   4
  + 2

5)   5
  + 4

6)   1
  + 3

7)   0
  + 3

8)   2
  + 1

9)   3
  + 2

10)   1
   + 5

11)   3
   + 4

12)   4
   + 0

13)   1
   + 5

14)   2
   + 2

15)   5
   + 2

16)   1
   + 4

17)   1
   + 5

18)   5
   + 1

19)   1
   + 3

20)   5
   + 5

21)   5
   + 0

22)   0
   + 3

23)   3
   + 3

24)   2
   + 3

25)   1
   + 3

26)   2
   + 1

27)   3
   + 3

28)   1
   + 4

29)   0
   + 5

30)   2
   + 3

31)   2
   + 4

32)   0
   + 1

33)   2
   + 5

34)   1
   + 4

35)   5
   + 3

36)   1
   + 0

37)   4
   + 3

38)   0
   + 1

39)   5
   + 1

40)   4
   + 3

41)   2
   + 5

42)   4
   + 4

43)   5
   + 0

44)   4
   + 3

45)   5
   + 3

46)   3
   + 5

47)   5
   + 5

48)   0
   + 2

49)   1
   + 1

50)   3
   + 3

51)   2
   + 4

52)   5
   + 5

53)   4
   + 4

54)   2
   + 0

55)   5
   + 5

56)   3
   + 3

57)   5
   + 1

58)   2
   + 2

59)   0
   + 2

60)   3
   + 5

Name:

Score:

/60

time   :

1) $\begin{array}{r} 5 \\ + \ 0 \\ \hline \end{array}$

2) $\begin{array}{r} 2 \\ + \ 1 \\ \hline \end{array}$

3) $\begin{array}{r} 0 \\ + \ 3 \\ \hline \end{array}$

4) $\begin{array}{r} 5 \\ + \ 0 \\ \hline \end{array}$

5) $\begin{array}{r} 2 \\ + \ 4 \\ \hline \end{array}$

6) $\begin{array}{r} 5 \\ + \ 3 \\ \hline \end{array}$

7) $\begin{array}{r} 1 \\ + \ 3 \\ \hline \end{array}$

8) $\begin{array}{r} 0 \\ + \ 2 \\ \hline \end{array}$

9) $\begin{array}{r} 5 \\ + \ 0 \\ \hline \end{array}$

10) $\begin{array}{r} 3 \\ + \ 1 \\ \hline \end{array}$

11) $\begin{array}{r} 2 \\ + \ 0 \\ \hline \end{array}$

12) $\begin{array}{r} 0 \\ + \ 1 \\ \hline \end{array}$

13) $\begin{array}{r} 3 \\ + \ 5 \\ \hline \end{array}$

14) $\begin{array}{r} 5 \\ + \ 0 \\ \hline \end{array}$

15) $\begin{array}{r} 4 \\ + \ 1 \\ \hline \end{array}$

16) $\begin{array}{r} 3 \\ + \ 0 \\ \hline \end{array}$

17) $\begin{array}{r} 1 \\ + \ 1 \\ \hline \end{array}$

18) $\begin{array}{r} 3 \\ + \ 5 \\ \hline \end{array}$

19) $\begin{array}{r} 5 \\ + \ 3 \\ \hline \end{array}$

20) $\begin{array}{r} 2 \\ + \ 4 \\ \hline \end{array}$

21) $\begin{array}{r} 3 \\ + \ 0 \\ \hline \end{array}$

22) $\begin{array}{r} 1 \\ + \ 5 \\ \hline \end{array}$

23) $\begin{array}{r} 4 \\ + \ 3 \\ \hline \end{array}$

24) $\begin{array}{r} 5 \\ + \ 5 \\ \hline \end{array}$

25) $\begin{array}{r} 3 \\ + \ 1 \\ \hline \end{array}$

26) $\begin{array}{r} 4 \\ + \ 2 \\ \hline \end{array}$

27) $\begin{array}{r} 3 \\ + \ 3 \\ \hline \end{array}$

28) $\begin{array}{r} 2 \\ + \ 0 \\ \hline \end{array}$

29) $\begin{array}{r} 5 \\ + \ 4 \\ \hline \end{array}$

30) $\begin{array}{r} 0 \\ + \ 5 \\ \hline \end{array}$

31) $\begin{array}{r} 4 \\ + \ 3 \\ \hline \end{array}$

32) $\begin{array}{r} 3 \\ + \ 0 \\ \hline \end{array}$

33) $\begin{array}{r} 0 \\ + \ 1 \\ \hline \end{array}$

34) $\begin{array}{r} 5 \\ + \ 2 \\ \hline \end{array}$

35) $\begin{array}{r} 5 \\ + \ 3 \\ \hline \end{array}$

36) $\begin{array}{r} 0 \\ + \ 0 \\ \hline \end{array}$

37) $\begin{array}{r} 5 \\ + \ 1 \\ \hline \end{array}$

38) $\begin{array}{r} 0 \\ + \ 4 \\ \hline \end{array}$

39) $\begin{array}{r} 5 \\ + \ 2 \\ \hline \end{array}$

40) $\begin{array}{r} 1 \\ + \ 5 \\ \hline \end{array}$

41) $\begin{array}{r} 3 \\ + \ 4 \\ \hline \end{array}$

42) $\begin{array}{r} 3 \\ + \ 0 \\ \hline \end{array}$

43) $\begin{array}{r} 4 \\ + \ 1 \\ \hline \end{array}$

44) $\begin{array}{r} 4 \\ + \ 1 \\ \hline \end{array}$

45) $\begin{array}{r} 0 \\ + \ 4 \\ \hline \end{array}$

46) $\begin{array}{r} 2 \\ + \ 0 \\ \hline \end{array}$

47) $\begin{array}{r} 3 \\ + \ 2 \\ \hline \end{array}$

48) $\begin{array}{r} 2 \\ + \ 3 \\ \hline \end{array}$

49) $\begin{array}{r} 4 \\ + \ 1 \\ \hline \end{array}$

50) $\begin{array}{r} 2 \\ + \ 3 \\ \hline \end{array}$

51) $\begin{array}{r} 0 \\ + \ 0 \\ \hline \end{array}$

52) $\begin{array}{r} 5 \\ + \ 0 \\ \hline \end{array}$

53) $\begin{array}{r} 4 \\ + \ 3 \\ \hline \end{array}$

54) $\begin{array}{r} 0 \\ + \ 1 \\ \hline \end{array}$

55) $\begin{array}{r} 0 \\ + \ 2 \\ \hline \end{array}$

56) $\begin{array}{r} 5 \\ + \ 0 \\ \hline \end{array}$

57) $\begin{array}{r} 4 \\ + \ 5 \\ \hline \end{array}$

58) $\begin{array}{r} 3 \\ + \ 2 \\ \hline \end{array}$

59) $\begin{array}{r} 2 \\ + \ 3 \\ \hline \end{array}$

60) $\begin{array}{r} 1 \\ + \ 4 \\ \hline \end{array}$

Score:

/60

Name:

time   :

1)
$$0 + \square = 5$$

2)
$$\square + 3 = 7$$

3)
$$4 + \square = 9$$

4)
$$\square + 5 = 10$$

5)
$$1 + \square = 4$$

6)
$$\square + 3 = 3$$

7)
$$5 + \square = 5$$

8)
$$\square + 4 = 4$$

9)
$$1 + \square = 3$$

10)
$$\square + 4 = 6$$

11)
$$0 + \square = 2$$

12)
$$\square + 5 = 9$$

13)
$$5 + \square = 6$$

14)
$$\square + 5 = 8$$

15)
$$0 + \square = 1$$

16)
$$\square + 0 = 3$$

17)
$$5 + \square = 7$$

18)
$$\square + 5 = 6$$

19)
$$4 + \square = 6$$

20)
$$\square + 3 = 5$$

21)
$$2 + \square = 4$$

22)
$$\square + 2 = 3$$

23)
$$1 + \square = 3$$

24)
$$\square + 1 = 4$$

25)
$$4 + \square = 7$$

26)
$$\square + 1 = 3$$

27)
$$1 + \square = 5$$

28)
$$\square + 5 = 8$$

29)
$$1 + \square = 3$$

30)
$$\square + 1 = 1$$

31)
$$0 + \square = 1$$

32)
$$\square + 1 = 5$$

33)
$$3 + \square = 8$$

34)
$$\square + 5 = 5$$

35)
$$2 + \square = 2$$

36)
$$\square + 0 = 0$$

37)
$$3 + \square = 6$$

38)
$$\square + 2 = 7$$

39)
$$4 + \square = 5$$

40)
$$\square + 0 = 2$$

41)
$$4 + \square = 6$$

42)
$$\square + 3 = 8$$

43)
$$2 + \square = 5$$

44)
$$\square + 4 = 7$$

45)
$$3 + \square = 7$$

46)
$$\square + 5 = 10$$

47)
$$1 + \square = 1$$

48)
$$\square + 4 = 8$$

49)
$$5 + \square = 5$$

50)
$$\square + 2 = 5$$

51)
$$2 + \square = 7$$

52)
$$\square + 0 = 3$$

53)
$$4 + \square = 5$$

54)
$$\square + 0 = 3$$

55)
$$2 + \square = 4$$

56)
$$\square + 4 = 8$$

57)
$$3 + \square = 6$$

58)
$$\square + 2 = 3$$

59)
$$1 + \square = 4$$

60)
$$\square + 1 = 2$$

Score:

/60

Name:

time   :

1)
$$\begin{array}{r} 3 \\ + \square \\ \hline 6 \end{array}$$

2)
$$\begin{array}{r} \square \\ + 1 \\ \hline 5 \end{array}$$

3)
$$\begin{array}{r} 4 \\ + \square \\ \hline 8 \end{array}$$

4)
$$\begin{array}{r} \square \\ + 0 \\ \hline 5 \end{array}$$

5)
$$\begin{array}{r} 1 \\ + \square \\ \hline 6 \end{array}$$

6)
$$\begin{array}{r} \square \\ + 4 \\ \hline 5 \end{array}$$

7)
$$\begin{array}{r} 5 \\ + \square \\ \hline 7 \end{array}$$

8)
$$\begin{array}{r} \square \\ + 3 \\ \hline 5 \end{array}$$

9)
$$\begin{array}{r} 0 \\ + \square \\ \hline 5 \end{array}$$

10)
$$\begin{array}{r} \square \\ + 2 \\ \hline 6 \end{array}$$

11)
$$\begin{array}{r} 2 \\ + \square \\ \hline 7 \end{array}$$

12)
$$\begin{array}{r} \square \\ + 0 \\ \hline 0 \end{array}$$

13)
$$\begin{array}{r} 5 \\ + \square \\ \hline 6 \end{array}$$

14)
$$\begin{array}{r} \square \\ + 5 \\ \hline 10 \end{array}$$

15)
$$\begin{array}{r} 5 \\ + \square \\ \hline 8 \end{array}$$

16)
$$\begin{array}{r} \square \\ + 0 \\ \hline 3 \end{array}$$

17)
$$\begin{array}{r} 4 \\ + \square \\ \hline 9 \end{array}$$

18)
$$\begin{array}{r} \square \\ + 0 \\ \hline 4 \end{array}$$

19)
$$\begin{array}{r} 4 \\ + \square \\ \hline 4 \end{array}$$

20)
$$\begin{array}{r} \square \\ + 3 \\ \hline 4 \end{array}$$

21)
$$\begin{array}{r} 3 \\ + \square \\ \hline 3 \end{array}$$

22)
$$\begin{array}{r} \square \\ + 4 \\ \hline 5 \end{array}$$

23)
$$\begin{array}{r} 5 \\ + \square \\ \hline 5 \end{array}$$

24)
$$\begin{array}{r} \square \\ + 5 \\ \hline 7 \end{array}$$

25)
$$\begin{array}{r} 1 \\ + \square \\ \hline 4 \end{array}$$

26)
$$\begin{array}{r} \square \\ + 1 \\ \hline 4 \end{array}$$

27)
$$\begin{array}{r} 2 \\ + \square \\ \hline 4 \end{array}$$

28)
$$\begin{array}{r} \square \\ + 4 \\ \hline 6 \end{array}$$

29)
$$\begin{array}{r} 0 \\ + \square \\ \hline 0 \end{array}$$

30)
$$\begin{array}{r} \square \\ + 4 \\ \hline 5 \end{array}$$

31)
$$\begin{array}{r} 5 \\ + \square \\ \hline 6 \end{array}$$

32)
$$\begin{array}{r} \square \\ + 4 \\ \hline 5 \end{array}$$

33)
$$\begin{array}{r} 4 \\ + \square \\ \hline 9 \end{array}$$

34)
$$\begin{array}{r} \square \\ + 3 \\ \hline 3 \end{array}$$

35)
$$\begin{array}{r} 5 \\ + \square \\ \hline 7 \end{array}$$

36)
$$\begin{array}{r} \square \\ + 0 \\ \hline 0 \end{array}$$

37)
$$\begin{array}{r} 4 \\ + \square \\ \hline 9 \end{array}$$

38)
$$\begin{array}{r} \square \\ + 0 \\ \hline 1 \end{array}$$

39)
$$\begin{array}{r} 0 \\ + \square \\ \hline 0 \end{array}$$

40)
$$\begin{array}{r} \square \\ + 3 \\ \hline 6 \end{array}$$

41)
$$\begin{array}{r} 4 \\ + \square \\ \hline 4 \end{array}$$

42)
$$\begin{array}{r} \square \\ + 2 \\ \hline 3 \end{array}$$

43)
$$\begin{array}{r} 4 \\ + \square \\ \hline 8 \end{array}$$

44)
$$\begin{array}{r} \square \\ + 1 \\ \hline 6 \end{array}$$

45)
$$\begin{array}{r} 4 \\ + \square \\ \hline 5 \end{array}$$

46)
$$\begin{array}{r} \square \\ + 4 \\ \hline 5 \end{array}$$

47)
$$\begin{array}{r} 3 \\ + \square \\ \hline 7 \end{array}$$

48)
$$\begin{array}{r} \square \\ + 1 \\ \hline 3 \end{array}$$

49)
$$\begin{array}{r} 2 \\ + \square \\ \hline 5 \end{array}$$

50)
$$\begin{array}{r} \square \\ + 2 \\ \hline 7 \end{array}$$

51)
$$\begin{array}{r} 0 \\ + \square \\ \hline 0 \end{array}$$

52)
$$\begin{array}{r} \square \\ + 5 \\ \hline 9 \end{array}$$

53)
$$\begin{array}{r} 0 \\ + \square \\ \hline 3 \end{array}$$

54)
$$\begin{array}{r} \square \\ + 4 \\ \hline 6 \end{array}$$

55)
$$\begin{array}{r} 5 \\ + \square \\ \hline 6 \end{array}$$

56)
$$\begin{array}{r} \square \\ + 5 \\ \hline 10 \end{array}$$

57)
$$\begin{array}{r} 3 \\ + \square \\ \hline 7 \end{array}$$

58)
$$\begin{array}{r} \square \\ + 5 \\ \hline 10 \end{array}$$

59)
$$\begin{array}{r} 1 \\ + \square \\ \hline 6 \end{array}$$

60)
$$\begin{array}{r} \square \\ + 0 \\ \hline 5 \end{array}$$

Score:

/60

Name:

Time   :

1) 5
   +☐
  ───
   10

2) ☐
   + 0
  ───
    0

3) 3
   +☐
  ───
    5

4) ☐
   + 5
  ───
    6

5) 5
   +☐
  ───
   10

6) ☐
   + 1
  ───
    3

7) 1
   +☐
  ───
    2

8) ☐
   + 1
  ───
    4

9) 4
   +☐
  ───
    5

10) ☐
   + 1
  ───
    3

11) 4
   +☐
  ───
    4

12) ☐
   + 4
  ───
    4

13) 0
   +☐
  ───
    5

14) ☐
   + 3
  ───
    6

15) 5
   +☐
  ───
    7

16) ☐
   + 5
  ───
    5

17) 5
   +☐
  ───
   10

18) ☐
   + 3
  ───
    6

19) 1
   +☐
  ───
    1

20) ☐
   + 1
  ───
    2

21) 4
   +☐
  ───
    7

22) ☐
   + 1
  ───
    2

23) 2
   +☐
  ───
    3

24) ☐
   + 1
  ───
    3

25) 1
   +☐
  ───
    3

26) ☐
   + 4
  ───
    8

27) 0
   +☐
  ───
    1

28) ☐
   + 0
  ───
    5

29) 2
   +☐
  ───
    3

30) ☐
   + 0
  ───
    4

31) 1
   +☐
  ───
    2

32) ☐
   + 1
  ───
    3

33) 2
   +☐
  ───
    2

34) ☐
   + 2
  ───
    7

35) 2
   +☐
  ───
    4

36) ☐
   + 3
  ───
    8

37) 3
   +☐
  ───
    3

38) ☐
   + 5
  ───
    9

39) 4
   +☐
  ───
    5

40) ☐
   + 3
  ───
    7

41) 3
   +☐
  ───
    4

42) ☐
   + 5
  ───
    9

43) 1
   +☐
  ───
    4

44) ☐
   + 2
  ───
    6

45) 4
   +☐
  ───
    8

46) ☐
   + 1
  ───
    5

47) 5
   +☐
  ───
    6

48) ☐
   + 4
  ───
    4

49) 2
   +☐
  ───
    3

50) ☐
   + 3
  ───
    7

51) 3
   +☐
  ───
    6

52) ☐
   + 5
  ───
    8

53) 4
   +☐
  ───
    8

54) ☐
   + 3
  ───
    4

55) 5
   +☐
  ───
    5

56) ☐
   + 1
  ───
    6

57) 2
   +☐
  ───
    3

58) ☐
   + 5
  ───
    8

59) 0
   +☐
  ───
    3

60) ☐
   + 3
  ───
    5

Name:

Score:

/60

time   :

1)
   3
  +☐
  ___
   8

2)
   ☐
  + 0
  ___
   4

3)
   2
  +☐
  ___
   5

4)
   ☐
  + 0
  ___
   4

5)
   1
  +☐
  ___
   3

6)
   ☐
  + 5
  ___
   5

7)
   2
  +☐
  ___
   6

8)
   ☐
  + 2
  ___
   5

9)
   1
  +☐
  ___
   4

10)
   ☐
  + 0
  ___
   5

11)
   0
  +☐
  ___
   3

12)
   ☐
  + 3
  ___
   4

13)
   3
  +☐
  ___
   6

14)
   ☐
  + 0
  ___
   0

15)
   0
  +☐
  ___
   2

16)
   ☐
  + 4
  ___
   4

17)
   5
  +☐
  ___
   6

18)
   ☐
  + 4
  ___
   8

19)
   1
  +☐
  ___
   6

20)
   ☐
  + 1
  ___
   2

21)
   5
  +☐
  ___
   9

22)
   ☐
  + 4
  ___
   6

23)
   0
  +☐
  ___
   0

24)
   ☐
  + 2
  ___
   7

25)
   3
  +☐
  ___
   7

26)
   ☐
  + 1
  ___
   2

27)
   4
  +☐
  ___
   6

28)
   ☐
  + 0
  ___
   5

29)
   3
  +☐
  ___
   3

30)
   ☐
  + 2
  ___
   7

31)
   4
  +☐
  ___
   5

32)
   ☐
  + 5
  ___
   6

33)
   1
  +☐
  ___
   6

34)
   ☐
  + 4
  ___
   8

35)
   5
  +☐
  ___
   7

36)
   ☐
  + 4
  ___
   9

37)
   3
  +☐
  ___
   5

38)
   ☐
  + 0
  ___
   1

39)
   4
  +☐
  ___
   6

40)
   ☐
  + 0
  ___
   0

41)
   1
  +☐
  ___
   3

42)
   ☐
  + 3
  ___
   7

43)
   4
  +☐
  ___
   9

44)
   ☐
  + 4
  ___
   7

45)
   0
  +☐
  ___
   2

46)
   ☐
  + 3
  ___
   5

47)
   2
  +☐
  ___
   7

48)
   ☐
  + 3
  ___
   7

49)
   3
  +☐
  ___
   4

50)
   ☐
  + 5
  ___
   6

51)
   4
  +☐
  ___
   9

52)
   ☐
  + 1
  ___
   3

53)
   5
  +☐
  ___
   10

54)
   ☐
  + 4
  ___
   7

55)
   0
  +☐
  ___
   3

56)
   ☐
  + 1
  ___
   4

57)
   5
  +☐
  ___
   5

58)
   ☐
  + 4
  ___
   5

59)
   4
  +☐
  ___
   4

60)
   ☐
  + 2
  ___
   7

Page 14

Score: /60

Name:

time :

1)
$$\begin{array}{r} 1 \\ + \boxed{} \\ \hline 6 \end{array}$$

2)
$$\begin{array}{r} \boxed{} \\ + 5 \\ \hline 9 \end{array}$$

3)
$$\begin{array}{r} 5 \\ + \boxed{} \\ \hline 7 \end{array}$$

4)
$$\begin{array}{r} \boxed{} \\ + 0 \\ \hline 1 \end{array}$$

5)
$$\begin{array}{r} 0 \\ + \boxed{} \\ \hline 4 \end{array}$$

6)
$$\begin{array}{r} \boxed{} \\ + 1 \\ \hline 2 \end{array}$$

7)
$$\begin{array}{r} 2 \\ + \boxed{} \\ \hline 5 \end{array}$$

8)
$$\begin{array}{r} \boxed{} \\ + 4 \\ \hline 7 \end{array}$$

9)
$$\begin{array}{r} 5 \\ + \boxed{} \\ \hline 5 \end{array}$$

10)
$$\begin{array}{r} \boxed{} \\ + 1 \\ \hline 5 \end{array}$$

11)
$$\begin{array}{r} 4 \\ + \boxed{} \\ \hline 7 \end{array}$$

12)
$$\begin{array}{r} \boxed{} \\ + 4 \\ \hline 7 \end{array}$$

13)
$$\begin{array}{r} 1 \\ + \boxed{} \\ \hline 1 \end{array}$$

14)
$$\begin{array}{r} \boxed{} \\ + 3 \\ \hline 3 \end{array}$$

15)
$$\begin{array}{r} 0 \\ + \boxed{} \\ \hline 5 \end{array}$$

16)
$$\begin{array}{r} \boxed{} \\ + 3 \\ \hline 7 \end{array}$$

17)
$$\begin{array}{r} 5 \\ + \boxed{} \\ \hline 9 \end{array}$$

18)
$$\begin{array}{r} \boxed{} \\ + 2 \\ \hline 5 \end{array}$$

19)
$$\begin{array}{r} 0 \\ + \boxed{} \\ \hline 1 \end{array}$$

20)
$$\begin{array}{r} \boxed{} \\ + 0 \\ \hline 2 \end{array}$$

21)
$$\begin{array}{r} 4 \\ + \boxed{} \\ \hline 5 \end{array}$$

22)
$$\begin{array}{r} \boxed{} \\ + 3 \\ \hline 8 \end{array}$$

23)
$$\begin{array}{r} 5 \\ + \boxed{} \\ \hline 9 \end{array}$$

24)
$$\begin{array}{r} \boxed{} \\ + 2 \\ \hline 4 \end{array}$$

25)
$$\begin{array}{r} 1 \\ + \boxed{} \\ \hline 5 \end{array}$$

26)
$$\begin{array}{r} \boxed{} \\ + 5 \\ \hline 5 \end{array}$$

27)
$$\begin{array}{r} 0 \\ + \boxed{} \\ \hline 0 \end{array}$$

28)
$$\begin{array}{r} \boxed{} \\ + 0 \\ \hline 0 \end{array}$$

29)
$$\begin{array}{r} 0 \\ + \boxed{} \\ \hline 1 \end{array}$$

30)
$$\begin{array}{r} \boxed{} \\ + 0 \\ \hline 4 \end{array}$$

31)
$$\begin{array}{r} 1 \\ + \boxed{} \\ \hline 5 \end{array}$$

32)
$$\begin{array}{r} \boxed{} \\ + 3 \\ \hline 3 \end{array}$$

33)
$$\begin{array}{r} 3 \\ + \boxed{} \\ \hline 8 \end{array}$$

34)
$$\begin{array}{r} \boxed{} \\ + 4 \\ \hline 4 \end{array}$$

35)
$$\begin{array}{r} 2 \\ + \boxed{} \\ \hline 4 \end{array}$$

36)
$$\begin{array}{r} \boxed{} \\ + 2 \\ \hline 6 \end{array}$$

37)
$$\begin{array}{r} 4 \\ + \boxed{} \\ \hline 9 \end{array}$$

38)
$$\begin{array}{r} \boxed{} \\ + 1 \\ \hline 1 \end{array}$$

39)
$$\begin{array}{r} 3 \\ + \boxed{} \\ \hline 4 \end{array}$$

40)
$$\begin{array}{r} \boxed{} \\ + 4 \\ \hline 7 \end{array}$$

41)
$$\begin{array}{r} 3 \\ + \boxed{} \\ \hline 7 \end{array}$$

42)
$$\begin{array}{r} \boxed{} \\ + 0 \\ \hline 0 \end{array}$$

43)
$$\begin{array}{r} 5 \\ + \boxed{} \\ \hline 7 \end{array}$$

44)
$$\begin{array}{r} \boxed{} \\ + 0 \\ \hline 1 \end{array}$$

45)
$$\begin{array}{r} 0 \\ + \boxed{} \\ \hline 5 \end{array}$$

46)
$$\begin{array}{r} \boxed{} \\ + 3 \\ \hline 4 \end{array}$$

47)
$$\begin{array}{r} 1 \\ + \boxed{} \\ \hline 4 \end{array}$$

48)
$$\begin{array}{r} \boxed{} \\ + 3 \\ \hline 7 \end{array}$$

49)
$$\begin{array}{r} 5 \\ + \boxed{} \\ \hline 5 \end{array}$$

50)
$$\begin{array}{r} \boxed{} \\ + 5 \\ \hline 9 \end{array}$$

51)
$$\begin{array}{r} 3 \\ + \boxed{} \\ \hline 6 \end{array}$$

52)
$$\begin{array}{r} \boxed{} \\ + 1 \\ \hline 6 \end{array}$$

53)
$$\begin{array}{r} 4 \\ + \boxed{} \\ \hline 9 \end{array}$$

54)
$$\begin{array}{r} \boxed{} \\ + 3 \\ \hline 4 \end{array}$$

55)
$$\begin{array}{r} 3 \\ + \boxed{} \\ \hline 4 \end{array}$$

56)
$$\begin{array}{r} \boxed{} \\ + 2 \\ \hline 3 \end{array}$$

57)
$$\begin{array}{r} 3 \\ + \boxed{} \\ \hline 5 \end{array}$$

58)
$$\begin{array}{r} \boxed{} \\ + 3 \\ \hline 4 \end{array}$$

59)
$$\begin{array}{r} 1 \\ + \boxed{} \\ \hline 5 \end{array}$$

60)
$$\begin{array}{r} \boxed{} \\ + 1 \\ \hline 4 \end{array}$$

Page 15

Score: /60

Name:

time   :

1)
$$\begin{array}{r} 2 \\ +\ \square \\ \hline 2 \end{array}$$

2)
$$\begin{array}{r} \square \\ +\ 3 \\ \hline 8 \end{array}$$

3)
$$\begin{array}{r} 4 \\ +\ \square \\ \hline 4 \end{array}$$

4)
$$\begin{array}{r} \square \\ +\ 2 \\ \hline 4 \end{array}$$

5)
$$\begin{array}{r} 3 \\ +\ \square \\ \hline 6 \end{array}$$

6)
$$\begin{array}{r} \square \\ +\ 2 \\ \hline 5 \end{array}$$

7)
$$\begin{array}{r} 1 \\ +\ \square \\ \hline 1 \end{array}$$

8)
$$\begin{array}{r} \square \\ +\ 2 \\ \hline 4 \end{array}$$

9)
$$\begin{array}{r} 5 \\ +\ \square \\ \hline 10 \end{array}$$

10)
$$\begin{array}{r} \square \\ +\ 5 \\ \hline 5 \end{array}$$

11)
$$\begin{array}{r} 1 \\ +\ \square \\ \hline 6 \end{array}$$

12)
$$\begin{array}{r} \square \\ +\ 0 \\ \hline 2 \end{array}$$

13)
$$\begin{array}{r} 3 \\ +\ \square \\ \hline 4 \end{array}$$

14)
$$\begin{array}{r} \square \\ +\ 5 \\ \hline 10 \end{array}$$

15)
$$\begin{array}{r} 2 \\ +\ \square \\ \hline 2 \end{array}$$

16)
$$\begin{array}{r} \square \\ +\ 1 \\ \hline 2 \end{array}$$

17)
$$\begin{array}{r} 0 \\ +\ \square \\ \hline 5 \end{array}$$

18)
$$\begin{array}{r} \square \\ +\ 2 \\ \hline 7 \end{array}$$

19)
$$\begin{array}{r} 0 \\ +\ \square \\ \hline 4 \end{array}$$

20)
$$\begin{array}{r} \square \\ +\ 2 \\ \hline 6 \end{array}$$

21)
$$\begin{array}{r} 0 \\ +\ \square \\ \hline 0 \end{array}$$

22)
$$\begin{array}{r} \square \\ +\ 2 \\ \hline 6 \end{array}$$

23)
$$\begin{array}{r} 4 \\ +\ \square \\ \hline 6 \end{array}$$

24)
$$\begin{array}{r} \square \\ +\ 5 \\ \hline 8 \end{array}$$

25)
$$\begin{array}{r} 5 \\ +\ \square \\ \hline 9 \end{array}$$

26)
$$\begin{array}{r} \square \\ +\ 1 \\ \hline 6 \end{array}$$

27)
$$\begin{array}{r} 3 \\ +\ \square \\ \hline 7 \end{array}$$

28)
$$\begin{array}{r} \square \\ +\ 5 \\ \hline 7 \end{array}$$

29)
$$\begin{array}{r} 2 \\ +\ \square \\ \hline 7 \end{array}$$

30)
$$\begin{array}{r} \square \\ +\ 2 \\ \hline 6 \end{array}$$

31)
$$\begin{array}{r} 3 \\ +\ \square \\ \hline 4 \end{array}$$

32)
$$\begin{array}{r} \square \\ +\ 2 \\ \hline 4 \end{array}$$

33)
$$\begin{array}{r} 0 \\ +\ \square \\ \hline 1 \end{array}$$

34)
$$\begin{array}{r} \square \\ +\ 1 \\ \hline 1 \end{array}$$

35)
$$\begin{array}{r} 5 \\ +\ \square \\ \hline 5 \end{array}$$

36)
$$\begin{array}{r} \square \\ +\ 5 \\ \hline 5 \end{array}$$

37)
$$\begin{array}{r} 0 \\ +\ \square \\ \hline 5 \end{array}$$

38)
$$\begin{array}{r} \square \\ +\ 3 \\ \hline 7 \end{array}$$

39)
$$\begin{array}{r} 0 \\ +\ \square \\ \hline 5 \end{array}$$

40)
$$\begin{array}{r} \square \\ +\ 4 \\ \hline 6 \end{array}$$

41)
$$\begin{array}{r} 4 \\ +\ \square \\ \hline 9 \end{array}$$

42)
$$\begin{array}{r} \square \\ +\ 0 \\ \hline 1 \end{array}$$

43)
$$\begin{array}{r} 5 \\ +\ \square \\ \hline 9 \end{array}$$

44)
$$\begin{array}{r} \square \\ +\ 2 \\ \hline 2 \end{array}$$

45)
$$\begin{array}{r} 3 \\ +\ \square \\ \hline 6 \end{array}$$

46)
$$\begin{array}{r} \square \\ +\ 1 \\ \hline 5 \end{array}$$

47)
$$\begin{array}{r} 5 \\ +\ \square \\ \hline 9 \end{array}$$

48)
$$\begin{array}{r} \square \\ +\ 2 \\ \hline 3 \end{array}$$

49)
$$\begin{array}{r} 1 \\ +\ \square \\ \hline 3 \end{array}$$

50)
$$\begin{array}{r} \square \\ +\ 1 \\ \hline 1 \end{array}$$

51)
$$\begin{array}{r} 0 \\ +\ \square \\ \hline 4 \end{array}$$

52)
$$\begin{array}{r} \square \\ +\ 1 \\ \hline 1 \end{array}$$

53)
$$\begin{array}{r} 2 \\ +\ \square \\ \hline 4 \end{array}$$

54)
$$\begin{array}{r} \square \\ +\ 5 \\ \hline 10 \end{array}$$

55)
$$\begin{array}{r} 1 \\ +\ \square \\ \hline 4 \end{array}$$

56)
$$\begin{array}{r} \square \\ +\ 4 \\ \hline 5 \end{array}$$

57)
$$\begin{array}{r} 3 \\ +\ \square \\ \hline 5 \end{array}$$

58)
$$\begin{array}{r} \square \\ +\ 2 \\ \hline 5 \end{array}$$

59)
$$\begin{array}{r} 2 \\ +\ \square \\ \hline 4 \end{array}$$

60)
$$\begin{array}{r} \square \\ +\ 1 \\ \hline 5 \end{array}$$

Score:

/60

Name:

time   :

1) $\begin{array}{r} 1 \\ + \square \\ \hline 1 \end{array}$

2) $\begin{array}{r} \square \\ + 2 \\ \hline 6 \end{array}$

3) $\begin{array}{r} 4 \\ + \square \\ \hline 6 \end{array}$

4) $\begin{array}{r} \square \\ + 5 \\ \hline 6 \end{array}$

5) $\begin{array}{r} 3 \\ + \square \\ \hline 8 \end{array}$

6) $\begin{array}{r} \square \\ + 0 \\ \hline 1 \end{array}$

7) $\begin{array}{r} 0 \\ + \square \\ \hline 1 \end{array}$

8) $\begin{array}{r} \square \\ + 1 \\ \hline 4 \end{array}$

9) $\begin{array}{r} 3 \\ + \square \\ \hline 8 \end{array}$

10) $\begin{array}{r} \square \\ + 4 \\ \hline 4 \end{array}$

11) $\begin{array}{r} 0 \\ + \square \\ \hline 3 \end{array}$

12) $\begin{array}{r} \square \\ + 2 \\ \hline 4 \end{array}$

13) $\begin{array}{r} 0 \\ + \square \\ \hline 3 \end{array}$

14) $\begin{array}{r} \square \\ + 3 \\ \hline 5 \end{array}$

15) $\begin{array}{r} 1 \\ + \square \\ \hline 1 \end{array}$

16) $\begin{array}{r} \square \\ + 2 \\ \hline 5 \end{array}$

17) $\begin{array}{r} 4 \\ + \square \\ \hline 9 \end{array}$

18) $\begin{array}{r} \square \\ + 0 \\ \hline 4 \end{array}$

19) $\begin{array}{r} 2 \\ + \square \\ \hline 7 \end{array}$

20) $\begin{array}{r} \square \\ + 2 \\ \hline 6 \end{array}$

21) $\begin{array}{r} 3 \\ + \square \\ \hline 8 \end{array}$

22) $\begin{array}{r} \square \\ + 1 \\ \hline 5 \end{array}$

23) $\begin{array}{r} 0 \\ + \square \\ \hline 1 \end{array}$

24) $\begin{array}{r} \square \\ + 5 \\ \hline 6 \end{array}$

25) $\begin{array}{r} 5 \\ + \square \\ \hline 10 \end{array}$

26) $\begin{array}{r} \square \\ + 1 \\ \hline 2 \end{array}$

27) $\begin{array}{r} 1 \\ + \square \\ \hline 3 \end{array}$

28) $\begin{array}{r} \square \\ + 4 \\ \hline 6 \end{array}$

29) $\begin{array}{r} 4 \\ + \square \\ \hline 8 \end{array}$

30) $\begin{array}{r} \square \\ + 3 \\ \hline 5 \end{array}$

31) $\begin{array}{r} 5 \\ + \square \\ \hline 9 \end{array}$

32) $\begin{array}{r} \square \\ + 3 \\ \hline 6 \end{array}$

33) $\begin{array}{r} 1 \\ + \square \\ \hline 6 \end{array}$

34) $\begin{array}{r} \square \\ + 2 \\ \hline 3 \end{array}$

35) $\begin{array}{r} 1 \\ + \square \\ \hline 5 \end{array}$

36) $\begin{array}{r} \square \\ + 1 \\ \hline 3 \end{array}$

37) $\begin{array}{r} 3 \\ + \square \\ \hline 6 \end{array}$

38) $\begin{array}{r} \square \\ + 4 \\ \hline 9 \end{array}$

39) $\begin{array}{r} 3 \\ + \square \\ \hline 6 \end{array}$

40) $\begin{array}{r} \square \\ + 1 \\ \hline 5 \end{array}$

41) $\begin{array}{r} 0 \\ + \square \\ \hline 5 \end{array}$

42) $\begin{array}{r} \square \\ + 3 \\ \hline 5 \end{array}$

43) $\begin{array}{r} 0 \\ + \square \\ \hline 1 \end{array}$

44) $\begin{array}{r} \square \\ + 0 \\ \hline 3 \end{array}$

45) $\begin{array}{r} 1 \\ + \square \\ \hline 1 \end{array}$

46) $\begin{array}{r} \square \\ + 0 \\ \hline 4 \end{array}$

47) $\begin{array}{r} 4 \\ + \square \\ \hline 5 \end{array}$

48) $\begin{array}{r} \square \\ + 1 \\ \hline 4 \end{array}$

49) $\begin{array}{r} 0 \\ + \square \\ \hline 1 \end{array}$

50) $\begin{array}{r} \square \\ + 0 \\ \hline 3 \end{array}$

51) $\begin{array}{r} 0 \\ + \square \\ \hline 5 \end{array}$

52) $\begin{array}{r} \square \\ + 3 \\ \hline 6 \end{array}$

53) $\begin{array}{r} 2 \\ + \square \\ \hline 2 \end{array}$

54) $\begin{array}{r} \square \\ + 5 \\ \hline 7 \end{array}$

55) $\begin{array}{r} 5 \\ + \square \\ \hline 9 \end{array}$

56) $\begin{array}{r} \square \\ + 0 \\ \hline 0 \end{array}$

57) $\begin{array}{r} 5 \\ + \square \\ \hline 6 \end{array}$

58) $\begin{array}{r} \square \\ + 3 \\ \hline 5 \end{array}$

59) $\begin{array}{r} 0 \\ + \square \\ \hline 3 \end{array}$

60) $\begin{array}{r} \square \\ + 3 \\ \hline 3 \end{array}$

Score:

/60

Name:

time   :

1)
$$\begin{array}{r} 1 \\ + \square \\ \hline 6 \end{array}$$

2)
$$\begin{array}{r} \square \\ + 1 \\ \hline 2 \end{array}$$

3)
$$\begin{array}{r} 1 \\ + \square \\ \hline 2 \end{array}$$

4)
$$\begin{array}{r} \square \\ + 1 \\ \hline 3 \end{array}$$

5)
$$\begin{array}{r} 5 \\ + \square \\ \hline 8 \end{array}$$

6)
$$\begin{array}{r} \square \\ + 2 \\ \hline 7 \end{array}$$

7)
$$\begin{array}{r} 5 \\ + \square \\ \hline 10 \end{array}$$

8)
$$\begin{array}{r} \square \\ + 1 \\ \hline 4 \end{array}$$

9)
$$\begin{array}{r} 4 \\ + \square \\ \hline 6 \end{array}$$

10)
$$\begin{array}{r} \square \\ + 2 \\ \hline 6 \end{array}$$

11)
$$\begin{array}{r} 4 \\ + \square \\ \hline 5 \end{array}$$

12)
$$\begin{array}{r} \square \\ + 1 \\ \hline 2 \end{array}$$

13)
$$\begin{array}{r} 3 \\ + \square \\ \hline 4 \end{array}$$

14)
$$\begin{array}{r} \square \\ + 5 \\ \hline 8 \end{array}$$

15)
$$\begin{array}{r} 0 \\ + \square \\ \hline 5 \end{array}$$

16)
$$\begin{array}{r} \square \\ + 0 \\ \hline 0 \end{array}$$

17)
$$\begin{array}{r} 2 \\ + \square \\ \hline 3 \end{array}$$

18)
$$\begin{array}{r} \square \\ + 4 \\ \hline 4 \end{array}$$

19)
$$\begin{array}{r} 3 \\ + \square \\ \hline 8 \end{array}$$

20)
$$\begin{array}{r} \square \\ + 0 \\ \hline 0 \end{array}$$

21)
$$\begin{array}{r} 4 \\ + \square \\ \hline 7 \end{array}$$

22)
$$\begin{array}{r} \square \\ + 2 \\ \hline 5 \end{array}$$

23)
$$\begin{array}{r} 0 \\ + \square \\ \hline 0 \end{array}$$

24)
$$\begin{array}{r} \square \\ + 4 \\ \hline 6 \end{array}$$

25)
$$\begin{array}{r} 0 \\ + \square \\ \hline 1 \end{array}$$

26)
$$\begin{array}{r} \square \\ + 0 \\ \hline 4 \end{array}$$

27)
$$\begin{array}{r} 2 \\ + \square \\ \hline 2 \end{array}$$

28)
$$\begin{array}{r} \square \\ + 5 \\ \hline 10 \end{array}$$

29)
$$\begin{array}{r} 0 \\ + \square \\ \hline 0 \end{array}$$

30)
$$\begin{array}{r} \square \\ + 3 \\ \hline 7 \end{array}$$

31)
$$\begin{array}{r} 1 \\ + \square \\ \hline 4 \end{array}$$

32)
$$\begin{array}{r} \square \\ + 0 \\ \hline 3 \end{array}$$

33)
$$\begin{array}{r} 0 \\ + \square \\ \hline 3 \end{array}$$

34)
$$\begin{array}{r} \square \\ + 2 \\ \hline 4 \end{array}$$

35)
$$\begin{array}{r} 1 \\ + \square \\ \hline 2 \end{array}$$

36)
$$\begin{array}{r} \square \\ + 3 \\ \hline 4 \end{array}$$

37)
$$\begin{array}{r} 0 \\ + \square \\ \hline 0 \end{array}$$

38)
$$\begin{array}{r} \square \\ + 4 \\ \hline 4 \end{array}$$

39)
$$\begin{array}{r} 3 \\ + \square \\ \hline 3 \end{array}$$

40)
$$\begin{array}{r} \square \\ + 1 \\ \hline 4 \end{array}$$

41)
$$\begin{array}{r} 3 \\ + \square \\ \hline 5 \end{array}$$

42)
$$\begin{array}{r} \square \\ + 3 \\ \hline 6 \end{array}$$

43)
$$\begin{array}{r} 1 \\ + \square \\ \hline 4 \end{array}$$

44)
$$\begin{array}{r} \square \\ + 2 \\ \hline 3 \end{array}$$

45)
$$\begin{array}{r} 1 \\ + \square \\ \hline 2 \end{array}$$

46)
$$\begin{array}{r} \square \\ + 3 \\ \hline 5 \end{array}$$

47)
$$\begin{array}{r} 3 \\ + \square \\ \hline 6 \end{array}$$

48)
$$\begin{array}{r} \square \\ + 0 \\ \hline 5 \end{array}$$

49)
$$\begin{array}{r} 5 \\ + \square \\ \hline 8 \end{array}$$

50)
$$\begin{array}{r} \square \\ + 0 \\ \hline 4 \end{array}$$

51)
$$\begin{array}{r} 2 \\ + \square \\ \hline 2 \end{array}$$

52)
$$\begin{array}{r} \square \\ + 3 \\ \hline 4 \end{array}$$

53)
$$\begin{array}{r} 0 \\ + \square \\ \hline 3 \end{array}$$

54)
$$\begin{array}{r} \square \\ + 5 \\ \hline 10 \end{array}$$

55)
$$\begin{array}{r} 2 \\ + \square \\ \hline 5 \end{array}$$

56)
$$\begin{array}{r} \square \\ + 4 \\ \hline 6 \end{array}$$

57)
$$\begin{array}{r} 5 \\ + \square \\ \hline 8 \end{array}$$

58)
$$\begin{array}{r} \square \\ + 3 \\ \hline 4 \end{array}$$

59)
$$\begin{array}{r} 1 \\ + \square \\ \hline 5 \end{array}$$

60)
$$\begin{array}{r} \square \\ + 2 \\ \hline 7 \end{array}$$

Score:

/60

Name:

time   :

1) $\begin{array}{r} 2 \\ + \square \\ \hline 5 \end{array}$

2) $\begin{array}{r} \square \\ + 3 \\ \hline 4 \end{array}$

3) $\begin{array}{r} 3 \\ + \square \\ \hline 8 \end{array}$

4) $\begin{array}{r} \square \\ + 2 \\ \hline 2 \end{array}$

5) $\begin{array}{r} 3 \\ + \square \\ \hline 8 \end{array}$

6) $\begin{array}{r} \square \\ + 2 \\ \hline 4 \end{array}$

7) $\begin{array}{r} 3 \\ + \square \\ \hline 6 \end{array}$

8) $\begin{array}{r} \square \\ + 4 \\ \hline 5 \end{array}$

9) $\begin{array}{r} 2 \\ + \square \\ \hline 2 \end{array}$

10) $\begin{array}{r} \square \\ + 2 \\ \hline 5 \end{array}$

11) $\begin{array}{r} 2 \\ + \square \\ \hline 3 \end{array}$

12) $\begin{array}{r} \square \\ + 5 \\ \hline 8 \end{array}$

13) $\begin{array}{r} 2 \\ + \square \\ \hline 4 \end{array}$

14) $\begin{array}{r} \square \\ + 3 \\ \hline 5 \end{array}$

15) $\begin{array}{r} 1 \\ + \square \\ \hline 1 \end{array}$

16) $\begin{array}{r} \square \\ + 3 \\ \hline 7 \end{array}$

17) $\begin{array}{r} 0 \\ + \square \\ \hline 0 \end{array}$

18) $\begin{array}{r} \square \\ + 2 \\ \hline 3 \end{array}$

19) $\begin{array}{r} 2 \\ + \square \\ \hline 5 \end{array}$

20) $\begin{array}{r} \square \\ + 5 \\ \hline 7 \end{array}$

21) $\begin{array}{r} 2 \\ + \square \\ \hline 4 \end{array}$

22) $\begin{array}{r} \square \\ + 4 \\ \hline 4 \end{array}$

23) $\begin{array}{r} 0 \\ + \square \\ \hline 4 \end{array}$

24) $\begin{array}{r} \square \\ + 2 \\ \hline 5 \end{array}$

25) $\begin{array}{r} 5 \\ + \square \\ \hline 8 \end{array}$

26) $\begin{array}{r} \square \\ + 0 \\ \hline 0 \end{array}$

27) $\begin{array}{r} 5 \\ + \square \\ \hline 5 \end{array}$

28) $\begin{array}{r} \square \\ + 2 \\ \hline 7 \end{array}$

29) $\begin{array}{r} 3 \\ + \square \\ \hline 5 \end{array}$

30) $\begin{array}{r} \square \\ + 5 \\ \hline 7 \end{array}$

31) $\begin{array}{r} 0 \\ + \square \\ \hline 4 \end{array}$

32) $\begin{array}{r} \square \\ + 5 \\ \hline 6 \end{array}$

33) $\begin{array}{r} 4 \\ + \square \\ \hline 9 \end{array}$

34) $\begin{array}{r} \square \\ + 2 \\ \hline 5 \end{array}$

35) $\begin{array}{r} 4 \\ + \square \\ \hline 9 \end{array}$

36) $\begin{array}{r} \square \\ + 3 \\ \hline 3 \end{array}$

37) $\begin{array}{r} 0 \\ + \square \\ \hline 1 \end{array}$

38) $\begin{array}{r} \square \\ + 4 \\ \hline 5 \end{array}$

39) $\begin{array}{r} 2 \\ + \square \\ \hline 6 \end{array}$

40) $\begin{array}{r} \square \\ + 1 \\ \hline 3 \end{array}$

41) $\begin{array}{r} 2 \\ + \square \\ \hline 7 \end{array}$

42) $\begin{array}{r} \square \\ + 0 \\ \hline 5 \end{array}$

43) $\begin{array}{r} 5 \\ + \square \\ \hline 10 \end{array}$

44) $\begin{array}{r} \square \\ + 4 \\ \hline 4 \end{array}$

45) $\begin{array}{r} 4 \\ + \square \\ \hline 4 \end{array}$

46) $\begin{array}{r} \square \\ + 2 \\ \hline 5 \end{array}$

47) $\begin{array}{r} 4 \\ + \square \\ \hline 4 \end{array}$

48) $\begin{array}{r} \square \\ + 2 \\ \hline 7 \end{array}$

49) $\begin{array}{r} 4 \\ + \square \\ \hline 5 \end{array}$

50) $\begin{array}{r} \square \\ + 0 \\ \hline 3 \end{array}$

51) $\begin{array}{r} 4 \\ + \square \\ \hline 4 \end{array}$

52) $\begin{array}{r} \square \\ + 2 \\ \hline 6 \end{array}$

53) $\begin{array}{r} 3 \\ + \square \\ \hline 7 \end{array}$

54) $\begin{array}{r} \square \\ + 5 \\ \hline 9 \end{array}$

55) $\begin{array}{r} 0 \\ + \square \\ \hline 0 \end{array}$

56) $\begin{array}{r} \square \\ + 1 \\ \hline 3 \end{array}$

57) $\begin{array}{r} 4 \\ + \square \\ \hline 6 \end{array}$

58) $\begin{array}{r} \square \\ + 5 \\ \hline 9 \end{array}$

59) $\begin{array}{r} 0 \\ + \square \\ \hline 5 \end{array}$

60) $\begin{array}{r} \square \\ + 4 \\ \hline 9 \end{array}$

Score:

/60

Name:

time   :

1) 3
  + □
  ——
    8

2) □
  + 5
  ——
   10

3) 2
  + □
  ——
    3

4) □
  + 2
  ——
    4

5) 1
  + □
  ——
    6

6) □
  + 3
  ——
    8

7) 2
  + □
  ——
    7

8) □
  + 4
  ——
    4

9) 2
  + □
  ——
    4

10) □
   + 1
   ——
     1

11) 3
   + □
   ——
     8

12) □
   + 2
   ——
     2

13) 4
   + □
   ——
     7

14) □
   + 4
   ——
     7

15) 2
   + □
   ——
     7

16) □
   + 5
   ——
     9

17) 0
   + □
   ——
     1

18) □
   + 5
   ——
    10

19) 3
   + □
   ——
     3

20) □
   + 5
   ——
    10

21) 1
   + □
   ——
     4

22) □
   + 0
   ——
     5

23) 3
   + □
   ——
     7

24) □
   + 3
   ——
     4

25) 3
   + □
   ——
     7

26) □
   + 2
   ——
     2

27) 5
   + □
   ——
     7

28) □
   + 1
   ——
     4

29) 4
   + □
   ——
     6

30) □
   + 3
   ——
     6

31) 2
   + □
   ——
     2

32) □
   + 5
   ——
     8

33) 1
   + □
   ——
     5

34) □
   + 5
   ——
    10

35) 4
   + □
   ——
     6

36) □
   + 4
   ——
     4

37) 0
   + □
   ——
     3

38) □
   + 2
   ——
     5

39) 1
   + □
   ——
     6

40) □
   + 3
   ——
     8

41) 4
   + □
   ——
     4

42) □
   + 2
   ——
     4

43) 0
   + □
   ——
     5

44) □
   + 2
   ——
     5

45) 5
   + □
   ——
    10

46) □
   + 1
   ——
     4

47) 5
   + □
   ——
     6

48) □
   + 1
   ——
     5

49) 0
   + □
   ——
     5

50) □
   + 5
   ——
     9

51) 3
   + □
   ——
     4

52) □
   + 0
   ——
     4

53) 5
   + □
   ——
    10

54) □
   + 3
   ——
     8

55) 2
   + □
   ——
     7

56) □
   + 0
   ——
     5

57) 4
   + □
   ——
     9

58) □
   + 5
   ——
     6

59) 0
   + □
   ——
     2

60) □
   + 3
   ——
     3

Name: _____

Score:

/60

time   :

1)   1
   + 7

2)   6
   + 3

3)   0
   + 4

4)   5
   + 0

5)   1
   + 7

6)   0
   + 2

7)   3
   + 0

8)   0
   + 0

9)   7
   + 0

10)   3
    + 3

11)   6
    + 1

12)   6
    + 6

13)   2
    + 2

14)   4
    + 1

15)   1
    + 2

16)   2
    + 2

17)   2
    + 7

18)   7
    + 3

19)   4
    + 3

20)   5
    + 1

21)   0
    + 3

22)   7
    + 5

23)   1
    + 2

24)   0
    + 0

25)   4
    + 1

26)   6
    + 7

27)   5
    + 5

28)   5
    + 7

29)   7
    + 7

30)   0
    + 3

31)   4
    + 6

32)   0
    + 4

33)   5
    + 0

34)   3
    + 1

35)   0
    + 0

36)   1
    + 5

37)   4
    + 5

38)   5
    + 7

39)   7
    + 5

40)   3
    + 0

41)   3
    + 2

42)   3
    + 0

43)   0
    + 5

44)   4
    + 0

45)   7
    + 6

46)   0
    + 3

47)   4
    + 6

48)   2
    + 2

49)   7
    + 0

50)   1
    + 4

51)   0
    + 2

52)   1
    + 5

53)   4
    + 0

54)   2
    + 0

55)   3
    + 7

56)   3
    + 1

57)   2
    + 3

58)   5
    + 5

59)   3
    + 4

60)   1
    + 6

Name:

Score:

160

Time   :

1)   0
   + 0

2)   6
   + 5

3)   6
   + 0

4)   1
   + 6

5)   6
   + 6

6)   0
   + 6

7)   4
   + 2

8)   7
   + 1

9)   3
   + 7

10)   6
   + 1

11)   7
   + 3

12)   7
   + 1

13)   6
   + 5

14)   0
   + 2

15)   3
   + 6

16)   1
   + 4

17)   3
   + 2

18)   5
   + 4

19)   6
   + 4

20)   0
   + 5

21)   7
   + 7

22)   5
   + 6

23)   4
   + 4

24)   5
   + 6

25)   2
   + 6

26)   7
   + 5

27)   3
   + 3

28)   5
   + 1

29)   0
   + 4

30)   4
   + 2

31)   0
   + 3

32)   7
   + 1

33)   1
   + 7

34)   3
   + 3

35)   5
   + 5

36)   4
   + 3

37)   2
   + 4

38)   2
   + 0

39)   2
   + 4

40)   2
   + 2

41)   4
   + 5

42)   0
   + 2

43)   7
   + 3

44)   1
   + 2

45)   2
   + 5

46)   4
   + 0

47)   4
   + 0

48)   0
   + 6

49)   2
   + 6

50)   7
   + 3

51)   7
   + 1

52)   7
   + 4

53)   1
   + 0

54)   4
   + 4

55)   4
   + 4

56)   3
   + 7

57)   6
   + 1

58)   6
   + 4

59)   3
   + 4

60)   5
   + 0

Name:

Score: /60

Time   :

1)
$$\begin{array}{r} 1 \\ + 4 \\ \hline \end{array}$$

2)
$$\begin{array}{r} 3 \\ + 3 \\ \hline \end{array}$$

3)
$$\begin{array}{r} 1 \\ + 5 \\ \hline \end{array}$$

4)
$$\begin{array}{r} 1 \\ + 2 \\ \hline \end{array}$$

5)
$$\begin{array}{r} 4 \\ + 7 \\ \hline \end{array}$$

6)
$$\begin{array}{r} 4 \\ + 0 \\ \hline \end{array}$$

7)
$$\begin{array}{r} 4 \\ + 2 \\ \hline \end{array}$$

8)
$$\begin{array}{r} 7 \\ + 6 \\ \hline \end{array}$$

9)
$$\begin{array}{r} 6 \\ + 1 \\ \hline \end{array}$$

10)
$$\begin{array}{r} 0 \\ + 3 \\ \hline \end{array}$$

11)
$$\begin{array}{r} 7 \\ + 6 \\ \hline \end{array}$$

12)
$$\begin{array}{r} 6 \\ + 6 \\ \hline \end{array}$$

13)
$$\begin{array}{r} 0 \\ + 5 \\ \hline \end{array}$$

14)
$$\begin{array}{r} 0 \\ + 5 \\ \hline \end{array}$$

15)
$$\begin{array}{r} 0 \\ + 0 \\ \hline \end{array}$$

16)
$$\begin{array}{r} 1 \\ + 5 \\ \hline \end{array}$$

17)
$$\begin{array}{r} 5 \\ + 4 \\ \hline \end{array}$$

18)
$$\begin{array}{r} 7 \\ + 0 \\ \hline \end{array}$$

19)
$$\begin{array}{r} 4 \\ + 2 \\ \hline \end{array}$$

20)
$$\begin{array}{r} 0 \\ + 0 \\ \hline \end{array}$$

21)
$$\begin{array}{r} 6 \\ + 2 \\ \hline \end{array}$$

22)
$$\begin{array}{r} 6 \\ + 4 \\ \hline \end{array}$$

23)
$$\begin{array}{r} 5 \\ + 6 \\ \hline \end{array}$$

24)
$$\begin{array}{r} 4 \\ + 1 \\ \hline \end{array}$$

25)
$$\begin{array}{r} 6 \\ + 4 \\ \hline \end{array}$$

26)
$$\begin{array}{r} 2 \\ + 5 \\ \hline \end{array}$$

27)
$$\begin{array}{r} 2 \\ + 5 \\ \hline \end{array}$$

28)
$$\begin{array}{r} 2 \\ + 6 \\ \hline \end{array}$$

29)
$$\begin{array}{r} 1 \\ + 0 \\ \hline \end{array}$$

30)
$$\begin{array}{r} 0 \\ + 4 \\ \hline \end{array}$$

31)
$$\begin{array}{r} 5 \\ + 7 \\ \hline \end{array}$$

32)
$$\begin{array}{r} 7 \\ + 0 \\ \hline \end{array}$$

33)
$$\begin{array}{r} 2 \\ + 4 \\ \hline \end{array}$$

34)
$$\begin{array}{r} 5 \\ + 2 \\ \hline \end{array}$$

35)
$$\begin{array}{r} 7 \\ + 1 \\ \hline \end{array}$$

36)
$$\begin{array}{r} 0 \\ + 6 \\ \hline \end{array}$$

37)
$$\begin{array}{r} 6 \\ + 7 \\ \hline \end{array}$$

38)
$$\begin{array}{r} 2 \\ + 5 \\ \hline \end{array}$$

39)
$$\begin{array}{r} 3 \\ + 2 \\ \hline \end{array}$$

40)
$$\begin{array}{r} 6 \\ + 0 \\ \hline \end{array}$$

41)
$$\begin{array}{r} 7 \\ + 1 \\ \hline \end{array}$$

42)
$$\begin{array}{r} 2 \\ + 5 \\ \hline \end{array}$$

43)
$$\begin{array}{r} 0 \\ + 3 \\ \hline \end{array}$$

44)
$$\begin{array}{r} 2 \\ + 5 \\ \hline \end{array}$$

45)
$$\begin{array}{r} 7 \\ + 4 \\ \hline \end{array}$$

46)
$$\begin{array}{r} 7 \\ + 5 \\ \hline \end{array}$$

47)
$$\begin{array}{r} 4 \\ + 1 \\ \hline \end{array}$$

48)
$$\begin{array}{r} 0 \\ + 2 \\ \hline \end{array}$$

49)
$$\begin{array}{r} 5 \\ + 7 \\ \hline \end{array}$$

50)
$$\begin{array}{r} 6 \\ + 1 \\ \hline \end{array}$$

51)
$$\begin{array}{r} 1 \\ + 5 \\ \hline \end{array}$$

52)
$$\begin{array}{r} 3 \\ + 1 \\ \hline \end{array}$$

53)
$$\begin{array}{r} 2 \\ + 6 \\ \hline \end{array}$$

54)
$$\begin{array}{r} 3 \\ + 3 \\ \hline \end{array}$$

55)
$$\begin{array}{r} 3 \\ + 0 \\ \hline \end{array}$$

56)
$$\begin{array}{r} 2 \\ + 3 \\ \hline \end{array}$$

57)
$$\begin{array}{r} 1 \\ + 6 \\ \hline \end{array}$$

58)
$$\begin{array}{r} 3 \\ + 4 \\ \hline \end{array}$$

59)
$$\begin{array}{r} 3 \\ + 6 \\ \hline \end{array}$$

60)
$$\begin{array}{r} 0 \\ + 6 \\ \hline \end{array}$$

Name:

Score:

/60

time   :

1)
$$\begin{array}{r} 0 \\ + 6 \\ \hline \end{array}$$

2)
$$\begin{array}{r} 7 \\ + 5 \\ \hline \end{array}$$

3)
$$\begin{array}{r} 7 \\ + 3 \\ \hline \end{array}$$

4)
$$\begin{array}{r} 4 \\ + 1 \\ \hline \end{array}$$

5)
$$\begin{array}{r} 4 \\ + 2 \\ \hline \end{array}$$

6)
$$\begin{array}{r} 3 \\ + 0 \\ \hline \end{array}$$

7)
$$\begin{array}{r} 2 \\ + 7 \\ \hline \end{array}$$

8)
$$\begin{array}{r} 2 \\ + 1 \\ \hline \end{array}$$

9)
$$\begin{array}{r} 3 \\ + 0 \\ \hline \end{array}$$

10)
$$\begin{array}{r} 0 \\ + 1 \\ \hline \end{array}$$

11)
$$\begin{array}{r} 4 \\ + 6 \\ \hline \end{array}$$

12)
$$\begin{array}{r} 0 \\ + 5 \\ \hline \end{array}$$

13)
$$\begin{array}{r} 2 \\ + 3 \\ \hline \end{array}$$

14)
$$\begin{array}{r} 4 \\ + 4 \\ \hline \end{array}$$

15)
$$\begin{array}{r} 2 \\ + 7 \\ \hline \end{array}$$

16)
$$\begin{array}{r} 7 \\ + 2 \\ \hline \end{array}$$

17)
$$\begin{array}{r} 4 \\ + 3 \\ \hline \end{array}$$

18)
$$\begin{array}{r} 1 \\ + 4 \\ \hline \end{array}$$

19)
$$\begin{array}{r} 2 \\ + 3 \\ \hline \end{array}$$

20)
$$\begin{array}{r} 6 \\ + 6 \\ \hline \end{array}$$

21)
$$\begin{array}{r} 5 \\ + 6 \\ \hline \end{array}$$

22)
$$\begin{array}{r} 1 \\ + 2 \\ \hline \end{array}$$

23)
$$\begin{array}{r} 2 \\ + 6 \\ \hline \end{array}$$

24)
$$\begin{array}{r} 6 \\ + 1 \\ \hline \end{array}$$

25)
$$\begin{array}{r} 6 \\ + 3 \\ \hline \end{array}$$

26)
$$\begin{array}{r} 1 \\ + 0 \\ \hline \end{array}$$

27)
$$\begin{array}{r} 3 \\ + 1 \\ \hline \end{array}$$

28)
$$\begin{array}{r} 1 \\ + 7 \\ \hline \end{array}$$

29)
$$\begin{array}{r} 0 \\ + 0 \\ \hline \end{array}$$

30)
$$\begin{array}{r} 7 \\ + 3 \\ \hline \end{array}$$

31)
$$\begin{array}{r} 3 \\ + 6 \\ \hline \end{array}$$

32)
$$\begin{array}{r} 4 \\ + 5 \\ \hline \end{array}$$

33)
$$\begin{array}{r} 1 \\ + 5 \\ \hline \end{array}$$

34)
$$\begin{array}{r} 1 \\ + 0 \\ \hline \end{array}$$

35)
$$\begin{array}{r} 2 \\ + 1 \\ \hline \end{array}$$

36)
$$\begin{array}{r} 0 \\ + 7 \\ \hline \end{array}$$

37)
$$\begin{array}{r} 5 \\ + 0 \\ \hline \end{array}$$

38)
$$\begin{array}{r} 1 \\ + 5 \\ \hline \end{array}$$

39)
$$\begin{array}{r} 2 \\ + 0 \\ \hline \end{array}$$

40)
$$\begin{array}{r} 3 \\ + 0 \\ \hline \end{array}$$

41)
$$\begin{array}{r} 2 \\ + 3 \\ \hline \end{array}$$

42)
$$\begin{array}{r} 1 \\ + 7 \\ \hline \end{array}$$

43)
$$\begin{array}{r} 4 \\ + 5 \\ \hline \end{array}$$

44)
$$\begin{array}{r} 2 \\ + 4 \\ \hline \end{array}$$

45)
$$\begin{array}{r} 6 \\ + 7 \\ \hline \end{array}$$

46)
$$\begin{array}{r} 6 \\ + 2 \\ \hline \end{array}$$

47)
$$\begin{array}{r} 1 \\ + 1 \\ \hline \end{array}$$

48)
$$\begin{array}{r} 3 \\ + 5 \\ \hline \end{array}$$

49)
$$\begin{array}{r} 2 \\ + 2 \\ \hline \end{array}$$

50)
$$\begin{array}{r} 0 \\ + 3 \\ \hline \end{array}$$

51)
$$\begin{array}{r} 7 \\ + 7 \\ \hline \end{array}$$

52)
$$\begin{array}{r} 6 \\ + 6 \\ \hline \end{array}$$

53)
$$\begin{array}{r} 4 \\ + 5 \\ \hline \end{array}$$

54)
$$\begin{array}{r} 3 \\ + 1 \\ \hline \end{array}$$

55)
$$\begin{array}{r} 2 \\ + 2 \\ \hline \end{array}$$

56)
$$\begin{array}{r} 6 \\ + 5 \\ \hline \end{array}$$

57)
$$\begin{array}{r} 0 \\ + 0 \\ \hline \end{array}$$

58)
$$\begin{array}{r} 3 \\ + 7 \\ \hline \end{array}$$

59)
$$\begin{array}{r} 4 \\ + 5 \\ \hline \end{array}$$

60)
$$\begin{array}{r} 3 \\ + 1 \\ \hline \end{array}$$

Name:

Score:

/60

time   :

1)   7
   + 4

2)   7
   + 4

3)   3
   + 6

4)   4
   + 7

5)   2
   + 6

6)   5
   + 4

7)   4
   + 5

8)   2
   + 2

9)   2
   + 2

10)   6
    + 3

11)   1
    + 4

12)   3
    + 6

13)   4
    + 0

14)   2
    + 7

15)   4
    + 3

16)   2
    + 5

17)   5
    + 0

18)   7
    + 7

19)   3
    + 4

20)   0
    + 3

21)   5
    + 1

22)   3
    + 2

23)   3
    + 2

24)   3
    + 4

25)   7
    + 2

26)   4
    + 6

27)   5
    + 0

28)   3
    + 5

29)   4
    + 0

30)   7
    + 3

31)   1
    + 0

32)   3
    + 2

33)   1
    + 1

34)   7
    + 0

35)   1
    + 6

36)   7
    + 5

37)   4
    + 7

38)   0
    + 0

39)   5
    + 2

40)   1
    + 7

41)   7
    + 2

42)   3
    + 5

43)   1
    + 1

44)   1
    + 3

45)   5
    + 0

46)   3
    + 5

47)   3
    + 3

48)   0
    + 3

49)   6
    + 4

50)   3
    + 2

51)   3
    + 6

52)   1
    + 3

53)   2
    + 4

54)   3
    + 7

55)   0
    + 3

56)   7
    + 7

57)   2
    + 7

58)   0
    + 4

59)   4
    + 7

60)   5
    + 0

Score:

/60

Name:

time   :

1)   1
   + 4

2)   1
   + 7

3)   2
   + 6

4)   4
   + 7

5)   4
   + 2

6)   0
   + 5

7)   3
   + 1

8)   5
   + 1

9)   0
   + 6

10)   0
    + 2

11)   6
    + 0

12)   7
    + 2

13)   0
    + 6

14)   6
    + 7

15)   4
    + 0

16)   6
    + 3

17)   7
    + 3

18)   1
    + 6

19)   5
    + 3

20)   2
    + 6

21)   5
    + 2

22)   0
    + 3

23)   4
    + 1

24)   3
    + 3

25)   2
    + 0

26)   7
    + 4

27)   3
    + 2

28)   0
    + 7

29)   1
    + 1

30)   3
    + 3

31)   7
    + 7

32)   1
    + 6

33)   5
    + 6

34)   2
    + 6

35)   4
    + 7

36)   7
    + 0

37)   2
    + 1

38)   6
    + 0

39)   7
    + 4

40)   6
    + 2

41)   7
    + 4

42)   4
    + 4

43)   3
    + 7

44)   3
    + 6

45)   1
    + 5

46)   7
    + 2

47)   2
    + 7

48)   5
    + 7

49)   2
    + 7

50)   0
    + 3

51)   5
    + 0

52)   4
    + 0

53)   4
    + 2

54)   2
    + 6

55)   6
    + 6

56)   3
    + 3

57)   6
    + 0

58)   7
    + 5

59)   1
    + 6

60)   5
    + 7

Name:

Score:

/60

Time   :

1)
```
   1
 + 6
```

2)
```
   1
 + 1
```

3)
```
   0
 + 4
```

4)
```
   2
 + 6
```

5)
```
   2
 + 6
```

6)
```
   2
 + 1
```

7)
```
   0
 + 4
```

8)
```
   0
 + 4
```

9)
```
   2
 + 2
```

10)
```
   5
 + 3
```

11)
```
   3
 + 6
```

12)
```
   7
 + 0
```

13)
```
   1
 + 6
```

14)
```
   5
 + 3
```

15)
```
   0
 + 3
```

16)
```
   0
 + 4
```

17)
```
   7
 + 7
```

18)
```
   0
 + 1
```

19)
```
   3
 + 0
```

20)
```
   1
 + 5
```

21)
```
   0
 + 1
```

22)
```
   7
 + 3
```

23)
```
   7
 + 0
```

24)
```
   6
 + 2
```

25)
```
   5
 + 1
```

26)
```
   5
 + 2
```

27)
```
   7
 + 6
```

28)
```
   7
 + 0
```

29)
```
   4
 + 3
```

30)
```
   4
 + 2
```

31)
```
   7
 + 7
```

32)
```
   1
 + 7
```

33)
```
   6
 + 2
```

34)
```
   7
 + 0
```

35)
```
   0
 + 4
```

36)
```
   7
 + 2
```

37)
```
   2
 + 1
```

38)
```
   7
 + 5
```

39)
```
   5
 + 7
```

40)
```
   7
 + 0
```

41)
```
   4
 + 4
```

42)
```
   2
 + 5
```

43)
```
   1
 + 0
```

44)
```
   5
 + 2
```

45)
```
   0
 + 1
```

46)
```
   5
 + 1
```

47)
```
   3
 + 5
```

48)
```
   0
 + 5
```

49)
```
   5
 + 4
```

50)
```
   6
 + 5
```

51)
```
   0
 + 5
```

52)
```
   4
 + 4
```

53)
```
   4
 + 6
```

54)
```
   7
 + 1
```

55)
```
   5
 + 3
```

56)
```
   3
 + 0
```

57)
```
   5
 + 7
```

58)
```
   2
 + 6
```

59)
```
   0
 + 6
```

60)
```
   0
 + 4
```

Name:

Score:

/60

time   :

1)   5
   + 3

2)   1
   + 4

3)   6
   + 3

4)   2
   + 3

5)   3
   + 1

6)   7
   + 3

7)   1
   + 1

8)   3
   + 5

9)   2
   + 6

10)   2
   + 7

11)   2
   + 4

12)   0
   + 6

13)   6
   + 3

14)   3
   + 7

15)   2
   + 2

16)   5
   + 6

17)   3
   + 5

18)   0
   + 6

19)   3
   + 6

20)   4
   + 5

21)   6
   + 4

22)   7
   + 7

23)   0
   + 0

24)   1
   + 7

25)   4
   + 4

26)   1
   + 6

27)   2
   + 6

28)   5
   + 2

29)   5
   + 1

30)   7
   + 3

31)   2
   + 4

32)   5
   + 3

33)   1
   + 3

34)   6
   + 7

35)   5
   + 6

36)   3
   + 6

37)   1
   + 3

38)   5
   + 2

39)   0
   + 1

40)   2
   + 7

41)   7
   + 7

42)   0
   + 5

43)   3
   + 7

44)   5
   + 5

45)   0
   + 6

46)   4
   + 1

47)   1
   + 2

48)   1
   + 6

49)   4
   + 3

50)   2
   + 0

51)   3
   + 5

52)   4
   + 4

53)   0
   + 0

54)   3
   + 7

55)   2
   + 0

56)   5
   + 7

57)   5
   + 4

58)   3
   + 4

59)   5
   + 4

60)   5
   + 1

Score:

/60

time   :

Name:

1) 7 + 1

2) 6 + 4

3) 4 + 4

4) 5 + 7

5) 3 + 5

6) 3 + 3

7) 6 + 5

8) 4 + 3

9) 6 + 5

10) 3 + 5

11) 2 + 6

12) 5 + 1

13) 7 + 1

14) 4 + 5

15) 1 + 4

16) 6 + 4

17) 4 + 4

18) 4 + 4

19) 7 + 2

20) 5 + 1

21) 7 + 6

22) 1 + 3

23) 3 + 1

24) 5 + 7

25) 4 + 5

26) 4 + 1

27) 2 + 0

28) 2 + 4

29) 5 + 4

30) 2 + 0

31) 3 + 5

32) 7 + 7

33) 7 + 0

34) 7 + 7

35) 3 + 5

36) 0 + 6

37) 1 + 0

38) 3 + 6

39) 4 + 7

40) 1 + 6

41) 0 + 7

42) 7 + 6

43) 5 + 0

44) 4 + 5

45) 1 + 6

46) 5 + 3

47) 1 + 6

48) 2 + 1

49) 6 + 7

50) 0 + 5

51) 3 + 7

52) 3 + 0

53) 1 + 5

54) 4 + 4

55) 7 + 5

56) 1 + 4

57) 5 + 7

58) 4 + 0

59) 3 + 5

60) 6 + 2

Name:

Score:

/60

time   :

1)   4
     + 7

2)   6
     + 7

3)   4
     + 5

4)   4
     + 1

5)   7
     + 7

6)   5
     + 5

7)   1
     + 1

8)   4
     + 1

9)   7
     + 7

10)   3
     + 5

11)   1
     + 3

12)   5
     + 3

13)   5
     + 5

14)   6
     + 7

15)   2
     + 5

16)   1
     + 3

17)   0
     + 6

18)   7
     + 1

19)   1
     + 0

20)   1
     + 6

21)   4
     + 5

22)   6
     + 5

23)   4
     + 5

24)   2
     + 7

25)   1
     + 3

26)   1
     + 2

27)   4
     + 2

28)   0
     + 0

29)   0
     + 1

30)   0
     + 5

31)   5
     + 0

32)   1
     + 6

33)   5
     + 7

34)   4
     + 4

35)   4
     + 4

36)   6
     + 3

37)   4
     + 7

38)   3
     + 1

39)   3
     + 5

40)   7
     + 5

41)   1
     + 7

42)   6
     + 2

43)   0
     + 5

44)   6
     + 5

45)   5
     + 6

46)   5
     + 6

47)   0
     + 1

48)   5
     + 3

49)   5
     + 3

50)   0
     + 0

51)   4
     + 0

52)   6
     + 5

53)   3
     + 6

54)   6
     + 1

55)   3
     + 1

56)   4
     + 4

57)   2
     + 4

58)   7
     + 3

59)   4
     + 1

60)   4
     + 6

Score: /60

Name:

time :

1) $5 + \square = 11$

2) $\square + 5 = 7$

3) $5 + \square = 5$

4) $\square + 7 = 11$

5) $6 + \square = 9$

6) $\square + 4 = 5$

7) $0 + \square = 4$

8) $\square + 6 = 8$

9) $6 + \square = 10$

10) $\square + 2 = 2$

11) $1 + \square = 8$

12) $\square + 1 = 5$

13) $1 + \square = 7$

14) $\square + 3 = 8$

15) $4 + \square = 8$

16) $\square + 7 = 13$

17) $7 + \square = 7$

18) $\square + 7 = 7$

19) $6 + \square = 6$

20) $\square + 7 = 8$

21) $7 + \square = 8$

22) $\square + 5 = 6$

23) $0 + \square = 7$

24) $\square + 6 = 7$

25) $7 + \square = 10$

26) $\square + 2 = 8$

27) $1 + \square = 2$

28) $\square + 6 = 12$

29) $2 + \square = 6$

30) $\square + 7 = 12$

31) $0 + \square = 3$

32) $\square + 2 = 4$

33) $3 + \square = 6$

34) $\square + 4 = 11$

35) $4 + \square = 10$

36) $\square + 2 = 4$

37) $0 + \square = 1$

38) $\square + 7 = 14$

39) $5 + \square = 5$

40) $\square + 1 = 2$

41) $3 + \square = 3$

42) $\square + 1 = 7$

43) $1 + \square = 1$

44) $\square + 4 = 9$

45) $5 + \square = 10$

46) $\square + 7 = 13$

47) $5 + \square = 5$

48) $\square + 1 = 6$

49) $7 + \square = 8$

50) $\square + 6 = 13$

51) $7 + \square = 14$

52) $\square + 6 = 6$

53) $1 + \square = 1$

54) $\square + 4 = 9$

55) $7 + \square = 13$

56) $\square + 7 = 13$

57) $0 + \square = 7$

58) $\square + 7 = 7$

59) $0 + \square = 3$

60) $\square + 1 = 5$

Score:

/60

Name:

time   :

1) 1
  + ☐
    2

2) ☐
  + 7
    9

3) 7
  + ☐
   14

4) ☐
  + 2
    5

5) 3
  + ☐
    3

6) ☐
  + 4
    8

7) 3
  + ☐
    7

8) ☐
  + 0
    6

9) 2
  + ☐
    4

10) ☐
   + 0
     6

11) 6
   + ☐
     6

12) ☐
   + 7
    11

13) 7
   + ☐
    14

14) ☐
   + 1
     7

15) 3
   + ☐
     8

16) ☐
   + 7
     8

17) 4
   + ☐
    10

18) ☐
   + 2
     8

19) 2
   + ☐
     4

20) ☐
   + 7
     8

21) 4
   + ☐
     8

22) ☐
   + 5
    12

23) 7
   + ☐
     9

24) ☐
   + 7
    11

25) 7
   + ☐
    13

26) ☐
   + 4
     8

27) 4
   + ☐
    10

28) ☐
   + 2
     2

29) 4
   + ☐
     9

30) ☐
   + 0
     5

31) 5
   + ☐
     9

32) ☐
   + 2
     2

33) 2
   + ☐
     4

34) ☐
   + 5
     5

35) 5
   + ☐
     9

36) ☐
   + 0
     7

37) 1
   + ☐
     5

38) ☐
   + 2
     3

39) 6
   + ☐
     6

40) ☐
   + 3
     8

41) 6
   + ☐
     9

42) ☐
   + 1
     8

43) 6
   + ☐
    13

44) ☐
   + 7
    12

45) 4
   + ☐
     5

46) ☐
   + 5
     6

47) 5
   + ☐
     8

48) ☐
   + 7
     8

49) 7
   + ☐
    11

50) ☐
   + 1
     2

51) 7
   + ☐
    10

52) ☐
   + 6
    13

53) 4
   + ☐
     8

54) ☐
   + 1
     3

55) 0
   + ☐
     6

56) ☐
   + 2
     6

57) 1
   + ☐
     7

58) ☐
   + 5
     7

59) 1
   + ☐
     1

60) ☐
   + 7
     7

Page 32

Score: /60

Name:

Time   :

1) $\begin{array}{r} 4 \\ + \square \\ \hline 9 \end{array}$

2) $\begin{array}{r} \square \\ + 7 \\ \hline 10 \end{array}$

3) $\begin{array}{r} 5 \\ + \square \\ \hline 11 \end{array}$

4) $\begin{array}{r} \square \\ + 3 \\ \hline 8 \end{array}$

5) $\begin{array}{r} 1 \\ + \square \\ \hline 7 \end{array}$

6) $\begin{array}{r} \square \\ + 0 \\ \hline 4 \end{array}$

7) $\begin{array}{r} 1 \\ + \square \\ \hline 4 \end{array}$

8) $\begin{array}{r} \square \\ + 5 \\ \hline 7 \end{array}$

9) $\begin{array}{r} 2 \\ + \square \\ \hline 3 \end{array}$

10) $\begin{array}{r} \square \\ + 4 \\ \hline 7 \end{array}$

11) $\begin{array}{r} 7 \\ + \square \\ \hline 14 \end{array}$

12) $\begin{array}{r} \square \\ + 4 \\ \hline 9 \end{array}$

13) $\begin{array}{r} 2 \\ + \square \\ \hline 3 \end{array}$

14) $\begin{array}{r} \square \\ + 0 \\ \hline 2 \end{array}$

15) $\begin{array}{r} 4 \\ + \square \\ \hline 6 \end{array}$

16) $\begin{array}{r} \square \\ + 3 \\ \hline 3 \end{array}$

17) $\begin{array}{r} 0 \\ + \square \\ \hline 0 \end{array}$

18) $\begin{array}{r} \square \\ + 3 \\ \hline 10 \end{array}$

19) $\begin{array}{r} 7 \\ + \square \\ \hline 7 \end{array}$

20) $\begin{array}{r} \square \\ + 0 \\ \hline 5 \end{array}$

21) $\begin{array}{r} 6 \\ + \square \\ \hline 9 \end{array}$

22) $\begin{array}{r} \square \\ + 1 \\ \hline 3 \end{array}$

23) $\begin{array}{r} 7 \\ + \square \\ \hline 10 \end{array}$

24) $\begin{array}{r} \square \\ + 7 \\ \hline 13 \end{array}$

25) $\begin{array}{r} 0 \\ + \square \\ \hline 1 \end{array}$

26) $\begin{array}{r} \square \\ + 3 \\ \hline 5 \end{array}$

27) $\begin{array}{r} 3 \\ + \square \\ \hline 10 \end{array}$

28) $\begin{array}{r} \square \\ + 1 \\ \hline 1 \end{array}$

29) $\begin{array}{r} 4 \\ + \square \\ \hline 4 \end{array}$

30) $\begin{array}{r} \square \\ + 4 \\ \hline 11 \end{array}$

31) $\begin{array}{r} 2 \\ + \square \\ \hline 6 \end{array}$

32) $\begin{array}{r} \square \\ + 1 \\ \hline 8 \end{array}$

33) $\begin{array}{r} 0 \\ + \square \\ \hline 5 \end{array}$

34) $\begin{array}{r} \square \\ + 4 \\ \hline 4 \end{array}$

35) $\begin{array}{r} 6 \\ + \square \\ \hline 9 \end{array}$

36) $\begin{array}{r} \square \\ + 1 \\ \hline 5 \end{array}$

37) $\begin{array}{r} 4 \\ + \square \\ \hline 4 \end{array}$

38) $\begin{array}{r} \square \\ + 1 \\ \hline 5 \end{array}$

39) $\begin{array}{r} 4 \\ + \square \\ \hline 9 \end{array}$

40) $\begin{array}{r} \square \\ + 0 \\ \hline 5 \end{array}$

41) $\begin{array}{r} 5 \\ + \square \\ \hline 6 \end{array}$

42) $\begin{array}{r} \square \\ + 3 \\ \hline 7 \end{array}$

43) $\begin{array}{r} 7 \\ + \square \\ \hline 7 \end{array}$

44) $\begin{array}{r} \square \\ + 7 \\ \hline 7 \end{array}$

45) $\begin{array}{r} 6 \\ + \square \\ \hline 10 \end{array}$

46) $\begin{array}{r} \square \\ + 1 \\ \hline 6 \end{array}$

47) $\begin{array}{r} 1 \\ + \square \\ \hline 4 \end{array}$

48) $\begin{array}{r} \square \\ + 4 \\ \hline 9 \end{array}$

49) $\begin{array}{r} 0 \\ + \square \\ \hline 3 \end{array}$

50) $\begin{array}{r} \square \\ + 0 \\ \hline 4 \end{array}$

51) $\begin{array}{r} 6 \\ + \square \\ \hline 11 \end{array}$

52) $\begin{array}{r} \square \\ + 7 \\ \hline 13 \end{array}$

53) $\begin{array}{r} 1 \\ + \square \\ \hline 6 \end{array}$

54) $\begin{array}{r} \square \\ + 7 \\ \hline 7 \end{array}$

55) $\begin{array}{r} 1 \\ + \square \\ \hline 5 \end{array}$

56) $\begin{array}{r} \square \\ + 5 \\ \hline 5 \end{array}$

57) $\begin{array}{r} 4 \\ + \square \\ \hline 4 \end{array}$

58) $\begin{array}{r} \square \\ + 3 \\ \hline 8 \end{array}$

59) $\begin{array}{r} 0 \\ + \square \\ \hline 6 \end{array}$

60) $\begin{array}{r} \square \\ + 4 \\ \hline 8 \end{array}$

Page 33

Score:

/60

Name:

Time   :

1)
$$\begin{array}{r} 1 \\ + \square \\ \hline 2 \end{array}$$

2)
$$\begin{array}{r} \square \\ + 1 \\ \hline 2 \end{array}$$

3)
$$\begin{array}{r} 2 \\ + \square \\ \hline 6 \end{array}$$

4)
$$\begin{array}{r} \square \\ + 1 \\ \hline 2 \end{array}$$

5)
$$\begin{array}{r} 7 \\ + \square \\ \hline 12 \end{array}$$

6)
$$\begin{array}{r} \square \\ + 5 \\ \hline 5 \end{array}$$

7)
$$\begin{array}{r} 4 \\ + \square \\ \hline 4 \end{array}$$

8)
$$\begin{array}{r} \square \\ + 0 \\ \hline 7 \end{array}$$

9)
$$\begin{array}{r} 0 \\ + \square \\ \hline 0 \end{array}$$

10)
$$\begin{array}{r} \square \\ + 1 \\ \hline 5 \end{array}$$

11)
$$\begin{array}{r} 4 \\ + \square \\ \hline 4 \end{array}$$

12)
$$\begin{array}{r} \square \\ + 2 \\ \hline 7 \end{array}$$

13)
$$\begin{array}{r} 6 \\ + \square \\ \hline 13 \end{array}$$

14)
$$\begin{array}{r} \square \\ + 4 \\ \hline 11 \end{array}$$

15)
$$\begin{array}{r} 3 \\ + \square \\ \hline 8 \end{array}$$

16)
$$\begin{array}{r} \square \\ + 4 \\ \hline 5 \end{array}$$

17)
$$\begin{array}{r} 0 \\ + \square \\ \hline 0 \end{array}$$

18)
$$\begin{array}{r} \square \\ + 7 \\ \hline 13 \end{array}$$

19)
$$\begin{array}{r} 6 \\ + \square \\ \hline 13 \end{array}$$

20)
$$\begin{array}{r} \square \\ + 2 \\ \hline 8 \end{array}$$

21)
$$\begin{array}{r} 6 \\ + \square \\ \hline 12 \end{array}$$

22)
$$\begin{array}{r} \square \\ + 2 \\ \hline 5 \end{array}$$

23)
$$\begin{array}{r} 4 \\ + \square \\ \hline 4 \end{array}$$

24)
$$\begin{array}{r} \square \\ + 7 \\ \hline 13 \end{array}$$

25)
$$\begin{array}{r} 6 \\ + \square \\ \hline 11 \end{array}$$

26)
$$\begin{array}{r} \square \\ + 7 \\ \hline 11 \end{array}$$

27)
$$\begin{array}{r} 1 \\ + \square \\ \hline 8 \end{array}$$

28)
$$\begin{array}{r} \square \\ + 5 \\ \hline 6 \end{array}$$

29)
$$\begin{array}{r} 0 \\ + \square \\ \hline 1 \end{array}$$

30)
$$\begin{array}{r} \square \\ + 4 \\ \hline 9 \end{array}$$

31)
$$\begin{array}{r} 7 \\ + \square \\ \hline 14 \end{array}$$

32)
$$\begin{array}{r} \square \\ + 7 \\ \hline 9 \end{array}$$

33)
$$\begin{array}{r} 5 \\ + \square \\ \hline 11 \end{array}$$

34)
$$\begin{array}{r} \square \\ + 4 \\ \hline 10 \end{array}$$

35)
$$\begin{array}{r} 0 \\ + \square \\ \hline 3 \end{array}$$

36)
$$\begin{array}{r} \square \\ + 2 \\ \hline 2 \end{array}$$

37)
$$\begin{array}{r} 2 \\ + \square \\ \hline 7 \end{array}$$

38)
$$\begin{array}{r} \square \\ + 0 \\ \hline 0 \end{array}$$

39)
$$\begin{array}{r} 0 \\ + \square \\ \hline 4 \end{array}$$

40)
$$\begin{array}{r} \square \\ + 7 \\ \hline 9 \end{array}$$

41)
$$\begin{array}{r} 7 \\ + \square \\ \hline 12 \end{array}$$

42)
$$\begin{array}{r} \square \\ + 0 \\ \hline 7 \end{array}$$

43)
$$\begin{array}{r} 0 \\ + \square \\ \hline 3 \end{array}$$

44)
$$\begin{array}{r} \square \\ + 4 \\ \hline 7 \end{array}$$

45)
$$\begin{array}{r} 0 \\ + \square \\ \hline 6 \end{array}$$

46)
$$\begin{array}{r} \square \\ + 0 \\ \hline 0 \end{array}$$

47)
$$\begin{array}{r} 1 \\ + \square \\ \hline 8 \end{array}$$

48)
$$\begin{array}{r} \square \\ + 0 \\ \hline 6 \end{array}$$

49)
$$\begin{array}{r} 4 \\ + \square \\ \hline 11 \end{array}$$

50)
$$\begin{array}{r} \square \\ + 1 \\ \hline 8 \end{array}$$

51)
$$\begin{array}{r} 4 \\ + \square \\ \hline 8 \end{array}$$

52)
$$\begin{array}{r} \square \\ + 3 \\ \hline 9 \end{array}$$

53)
$$\begin{array}{r} 4 \\ + \square \\ \hline 7 \end{array}$$

54)
$$\begin{array}{r} \square \\ + 6 \\ \hline 7 \end{array}$$

55)
$$\begin{array}{r} 1 \\ + \square \\ \hline 8 \end{array}$$

56)
$$\begin{array}{r} \square \\ + 6 \\ \hline 10 \end{array}$$

57)
$$\begin{array}{r} 2 \\ + \square \\ \hline 8 \end{array}$$

58)
$$\begin{array}{r} \square \\ + 7 \\ \hline 7 \end{array}$$

59)
$$\begin{array}{r} 6 \\ + \square \\ \hline 6 \end{array}$$

60)
$$\begin{array}{r} \square \\ + 1 \\ \hline 5 \end{array}$$

Score:

/60

Name:

time   :

1)
```
  1
+ ☐
───
  1
```

2)
```
  ☐
+ 5
───
 11
```

3)
```
  2
+ ☐
───
  6
```

4)
```
  ☐
+ 3
───
  5
```

5)
```
  7
+ ☐
───
 14
```

6)
```
  ☐
+ 6
───
  8
```

7)
```
  3
+ ☐
───
  3
```

8)
```
  ☐
+ 2
───
  4
```

9)
```
  6
+ ☐
───
 12
```

10)
```
  ☐
+ 2
───
  6
```

11)
```
  5
+ ☐
───
  6
```

12)
```
  ☐
+ 4
───
  8
```

13)
```
  3
+ ☐
───
  6
```

14)
```
  ☐
+ 4
───
  7
```

15)
```
  1
+ ☐
───
  3
```

16)
```
  ☐
+ 7
───
 11
```

17)
```
  2
+ ☐
───
  5
```

18)
```
  ☐
+ 0
───
  4
```

19)
```
  7
+ ☐
───
 10
```

20)
```
  ☐
+ 3
───
  6
```

21)
```
  2
+ ☐
───
  8
```

22)
```
  ☐
+ 4
───
  6
```

23)
```
  4
+ ☐
───
  7
```

24)
```
  ☐
+ 3
───
  3
```

25)
```
  7
+ ☐
───
 10
```

26)
```
  ☐
+ 5
───
 12
```

27)
```
  4
+ ☐
───
 10
```

28)
```
  ☐
+ 7
───
  7
```

29)
```
  4
+ ☐
───
  7
```

30)
```
  ☐
+ 6
───
  6
```

31)
```
  0
+ ☐
───
  3
```

32)
```
  ☐
+ 7
───
 10
```

33)
```
  3
+ ☐
───
  5
```

34)
```
  ☐
+ 4
───
  8
```

35)
```
  4
+ ☐
───
  7
```

36)
```
  ☐
+ 1
───
  2
```

37)
```
  2
+ ☐
───
  9
```

38)
```
  ☐
+ 4
───
 11
```

39)
```
  6
+ ☐
───
  8
```

40)
```
  ☐
+ 7
───
  8
```

41)
```
  7
+ ☐
───
  7
```

42)
```
  ☐
+ 4
───
 10
```

43)
```
  3
+ ☐
───
  9
```

44)
```
  ☐
+ 1
───
  7
```

45)
```
  3
+ ☐
───
  9
```

46)
```
  ☐
+ 2
───
  6
```

47)
```
  6
+ ☐
───
  8
```

48)
```
  ☐
+ 3
───
 10
```

49)
```
  1
+ ☐
───
  5
```

50)
```
  ☐
+ 1
───
  7
```

51)
```
  0
+ ☐
───
  0
```

52)
```
  ☐
+ 1
───
  5
```

53)
```
  1
+ ☐
───
  6
```

54)
```
  ☐
+ 1
───
  1
```

55)
```
  1
+ ☐
───
  5
```

56)
```
  ☐
+ 5
───
  6
```

57)
```
  3
+ ☐
───
 10
```

58)
```
  ☐
+ 5
───
  7
```

59)
```
  5
+ ☐
───
  6
```

60)
```
  ☐
+ 0
───
  0
```

Name:

Score:

/60

time   :

1)   3
   +☐
    10

2)   ☐
   + 7
    11

3)   0
   +☐
    3

4)   ☐
   + 4
    4

5)   6
   +☐
    6

6)   ☐
   + 3
    3

7)   5
   +☐
    12

8)   ☐
   + 0
    5

9)   6
   +☐
    10

10)   ☐
   + 7
    9

11)   7
   +☐
    14

12)   ☐
   + 4
    9

13)   5
   +☐
    8

14)   ☐
   + 6
    9

15)   2
   +☐
    6

16)   ☐
   + 5
    10

17)   4
   +☐
    10

18)   ☐
   + 0
    0

19)   0
   +☐
    5

20)   ☐
   + 5
    11

21)   7
   +☐
    9

22)   ☐
   + 5
    9

23)   1
   +☐
    7

24)   ☐
   + 0
    7

25)   4
   +☐
    9

26)   ☐
   + 1
    8

27)   5
   +☐
    11

28)   ☐
   + 5
    8

29)   6
   +☐
    13

30)   ☐
   + 5
    8

31)   4
   +☐
    7

32)   ☐
   + 7
    10

33)   5
   +☐
    8

34)   ☐
   + 6
    8

35)   6
   +☐
    9

36)   ☐
   + 4
    7

37)   0
   +☐
    4

38)   ☐
   + 6
    11

39)   2
   +☐
    8

40)   ☐
   + 7
    9

41)   3
   +☐
    8

42)   ☐
   + 6
    12

43)   3
   +☐
    4

44)   ☐
   + 3
    6

45)   0
   +☐
    5

46)   ☐
   + 2
    7

47)   5
   +☐
    12

48)   ☐
   + 7
    7

49)   0
   +☐
    7

50)   ☐
   + 5
    8

51)   2
   +☐
    9

52)   ☐
   + 1
    2

53)   7
   +☐
    9

54)   ☐
   + 6
    12

55)   2
   +☐
    4

56)   ☐
   + 3
    8

57)   4
   +☐
    11

58)   ☐
   + 3
    5

59)   1
   +☐
    3

60)   ☐
   + 6
    8

Score: /60

Name:

time   :

1) $5 + \square = 7$

2) $\square + 1 = 2$

3) $1 + \square = 7$

4) $\square + 2 = 9$

5) $7 + \square = 11$

6) $\square + 3 = 9$

7) $6 + \square = 7$

8) $\square + 4 = 10$

9) $6 + \square = 10$

10) $\square + 2 = 3$

11) $1 + \square = 4$

12) $\square + 4 = 11$

13) $5 + \square = 10$

14) $\square + 7 = 12$

15) $0 + \square = 2$

16) $\square + 4 = 10$

17) $1 + \square = 7$

18) $\square + 0 = 3$

19) $6 + \square = 10$

20) $\square + 3 = 3$

21) $0 + \square = 5$

22) $\square + 3 = 3$

23) $0 + \square = 3$

24) $\square + 5 = 6$

25) $2 + \square = 6$

26) $\square + 5 = 10$

27) $7 + \square = 13$

28) $\square + 0 = 5$

29) $4 + \square = 4$

30) $\square + 4 = 11$

31) $2 + \square = 8$

32) $\square + 3 = 10$

33) $1 + \square = 2$

34) $\square + 3 = 5$

35) $6 + \square = 9$

36) $\square + 1 = 2$

37) $1 + \square = 6$

38) $\square + 4 = 10$

39) $2 + \square = 3$

40) $\square + 0 = 3$

41) $3 + \square = 6$

42) $\square + 7 = 11$

43) $6 + \square = 7$

44) $\square + 0 = 6$

45) $3 + \square = 5$

46) $\square + 5 = 7$

47) $7 + \square = 12$

48) $\square + 6 = 11$

49) $1 + \square = 5$

50) $\square + 5 = 10$

51) $0 + \square = 6$

52) $\square + 3 = 7$

53) $4 + \square = 4$

54) $\square + 7 = 12$

55) $3 + \square = 9$

56) $\square + 2 = 8$

57) $0 + \square = 7$

58) $\square + 5 = 7$

59) $6 + \square = 13$

60) $\square + 3 = 6$

Page 37

Score: /60

Name:

time   :

1) 4 + □ = 10

2) □ + 0 = 1

3) 5 + □ = 5

4) □ + 0 = 1

5) 4 + □ = 10

6) □ + 0 = 5

7) 3 + □ = 8

8) □ + 6 = 13

9) 6 + □ = 9

10) □ + 0 = 6

11) 0 + □ = 6

12) □ + 2 = 7

13) 1 + □ = 1

14) □ + 6 = 8

15) 3 + □ = 8

16) □ + 6 = 7

17) 7 + □ = 11

18) □ + 1 = 3

19) 0 + □ = 1

20) □ + 4 = 8

21) 6 + □ = 7

22) □ + 3 = 8

23) 6 + □ = 12

24) □ + 7 = 14

25) 3 + □ = 9

26) □ + 2 = 7

27) 0 + □ = 4

28) □ + 6 = 12

29) 5 + □ = 5

30) □ + 6 = 13

31) 2 + □ = 3

32) □ + 4 = 7

33) 0 + □ = 7

34) □ + 2 = 6

35) 1 + □ = 4

36) □ + 5 = 7

37) 7 + □ = 8

38) □ + 0 = 0

39) 0 + □ = 6

40) □ + 4 = 10

41) 4 + □ = 11

42) □ + 7 = 14

43) 7 + □ = 10

44) □ + 6 = 7

45) 1 + □ = 7

46) □ + 1 = 1

47) 1 + □ = 7

48) □ + 4 = 5

49) 5 + □ = 5

50) □ + 1 = 5

51) 3 + □ = 4

52) □ + 5 = 6

53) 1 + □ = 1

54) □ + 7 = 14

55) 1 + □ = 2

56) □ + 2 = 6

57) 3 + □ = 7

58) □ + 3 = 8

59) 0 + □ = 7

60) □ + 1 = 2

Page 38

Score:

/60

Name:

time   :

1)
$$\begin{array}{r} 1 \\ + \square \\ \hline 8 \end{array}$$

2)
$$\begin{array}{r} \square \\ + 7 \\ \hline 14 \end{array}$$

3)
$$\begin{array}{r} 0 \\ + \square \\ \hline 2 \end{array}$$

4)
$$\begin{array}{r} \square \\ + 5 \\ \hline 8 \end{array}$$

5)
$$\begin{array}{r} 3 \\ + \square \\ \hline 3 \end{array}$$

6)
$$\begin{array}{r} \square \\ + 5 \\ \hline 11 \end{array}$$

7)
$$\begin{array}{r} 7 \\ + \square \\ \hline 13 \end{array}$$

8)
$$\begin{array}{r} \square \\ + 2 \\ \hline 5 \end{array}$$

9)
$$\begin{array}{r} 0 \\ + \square \\ \hline 6 \end{array}$$

10)
$$\begin{array}{r} \square \\ + 2 \\ \hline 3 \end{array}$$

11)
$$\begin{array}{r} 1 \\ + \square \\ \hline 1 \end{array}$$

12)
$$\begin{array}{r} \square \\ + 0 \\ \hline 5 \end{array}$$

13)
$$\begin{array}{r} 5 \\ + \square \\ \hline 6 \end{array}$$

14)
$$\begin{array}{r} \square \\ + 1 \\ \hline 1 \end{array}$$

15)
$$\begin{array}{r} 7 \\ + \square \\ \hline 11 \end{array}$$

16)
$$\begin{array}{r} \square \\ + 5 \\ \hline 7 \end{array}$$

17)
$$\begin{array}{r} 2 \\ + \square \\ \hline 4 \end{array}$$

18)
$$\begin{array}{r} \square \\ + 3 \\ \hline 8 \end{array}$$

19)
$$\begin{array}{r} 5 \\ + \square \\ \hline 8 \end{array}$$

20)
$$\begin{array}{r} \square \\ + 5 \\ \hline 11 \end{array}$$

21)
$$\begin{array}{r} 5 \\ + \square \\ \hline 5 \end{array}$$

22)
$$\begin{array}{r} \square \\ + 3 \\ \hline 8 \end{array}$$

23)
$$\begin{array}{r} 1 \\ + \square \\ \hline 1 \end{array}$$

24)
$$\begin{array}{r} \square \\ + 1 \\ \hline 3 \end{array}$$

25)
$$\begin{array}{r} 7 \\ + \square \\ \hline 11 \end{array}$$

26)
$$\begin{array}{r} \square \\ + 1 \\ \hline 8 \end{array}$$

27)
$$\begin{array}{r} 5 \\ + \square \\ \hline 11 \end{array}$$

28)
$$\begin{array}{r} \square \\ + 1 \\ \hline 6 \end{array}$$

29)
$$\begin{array}{r} 4 \\ + \square \\ \hline 4 \end{array}$$

30)
$$\begin{array}{r} \square \\ + 6 \\ \hline 10 \end{array}$$

31)
$$\begin{array}{r} 5 \\ + \square \\ \hline 11 \end{array}$$

32)
$$\begin{array}{r} \square \\ + 7 \\ \hline 9 \end{array}$$

33)
$$\begin{array}{r} 7 \\ + \square \\ \hline 9 \end{array}$$

34)
$$\begin{array}{r} \square \\ + 7 \\ \hline 12 \end{array}$$

35)
$$\begin{array}{r} 1 \\ + \square \\ \hline 1 \end{array}$$

36)
$$\begin{array}{r} \square \\ + 1 \\ \hline 3 \end{array}$$

37)
$$\begin{array}{r} 0 \\ + \square \\ \hline 3 \end{array}$$

38)
$$\begin{array}{r} \square \\ + 6 \\ \hline 6 \end{array}$$

39)
$$\begin{array}{r} 6 \\ + \square \\ \hline 13 \end{array}$$

40)
$$\begin{array}{r} \square \\ + 4 \\ \hline 9 \end{array}$$

41)
$$\begin{array}{r} 4 \\ + \square \\ \hline 8 \end{array}$$

42)
$$\begin{array}{r} \square \\ + 1 \\ \hline 4 \end{array}$$

43)
$$\begin{array}{r} 7 \\ + \square \\ \hline 8 \end{array}$$

44)
$$\begin{array}{r} \square \\ + 6 \\ \hline 9 \end{array}$$

45)
$$\begin{array}{r} 4 \\ + \square \\ \hline 6 \end{array}$$

46)
$$\begin{array}{r} \square \\ + 3 \\ \hline 8 \end{array}$$

47)
$$\begin{array}{r} 4 \\ + \square \\ \hline 6 \end{array}$$

48)
$$\begin{array}{r} \square \\ + 7 \\ \hline 14 \end{array}$$

49)
$$\begin{array}{r} 7 \\ + \square \\ \hline 13 \end{array}$$

50)
$$\begin{array}{r} \square \\ + 2 \\ \hline 5 \end{array}$$

51)
$$\begin{array}{r} 6 \\ + \square \\ \hline 7 \end{array}$$

52)
$$\begin{array}{r} \square \\ + 4 \\ \hline 4 \end{array}$$

53)
$$\begin{array}{r} 5 \\ + \square \\ \hline 9 \end{array}$$

54)
$$\begin{array}{r} \square \\ + 3 \\ \hline 9 \end{array}$$

55)
$$\begin{array}{r} 4 \\ + \square \\ \hline 11 \end{array}$$

56)
$$\begin{array}{r} \square \\ + 7 \\ \hline 12 \end{array}$$

57)
$$\begin{array}{r} 7 \\ + \square \\ \hline 8 \end{array}$$

58)
$$\begin{array}{r} \square \\ + 7 \\ \hline 9 \end{array}$$

59)
$$\begin{array}{r} 6 \\ + \square \\ \hline 8 \end{array}$$

60)
$$\begin{array}{r} \square \\ + 6 \\ \hline 11 \end{array}$$

Name:

Score:

/60

time   :

1)
```
    4
  + □
  ───
    4
```

2)
```
    □
  + 4
  ───
    4
```

3)
```
    5
  + □
  ───
   12
```

4)
```
    □
  + 2
  ───
    7
```

5)
```
    5
  + □
  ───
   10
```

6)
```
    □
  + 7
  ───
   13
```

7)
```
    2
  + □
  ───
    5
```

8)
```
    □
  + 1
  ───
    5
```

9)
```
    4
  + □
  ───
    4
```

10)
```
    □
  + 5
  ───
   12
```

11)
```
    4
  + □
  ───
    8
```

12)
```
    □
  + 1
  ───
    8
```

13)
```
    3
  + □
  ───
    4
```

14)
```
    □
  + 5
  ───
    8
```

15)
```
    3
  + □
  ───
    4
```

16)
```
    □
  + 5
  ───
    7
```

17)
```
    6
  + □
  ───
   13
```

18)
```
    □
  + 2
  ───
    5
```

19)
```
    6
  + □
  ───
    7
```

20)
```
    □
  + 6
  ───
   13
```

21)
```
    7
  + □
  ───
    9
```

22)
```
    □
  + 6
  ───
   12
```

23)
```
    1
  + □
  ───
    5
```

24)
```
    □
  + 4
  ───
    5
```

25)
```
    6
  + □
  ───
   11
```

26)
```
    □
  + 5
  ───
    8
```

27)
```
    6
  + □
  ───
    7
```

28)
```
    □
  + 0
  ───
    7
```

29)
```
    3
  + □
  ───
    8
```

30)
```
    □
  + 7
  ───
   11
```

31)
```
    0
  + □
  ───
    3
```

32)
```
    □
  + 5
  ───
   12
```

33)
```
    4
  + □
  ───
   11
```

34)
```
    □
  + 1
  ───
    8
```

35)
```
    2
  + □
  ───
    4
```

36)
```
    □
  + 7
  ───
   10
```

37)
```
    0
  + □
  ───
    0
```

38)
```
    □
  + 3
  ───
    8
```

39)
```
    1
  + □
  ───
    7
```

40)
```
    □
  + 7
  ───
   10
```

41)
```
    3
  + □
  ───
   10
```

42)
```
    □
  + 3
  ───
    7
```

43)
```
    2
  + □
  ───
    2
```

44)
```
    □
  + 4
  ───
    8
```

45)
```
    6
  + □
  ───
   10
```

46)
```
    □
  + 7
  ───
   14
```

47)
```
    7
  + □
  ───
   13
```

48)
```
    □
  + 5
  ───
    5
```

49)
```
    0
  + □
  ───
    7
```

50)
```
    □
  + 3
  ───
    9
```

51)
```
    3
  + □
  ───
    6
```

52)
```
    □
  + 5
  ───
    7
```

53)
```
    5
  + □
  ───
    7
```

54)
```
    □
  + 6
  ───
   11
```

55)
```
    1
  + □
  ───
    3
```

56)
```
    □
  + 1
  ───
    2
```

57)
```
    1
  + □
  ───
    5
```

58)
```
    □
  + 5
  ───
    8
```

59)
```
    0
  + □
  ───
    2
```

60)
```
    □
  + 1
  ───
    6
```

Name:

Score:

/60

time   :

1)
$$\begin{array}{r} 0 \\ + 7 \\ \hline \end{array}$$

2)
$$\begin{array}{r} 2 \\ + 2 \\ \hline \end{array}$$

3)
$$\begin{array}{r} 9 \\ + 3 \\ \hline \end{array}$$

4)
$$\begin{array}{r} 0 \\ + 7 \\ \hline \end{array}$$

5)
$$\begin{array}{r} 8 \\ + 3 \\ \hline \end{array}$$

6)
$$\begin{array}{r} 0 \\ + 0 \\ \hline \end{array}$$

7)
$$\begin{array}{r} 4 \\ + 4 \\ \hline \end{array}$$

8)
$$\begin{array}{r} 6 \\ + 8 \\ \hline \end{array}$$

9)
$$\begin{array}{r} 8 \\ + 6 \\ \hline \end{array}$$

10)
$$\begin{array}{r} 0 \\ + 5 \\ \hline \end{array}$$

11)
$$\begin{array}{r} 0 \\ + 8 \\ \hline \end{array}$$

12)
$$\begin{array}{r} 9 \\ + 7 \\ \hline \end{array}$$

13)
$$\begin{array}{r} 9 \\ + 0 \\ \hline \end{array}$$

14)
$$\begin{array}{r} 1 \\ + 8 \\ \hline \end{array}$$

15)
$$\begin{array}{r} 5 \\ + 7 \\ \hline \end{array}$$

16)
$$\begin{array}{r} 0 \\ + 3 \\ \hline \end{array}$$

17)
$$\begin{array}{r} 6 \\ + 0 \\ \hline \end{array}$$

18)
$$\begin{array}{r} 9 \\ + 10 \\ \hline \end{array}$$

19)
$$\begin{array}{r} 0 \\ + 5 \\ \hline \end{array}$$

20)
$$\begin{array}{r} 6 \\ + 8 \\ \hline \end{array}$$

21)
$$\begin{array}{r} 2 \\ + 2 \\ \hline \end{array}$$

22)
$$\begin{array}{r} 2 \\ + 9 \\ \hline \end{array}$$

23)
$$\begin{array}{r} 2 \\ + 6 \\ \hline \end{array}$$

24)
$$\begin{array}{r} 0 \\ + 8 \\ \hline \end{array}$$

25)
$$\begin{array}{r} 1 \\ + 7 \\ \hline \end{array}$$

26)
$$\begin{array}{r} 9 \\ + 1 \\ \hline \end{array}$$

27)
$$\begin{array}{r} 2 \\ + 4 \\ \hline \end{array}$$

28)
$$\begin{array}{r} 3 \\ + 3 \\ \hline \end{array}$$

29)
$$\begin{array}{r} 9 \\ + 4 \\ \hline \end{array}$$

30)
$$\begin{array}{r} 8 \\ + 3 \\ \hline \end{array}$$

31)
$$\begin{array}{r} 10 \\ + 9 \\ \hline \end{array}$$

32)
$$\begin{array}{r} 5 \\ + 4 \\ \hline \end{array}$$

33)
$$\begin{array}{r} 7 \\ + 2 \\ \hline \end{array}$$

34)
$$\begin{array}{r} 2 \\ + 4 \\ \hline \end{array}$$

35)
$$\begin{array}{r} 9 \\ + 8 \\ \hline \end{array}$$

36)
$$\begin{array}{r} 8 \\ + 4 \\ \hline \end{array}$$

37)
$$\begin{array}{r} 4 \\ + 0 \\ \hline \end{array}$$

38)
$$\begin{array}{r} 4 \\ + 5 \\ \hline \end{array}$$

39)
$$\begin{array}{r} 7 \\ + 6 \\ \hline \end{array}$$

40)
$$\begin{array}{r} 1 \\ + 0 \\ \hline \end{array}$$

41)
$$\begin{array}{r} 4 \\ + 2 \\ \hline \end{array}$$

42)
$$\begin{array}{r} 8 \\ + 0 \\ \hline \end{array}$$

43)
$$\begin{array}{r} 10 \\ + 1 \\ \hline \end{array}$$

44)
$$\begin{array}{r} 9 \\ + 4 \\ \hline \end{array}$$

45)
$$\begin{array}{r} 5 \\ + 9 \\ \hline \end{array}$$

46)
$$\begin{array}{r} 5 \\ + 7 \\ \hline \end{array}$$

47)
$$\begin{array}{r} 3 \\ + 1 \\ \hline \end{array}$$

48)
$$\begin{array}{r} 3 \\ + 7 \\ \hline \end{array}$$

49)
$$\begin{array}{r} 5 \\ + 6 \\ \hline \end{array}$$

50)
$$\begin{array}{r} 8 \\ + 0 \\ \hline \end{array}$$

51)
$$\begin{array}{r} 6 \\ + 5 \\ \hline \end{array}$$

52)
$$\begin{array}{r} 4 \\ + 3 \\ \hline \end{array}$$

53)
$$\begin{array}{r} 2 \\ + 4 \\ \hline \end{array}$$

54)
$$\begin{array}{r} 6 \\ + 7 \\ \hline \end{array}$$

55)
$$\begin{array}{r} 7 \\ + 9 \\ \hline \end{array}$$

56)
$$\begin{array}{r} 1 \\ + 1 \\ \hline \end{array}$$

57)
$$\begin{array}{r} 2 \\ + 6 \\ \hline \end{array}$$

58)
$$\begin{array}{r} 0 \\ + 7 \\ \hline \end{array}$$

59)
$$\begin{array}{r} 6 \\ + 4 \\ \hline \end{array}$$

60)
$$\begin{array}{r} 5 \\ + 3 \\ \hline \end{array}$$

Score:

/60

Name:

Time   :

1)   4
    + 10

2)   9
    + 9

3)   0
    + 0

4)   1
    + 8

5)   6
    + 9

6)   9
    + 5

7)   6
    + 0

8)   4
    + 5

9)   4
    + 8

10)   5
    + 4

11)   1
    + 5

12)   5
    + 5

13)   9
    + 2

14)   10
    + 8

15)   7
    + 4

16)   0
    + 2

17)   8
    + 9

18)   8
    + 1

19)   3
    + 4

20)   3
    + 5

21)   9
    + 1

22)   9
    + 0

23)   0
    + 1

24)   9
    + 1

25)   2
    + 0

26)   4
    + 9

27)   3
    + 2

28)   4
    + 4

29)   0
    + 10

30)   2
    + 0

31)   8
    + 7

32)   3
    + 1

33)   10
    + 5

34)   1
    + 0

35)   1
    + 6

36)   6
    + 7

37)   0
    + 3

38)   5
    + 6

39)   2
    + 5

40)   4
    + 6

41)   9
    + 4

42)   0
    + 8

43)   2
    + 10

44)   1
    + 8

45)   10
    + 10

46)   8
    + 8

47)   3
    + 7

48)   1
    + 6

49)   6
    + 10

50)   3
    + 7

51)   0
    + 8

52)   1
    + 8

53)   3
    + 8

54)   7
    + 6

55)   10
    + 9

56)   4
    + 6

57)   10
    + 1

58)   0
    + 6

59)   7
    + 0

60)   5
    + 0

Score:

/60

Name:

time   :

1)
```
    0
+   0
```

2)
```
   10
+  10
```

3)
```
    5
+   0
```

4)
```
   10
+   2
```

5)
```
   10
+   8
```

6)
```
    9
+   1
```

7)
```
    6
+   3
```

8)
```
    7
+   9
```

9)
```
    0
+  10
```

10)
```
    8
+   2
```

11)
```
    6
+   5
```

12)
```
    4
+   2
```

13)
```
    7
+   2
```

14)
```
    6
+   8
```

15)
```
   10
+   8
```

16)
```
    6
+   8
```

17)
```
    5
+  10
```

18)
```
   10
+   7
```

19)
```
    6
+   9
```

20)
```
    3
+   4
```

21)
```
    3
+   5
```

22)
```
    5
+   0
```

23)
```
    5
+   4
```

24)
```
    1
+   6
```

25)
```
    2
+   7
```

26)
```
    5
+   1
```

27)
```
    9
+  10
```

28)
```
    5
+   9
```

29)
```
    9
+   1
```

30)
```
    3
+   7
```

31)
```
    2
+   6
```

32)
```
    7
+   4
```

33)
```
    2
+  10
```

34)
```
    1
+   4
```

35)
```
    1
+   0
```

36)
```
    3
+   4
```

37)
```
    8
+   0
```

38)
```
    9
+   2
```

39)
```
    2
+   5
```

40)
```
    6
+   5
```

41)
```
    8
+   7
```

42)
```
    9
+   1
```

43)
```
   10
+   9
```

44)
```
    2
+  10
```

45)
```
    0
+   3
```

46)
```
    1
+   1
```

47)
```
    0
+   1
```

48)
```
    7
+   8
```

49)
```
    6
+   4
```

50)
```
    7
+   3
```

51)
```
    8
+  10
```

52)
```
    3
+   0
```

53)
```
    5
+   9
```

54)
```
    5
+   5
```

55)
```
    6
+  10
```

56)
```
    2
+   3
```

57)
```
    0
+   8
```

58)
```
   10
+  10
```

59)
```
   10
+   0
```

60)
```
    3
+   2
```

Name:

Score:

/60

time   :

1)   0
    + 8

2)   3
    + 2

3)   1
    + 8

4)   1
    + 9

5)   2
    + 9

6)   5
    + 5

7)   3
    + 0

8)   5
    + 7

9)   9
    + 0

10)   3
    + 10

11)   6
    + 2

12)   0
    + 7

13)   7
    + 2

14)   2
    + 3

15)   6
    + 10

16)   10
    + 5

17)   1
    + 3

18)   4
    + 4

19)   3
    + 9

20)   2
    + 3

21)   7
    + 7

22)   5
    + 8

23)   5
    + 6

24)   5
    + 5

25)   8
    + 2

26)   4
    + 8

27)   9
    + 10

28)   1
    + 6

29)   8
    + 4

30)   10
    + 2

31)   10
    + 3

32)   2
    + 8

33)   0
    + 8

34)   0
    + 10

35)   6
    + 8

36)   8
    + 4

37)   5
    + 4

38)   0
    + 9

39)   7
    + 7

40)   5
    + 7

41)   1
    + 5

42)   7
    + 7

43)   2
    + 1

44)   4
    + 8

45)   1
    + 2

46)   8
    + 10

47)   6
    + 1

48)   10
    + 5

49)   4
    + 9

50)   1
    + 2

51)   0
    + 6

52)   0
    + 1

53)   9
    + 3

54)   5
    + 4

55)   1
    + 10

56)   1
    + 3

57)   4
    + 5

58)   1
    + 2

59)   0
    + 4

60)   4
    + 4

Name:

Score:

/60

Time   :

1)   1
    +   9

2)   5
    +   6

3)   6
    +   9

4)   0
    +   7

5)   2
    +   0

6)   3
    +   5

7)   6
    +   2

8)   9
    +   3

9)   10
    +   8

10)   5
    + 10

11)   4
    +   1

12)   5
    +   7

13)   8
    +   3

14)   5
    +   7

15)   2
    +   9

16)   4
    +   5

17)   0
    + 10

18)   3
    +   8

19)   1
    +   0

20)   6
    +   0

21)   9
    +   1

22)   7
    +   5

23)   10
    +   2

24)   4
    +   1

25)   10
    +   7

26)   5
    +   2

27)   1
    +   5

28)   4
    +   8

29)   2
    + 10

30)   2
    + 10

31)   4
    + 10

32)   3
    +   8

33)   3
    +   6

34)   10
    +   1

35)   6
    +   2

36)   7
    + 10

37)   7
    +   2

38)   2
    +   7

39)   1
    +   7

40)   1
    +   0

41)   9
    +   3

42)   2
    +   9

43)   6
    +   1

44)   2
    +   9

45)   8
    +   3

46)   2
    +   0

47)   1
    +   5

48)   5
    +   5

49)   5
    +   8

50)   3
    +   0

51)   5
    +   9

52)   1
    +   8

53)   8
    +   1

54)   0
    +   4

55)   7
    +   8

56)   5
    +   7

57)   2
    +   8

58)   5
    +   3

59)   2
    +   4

60)   10
    +   0

Name:

Score:

/60

time   :

1)   10
+ 7

2)   9
+ 7

3)   2
+ 6

4)   6
+ 1

5)   9
+ 0

6)   0
+ 7

7)   7
+ 7

8)   4
+ 5

9)   3
+ 0

10)   9
+ 1

11)   6
+ 0

12)   8
+ 2

13)   5
+ 0

14)   7
+ 8

15)   9
+ 0

16)   5
+ 6

17)   2
+ 10

18)   3
+ 7

19)   2
+ 9

20)   6
+ 7

21)   2
+ 7

22)   9
+ 1

23)   3
+ 7

24)   8
+ 1

25)   9
+ 1

26)   4
+ 6

27)   7
+ 5

28)   0
+ 5

29)   6
+ 3

30)   10
+ 5

31)   7
+ 10

32)   6
+ 7

33)   8
+ 1

34)   3
+ 7

35)   5
+ 1

36)   7
+ 3

37)   9
+ 2

38)   1
+ 1

39)   10
+ 10

40)   9
+ 4

41)   4
+ 0

42)   0
+ 3

43)   0
+ 7

44)   0
+ 3

45)   2
+ 7

46)   9
+ 9

47)   5
+ 5

48)   6
+ 8

49)   6
+ 5

50)   8
+ 5

51)   1
+ 3

52)   10
+ 5

53)   10
+ 4

54)   6
+ 6

55)   8
+ 10

56)   0
+ 10

57)   1
+ 10

58)   6
+ 8

59)   9
+ 7

60)   9
+ 1

Name:

Score:

/60

time   :

1)   1
   + 9

2)   3
   + 10

3)   8
   + 10

4)   4
   + 9

5)   8
   + 5

6)   8
   + 10

7)   5
   + 10

8)   8
   + 0

9)   7
   + 7

10)   8
    + 9

11)   10
    + 5

12)   10
    + 3

13)   6
    + 7

14)   9
    + 4

15)   2
    + 3

16)   0
    + 1

17)   8
    + 10

18)   8
    + 0

19)   4
    + 9

20)   4
    + 7

21)   3
    + 7

22)   1
    + 8

23)   4
    + 2

24)   10
    + 9

25)   1
    + 1

26)   0
    + 6

27)   5
    + 2

28)   4
    + 8

29)   5
    + 0

30)   0
    + 4

31)   2
    + 9

32)   7
    + 0

33)   8
    + 6

34)   5
    + 8

35)   6
    + 0

36)   8
    + 4

37)   6
    + 3

38)   6
    + 4

39)   10
    + 10

40)   3
    + 4

41)   5
    + 4

42)   8
    + 5

43)   5
    + 8

44)   5
    + 4

45)   2
    + 1

46)   8
    + 4

47)   10
    + 5

48)   1
    + 10

49)   5
    + 4

50)   5
    + 10

51)   3
    + 6

52)   8
    + 8

53)   1
    + 4

54)   10
    + 8

55)   3
    + 5

56)   7
    + 1

57)   7
    + 9

58)   1
    + 9

59)   9
    + 5

60)   4
    + 1

Name:

Score:

/60

time   :

1)   1
    +   1

2)   2
    +   5

3)   0
    +   2

4)   2
    + 10

5)   4
    + 10

6)   8
    +   9

7)   0
    +   1

8)   8
    +   4

9)   3
    +   7

10)   9
    +   8

11)   3
    +   8

12)   2
    +   5

13)   0
    +   2

14)   4
    +   0

15)   0
    +   5

16)   7
    +   9

17)   1
    +   8

18)   6
    +   3

19)   5
    +   4

20)   1
    +   9

21)   10
    +   2

22)   4
    +   1

23)   9
    + 10

24)   6
    +   8

25)   9
    +   0

26)   0
    +   1

27)   6
    +   4

28)   0
    + 10

29)   10
    +   0

30)   7
    + 10

31)   1
    +   6

32)   1
    +   8

33)   5
    +   4

34)   4
    +   5

35)   6
    +   9

36)   8
    +   6

37)   9
    +   2

38)   9
    +   2

39)   8
    +   4

40)   1
    +   6

41)   5
    +   0

42)   2
    +   5

43)   7
    +   3

44)   10
    +   1

45)   10
    +   8

46)   0
    +   3

47)   10
    +   0

48)   2
    +   3

49)   1
    +   5

50)   0
    +   8

51)   10
    +   7

52)   1
    +   9

53)   0
    + 10

54)   3
    +   8

55)   10
    +   3

56)   5
    +   7

57)   2
    +   0

58)   8
    +   2

59)   9
    + 10

60)   2
    +   1

Name:

Score:

/60

time   :

1)   8
    + 4

2)   0
    + 0

3)   6
    + 3

4)   7
    + 9

5)   7
    + 4

6)   1
    + 6

7)   0
    + 9

8)   9
    + 2

9)   4
    + 9

10)   10
    + 2

11)   10
    + 6

12)   9
    + 1

13)   5
    + 3

14)   9
    + 4

15)   2
    + 6

16)   4
    + 4

17)   0
    + 5

18)   4
    + 8

19)   3
    + 3

20)   9
    + 0

21)   9
    + 10

22)   2
    + 3

23)   0
    + 3

24)   5
    + 4

25)   2
    + 7

26)   8
    + 0

27)   7
    + 5

28)   8
    + 5

29)   4
    + 4

30)   7
    + 7

31)   3
    + 7

32)   5
    + 0

33)   8
    + 9

34)   8
    + 10

35)   6
    + 9

36)   7
    + 10

37)   2
    + 7

38)   9
    + 3

39)   5
    + 7

40)   1
    + 2

41)   2
    + 2

42)   1
    + 2

43)   0
    + 7

44)   8
    + 6

45)   0
    + 7

46)   6
    + 2

47)   5
    + 8

48)   2
    + 6

49)   7
    + 4

50)   9
    + 4

51)   3
    + 1

52)   6
    + 4

53)   5
    + 5

54)   3
    + 0

55)   1
    + 0

56)   6
    + 3

57)   8
    + 4

58)   0
    + 1

59)   7
    + 1

60)   6
    + 5

Name:

Score:

/60

time   :

1)   5
   + 2

2)   10
   + 5

3)   9
   + 2

4)   1
   + 4

5)   4
   + 2

6)   4
   + 10

7)   8
   + 3

8)   6
   + 4

9)   10
   + 2

10)   3
    + 9

11)   8
    + 1

12)   2
    + 9

13)   3
    + 4

14)   3
    + 5

15)   7
    + 4

16)   4
    + 10

17)   6
    + 9

18)   1
    + 10

19)   7
    + 9

20)   6
    + 2

21)   7
    + 10

22)   10
    + 1

23)   0
    + 9

24)   9
    + 7

25)   0
    + 1

26)   3
    + 6

27)   9
    + 10

28)   1
    + 10

29)   6
    + 3

30)   2
    + 4

31)   8
    + 6

32)   7
    + 9

33)   6
    + 6

34)   4
    + 6

35)   6
    + 2

36)   0
    + 2

37)   3
    + 1

38)   3
    + 1

39)   5
    + 10

40)   1
    + 10

41)   8
    + 6

42)   7
    + 2

43)   4
    + 7

44)   0
    + 8

45)   8
    + 2

46)   8
    + 0

47)   3
    + 10

48)   2
    + 4

49)   0
    + 1

50)   10
    + 8

51)   3
    + 9

52)   3
    + 3

53)   6
    + 9

54)   8
    + 5

55)   5
    + 3

56)   1
    + 6

57)   10
    + 7

58)   8
    + 1

59)   8
    + 1

60)   2
    + 1

Score:

/60

Name:

time　　:

1)
$$\begin{array}{r} \square \\ + \quad 3 \\ \hline 11 \end{array}$$

2)
$$\begin{array}{r} 4 \\ + \quad \square \\ \hline 6 \end{array}$$

3)
$$\begin{array}{r} \square \\ + \quad 4 \\ \hline 12 \end{array}$$

4)
$$\begin{array}{r} 7 \\ + \quad \square \\ \hline 7 \end{array}$$

5)
$$\begin{array}{r} \square \\ + \quad 7 \\ \hline 15 \end{array}$$

6)
$$\begin{array}{r} 3 \\ + \quad \square \\ \hline 4 \end{array}$$

7)
$$\begin{array}{r} \square \\ + \quad 1 \\ \hline 1 \end{array}$$

8)
$$\begin{array}{r} 0 \\ + \quad \square \\ \hline 4 \end{array}$$

9)
$$\begin{array}{r} \square \\ + \quad 3 \\ \hline 13 \end{array}$$

10)
$$\begin{array}{r} 7 \\ + \quad \square \\ \hline 8 \end{array}$$

11)
$$\begin{array}{r} \square \\ + \quad 5 \\ \hline 13 \end{array}$$

12)
$$\begin{array}{r} 6 \\ + \quad \square \\ \hline 16 \end{array}$$

13)
$$\begin{array}{r} \square \\ + \quad 10 \\ \hline 19 \end{array}$$

14)
$$\begin{array}{r} 9 \\ + \quad \square \\ \hline 18 \end{array}$$

15)
$$\begin{array}{r} \square \\ + \quad 7 \\ \hline 11 \end{array}$$

16)
$$\begin{array}{r} 8 \\ + \quad \square \\ \hline 18 \end{array}$$

17)
$$\begin{array}{r} \square \\ + \quad 0 \\ \hline 5 \end{array}$$

18)
$$\begin{array}{r} 5 \\ + \quad \square \\ \hline 14 \end{array}$$

19)
$$\begin{array}{r} \square \\ + \quad 1 \\ \hline 2 \end{array}$$

20)
$$\begin{array}{r} 7 \\ + \quad \square \\ \hline 15 \end{array}$$

21)
$$\begin{array}{r} \square \\ + \quad 6 \\ \hline 16 \end{array}$$

22)
$$\begin{array}{r} 0 \\ + \quad \square \\ \hline 1 \end{array}$$

23)
$$\begin{array}{r} \square \\ + \quad 9 \\ \hline 14 \end{array}$$

24)
$$\begin{array}{r} 3 \\ + \quad \square \\ \hline 7 \end{array}$$

25)
$$\begin{array}{r} \square \\ + \quad 2 \\ \hline 6 \end{array}$$

26)
$$\begin{array}{r} 4 \\ + \quad \square \\ \hline 7 \end{array}$$

27)
$$\begin{array}{r} \square \\ + \quad 8 \\ \hline 18 \end{array}$$

28)
$$\begin{array}{r} 2 \\ + \quad \square \\ \hline 10 \end{array}$$

29)
$$\begin{array}{r} \square \\ + \quad 8 \\ \hline 13 \end{array}$$

30)
$$\begin{array}{r} 0 \\ + \quad \square \\ \hline 2 \end{array}$$

31)
$$\begin{array}{r} \square \\ + \quad 3 \\ \hline 4 \end{array}$$

32)
$$\begin{array}{r} 2 \\ + \quad \square \\ \hline 5 \end{array}$$

33)
$$\begin{array}{r} \square \\ + \quad 3 \\ \hline 3 \end{array}$$

34)
$$\begin{array}{r} 2 \\ + \quad \square \\ \hline 9 \end{array}$$

35)
$$\begin{array}{r} \square \\ + \quad 5 \\ \hline 8 \end{array}$$

36)
$$\begin{array}{r} 5 \\ + \quad \square \\ \hline 7 \end{array}$$

37)
$$\begin{array}{r} \square \\ + \quad 7 \\ \hline 13 \end{array}$$

38)
$$\begin{array}{r} 10 \\ + \quad \square \\ \hline 19 \end{array}$$

39)
$$\begin{array}{r} \square \\ + \quad 10 \\ \hline 17 \end{array}$$

40)
$$\begin{array}{r} 7 \\ + \quad \square \\ \hline 10 \end{array}$$

41)
$$\begin{array}{r} \square \\ + \quad 9 \\ \hline 18 \end{array}$$

42)
$$\begin{array}{r} 4 \\ + \quad \square \\ \hline 4 \end{array}$$

43)
$$\begin{array}{r} \square \\ + \quad 2 \\ \hline 3 \end{array}$$

44)
$$\begin{array}{r} 8 \\ + \quad \square \\ \hline 11 \end{array}$$

45)
$$\begin{array}{r} \square \\ + \quad 8 \\ \hline 17 \end{array}$$

46)
$$\begin{array}{r} 2 \\ + \quad \square \\ \hline 11 \end{array}$$

47)
$$\begin{array}{r} \square \\ + \quad 4 \\ \hline 11 \end{array}$$

48)
$$\begin{array}{r} 10 \\ + \quad \square \\ \hline 20 \end{array}$$

49)
$$\begin{array}{r} \square \\ + \quad 1 \\ \hline 4 \end{array}$$

50)
$$\begin{array}{r} 1 \\ + \quad \square \\ \hline 8 \end{array}$$

51)
$$\begin{array}{r} \square \\ + \quad 1 \\ \hline 7 \end{array}$$

52)
$$\begin{array}{r} 9 \\ + \quad \square \\ \hline 13 \end{array}$$

53)
$$\begin{array}{r} \square \\ + \quad 8 \\ \hline 14 \end{array}$$

54)
$$\begin{array}{r} 0 \\ + \quad \square \\ \hline 1 \end{array}$$

55)
$$\begin{array}{r} \square \\ + \quad 9 \\ \hline 11 \end{array}$$

56)
$$\begin{array}{r} 10 \\ + \quad \square \\ \hline 12 \end{array}$$

57)
$$\begin{array}{r} \square \\ + \quad 0 \\ \hline 9 \end{array}$$

58)
$$\begin{array}{r} 5 \\ + \quad \square \\ \hline 8 \end{array}$$

59)
$$\begin{array}{r} \square \\ + \quad 1 \\ \hline 6 \end{array}$$

60)
$$\begin{array}{r} 7 \\ + \quad \square \\ \hline 12 \end{array}$$

Score:

/60

Name:

Time   :

1)
$$\boxed{} + 0 \over 7$$

2)
$$6 + \boxed{} \over 7$$

3)
$$\boxed{} + 9 \over 15$$

4)
$$3 + \boxed{} \over 5$$

5)
$$\boxed{} + 3 \over 12$$

6)
$$9 + \boxed{} \over 15$$

7)
$$\boxed{} + 7 \over 15$$

8)
$$8 + \boxed{} \over 8$$

9)
$$\boxed{} + 8 \over 10$$

10)
$$9 + \boxed{} \over 17$$

11)
$$\boxed{} + 8 \over 10$$

12)
$$2 + \boxed{} \over 6$$

13)
$$\boxed{} + 8 \over 13$$

14)
$$5 + \boxed{} \over 12$$

15)
$$\boxed{} + 3 \over 6$$

16)
$$2 + \boxed{} \over 11$$

17)
$$\boxed{} + 9 \over 14$$

18)
$$0 + \boxed{} \over 0$$

19)
$$\boxed{} + 6 \over 15$$

20)
$$2 + \boxed{} \over 5$$

21)
$$\boxed{} + 10 \over 16$$

22)
$$8 + \boxed{} \over 15$$

23)
$$\boxed{} + 2 \over 12$$

24)
$$1 + \boxed{} \over 11$$

25)
$$\boxed{} + 10 \over 20$$

26)
$$5 + \boxed{} \over 8$$

27)
$$\boxed{} + 3 \over 11$$

28)
$$7 + \boxed{} \over 16$$

29)
$$\boxed{} + 9 \over 13$$

30)
$$5 + \boxed{} \over 11$$

31)
$$\boxed{} + 4 \over 10$$

32)
$$6 + \boxed{} \over 15$$

33)
$$\boxed{} + 4 \over 13$$

34)
$$2 + \boxed{} \over 6$$

35)
$$\boxed{} + 6 \over 9$$

36)
$$7 + \boxed{} \over 9$$

37)
$$\boxed{} + 3 \over 7$$

38)
$$7 + \boxed{} \over 14$$

39)
$$\boxed{} + 10 \over 11$$

40)
$$8 + \boxed{} \over 16$$

41)
$$\boxed{} + 8 \over 15$$

42)
$$8 + \boxed{} \over 15$$

43)
$$\boxed{} + 1 \over 5$$

44)
$$1 + \boxed{} \over 5$$

45)
$$\boxed{} + 0 \over 5$$

46)
$$4 + \boxed{} \over 6$$

47)
$$\boxed{} + 10 \over 14$$

48)
$$9 + \boxed{} \over 12$$

49)
$$\boxed{} + 3 \over 10$$

50)
$$3 + \boxed{} \over 12$$

51)
$$\boxed{} + 3 \over 3$$

52)
$$5 + \boxed{} \over 6$$

53)
$$\boxed{} + 8 \over 13$$

54)
$$1 + \boxed{} \over 3$$

55)
$$\boxed{} + 2 \over 10$$

56)
$$4 + \boxed{} \over 6$$

57)
$$\boxed{} + 8 \over 14$$

58)
$$10 + \boxed{} \over 17$$

59)
$$\boxed{} + 7 \over 13$$

60)
$$9 + \boxed{} \over 19$$

Name: _____

Score: /60

time :

1)
```
  □
+ 7
---
 15
```

2)
```
  2
+ □
---
  3
```

3)
```
  □
+ 6
---
  6
```

4)
```
  5
+ □
---
 15
```

5)
```
  □
+ 4
---
 14
```

6)
```
  9
+ □
---
 13
```

7)
```
  □
+ 3
---
  8
```

8)
```
  3
+ □
---
 10
```

9)
```
  □
+ 5
---
  6
```

10)
```
  7
+ □
---
  8
```

11)
```
  □
+ 6
---
 11
```

12)
```
  9
+ □
---
 12
```

13)
```
  □
+ 2
---
  3
```

14)
```
  6
+ □
---
  8
```

15)
```
  □
+ 8
---
 10
```

16)
```
  3
+ □
---
 12
```

17)
```
  □
+ 8
---
 10
```

18)
```
  9
+ □
---
 12
```

19)
```
  □
+ 3
---
  9
```

20)
```
  0
+ □
---
  5
```

21)
```
  □
+ 8
---
 13
```

22)
```
  3
+ □
---
  8
```

23)
```
  □
+ 4
---
  4
```

24)
```
  7
+ □
---
  8
```

25)
```
  □
+ 4
---
  5
```

26)
```
  5
+ □
---
 13
```

27)
```
  □
+ 5
---
 15
```

28)
```
  2
+ □
---
  2
```

29)
```
  □
+ 7
---
 15
```

30)
```
  7
+ □
---
 13
```

31)
```
  □
+ 1
---
  1
```

32)
```
  1
+ □
---
  9
```

33)
```
  □
+ 0
---
  0
```

34)
```
  0
+ □
---
  9
```

35)
```
  □
+ 4
---
 11
```

36)
```
  0
+ □
---
  4
```

37)
```
  □
+ 0
---
 10
```

38)
```
  5
+ □
---
 15
```

39)
```
  □
+ 7
---
  7
```

40)
```
  2
+ □
---
  6
```

41)
```
  □
+ 1
---
 11
```

42)
```
 10
+ □
---
 10
```

43)
```
  □
+ 10
---
 19
```

44)
```
  8
+ □
---
  9
```

45)
```
  □
+ 7
---
 13
```

46)
```
  3
+ □
---
  7
```

47)
```
  □
+ 2
---
  4
```

48)
```
  2
+ □
---
  6
```

49)
```
  □
+ 6
---
 13
```

50)
```
  2
+ □
---
 10
```

51)
```
  □
+ 9
---
 11
```

52)
```
  7
+ □
---
  7
```

53)
```
  □
+ 2
---
  9
```

54)
```
  3
+ □
---
  8
```

55)
```
  □
+ 5
---
 13
```

56)
```
  7
+ □
---
  9
```

57)
```
  □
+ 7
---
 11
```

58)
```
  6
+ □
---
 10
```

59)
```
  □
+ 1
---
  3
```

60)
```
  1
+ □
---
  8
```

Score: /60

Name:

time :

1) □ + 8 = 12

2) 10 + □ = 13

3) □ + 5 = 11

4) 4 + □ = 12

5) □ + 7 = 14

6) 9 + □ = 12

7) □ + 10 = 13

8) 3 + □ = 5

9) □ + 4 = 5

10) 0 + □ = 4

11) □ + 3 = 12

12) 5 + □ = 11

13) □ + 2 = 3

14) 3 + □ = 5

15) □ + 6 = 6

16) 6 + □ = 8

17) □ + 6 = 15

18) 5 + □ = 15

19) □ + 2 = 4

20) 10 + □ = 20

21) □ + 0 = 4

22) 7 + □ = 13

23) □ + 1 = 5

24) 6 + □ = 10

25) □ + 9 = 17

26) 0 + □ = 2

27) □ + 8 = 9

28) 0 + □ = 2

29) □ + 2 = 11

30) 0 + □ = 2

31) □ + 10 = 11

32) 7 + □ = 10

33) □ + 3 = 12

34) 9 + □ = 14

35) □ + 7 = 9

36) 1 + □ = 3

37) □ + 9 = 14

38) 4 + □ = 10

39) □ + 0 = 9

40) 5 + □ = 10

41) □ + 6 = 6

42) 4 + □ = 13

43) □ + 7 = 11

44) 3 + □ = 12

45) □ + 2 = 6

46) 0 + □ = 1

47) □ + 7 = 9

48) 3 + □ = 10

49) □ + 9 = 10

50) 10 + □ = 10

51) □ + 0 = 1

52) 8 + □ = 15

53) □ + 1 = 10

54) 7 + □ = 10

55) □ + 9 = 13

56) 2 + □ = 2

57) □ + 10 = 17

58) 10 + □ = 12

59) □ + 0 = 4

60) 10 + □ = 14

Page 54

Score:

/60

Name:

time   :

1)
$$\begin{array}{r} \square \\ + \quad 3 \\ \hline 7 \end{array}$$

2)
$$\begin{array}{r} 8 \\ + \quad \square \\ \hline 8 \end{array}$$

3)
$$\begin{array}{r} \square \\ + \quad 10 \\ \hline 14 \end{array}$$

4)
$$\begin{array}{r} 4 \\ + \quad \square \\ \hline 10 \end{array}$$

5)
$$\begin{array}{r} \square \\ + \quad 5 \\ \hline 12 \end{array}$$

6)
$$\begin{array}{r} 3 \\ + \quad \square \\ \hline 12 \end{array}$$

7)
$$\begin{array}{r} \square \\ + \quad 5 \\ \hline 5 \end{array}$$

8)
$$\begin{array}{r} 4 \\ + \quad \square \\ \hline 12 \end{array}$$

9)
$$\begin{array}{r} \square \\ + \quad 1 \\ \hline 4 \end{array}$$

10)
$$\begin{array}{r} 7 \\ + \quad \square \\ \hline 12 \end{array}$$

11)
$$\begin{array}{r} \square \\ + \quad 0 \\ \hline 2 \end{array}$$

12)
$$\begin{array}{r} 8 \\ + \quad \square \\ \hline 9 \end{array}$$

13)
$$\begin{array}{r} \square \\ + \quad 3 \\ \hline 11 \end{array}$$

14)
$$\begin{array}{r} 6 \\ + \quad \square \\ \hline 9 \end{array}$$

15)
$$\begin{array}{r} \square \\ + \quad 8 \\ \hline 15 \end{array}$$

16)
$$\begin{array}{r} 1 \\ + \quad \square \\ \hline 1 \end{array}$$

17)
$$\begin{array}{r} \square \\ + \quad 4 \\ \hline 5 \end{array}$$

18)
$$\begin{array}{r} 9 \\ + \quad \square \\ \hline 17 \end{array}$$

19)
$$\begin{array}{r} \square \\ + \quad 7 \\ \hline 9 \end{array}$$

20)
$$\begin{array}{r} 7 \\ + \quad \square \\ \hline 8 \end{array}$$

21)
$$\begin{array}{r} \square \\ + \quad 1 \\ \hline 4 \end{array}$$

22)
$$\begin{array}{r} 7 \\ + \quad \square \\ \hline 8 \end{array}$$

23)
$$\begin{array}{r} \square \\ + \quad 9 \\ \hline 12 \end{array}$$

24)
$$\begin{array}{r} 2 \\ + \quad \square \\ \hline 7 \end{array}$$

25)
$$\begin{array}{r} \square \\ + \quad 5 \\ \hline 13 \end{array}$$

26)
$$\begin{array}{r} 10 \\ + \quad \square \\ \hline 20 \end{array}$$

27)
$$\begin{array}{r} \square \\ + \quad 9 \\ \hline 19 \end{array}$$

28)
$$\begin{array}{r} 10 \\ + \quad \square \\ \hline 17 \end{array}$$

29)
$$\begin{array}{r} \square \\ + \quad 1 \\ \hline 3 \end{array}$$

30)
$$\begin{array}{r} 0 \\ + \quad \square \\ \hline 2 \end{array}$$

31)
$$\begin{array}{r} \square \\ + \quad 10 \\ \hline 13 \end{array}$$

32)
$$\begin{array}{r} 2 \\ + \quad \square \\ \hline 4 \end{array}$$

33)
$$\begin{array}{r} \square \\ + \quad 8 \\ \hline 14 \end{array}$$

34)
$$\begin{array}{r} 10 \\ + \quad \square \\ \hline 20 \end{array}$$

35)
$$\begin{array}{r} \square \\ + \quad 6 \\ \hline 8 \end{array}$$

36)
$$\begin{array}{r} 1 \\ + \quad \square \\ \hline 2 \end{array}$$

37)
$$\begin{array}{r} \square \\ + \quad 3 \\ \hline 10 \end{array}$$

38)
$$\begin{array}{r} 5 \\ + \quad \square \\ \hline 14 \end{array}$$

39)
$$\begin{array}{r} \square \\ + \quad 0 \\ \hline 0 \end{array}$$

40)
$$\begin{array}{r} 0 \\ + \quad \square \\ \hline 0 \end{array}$$

41)
$$\begin{array}{r} \square \\ + \quad 1 \\ \hline 10 \end{array}$$

42)
$$\begin{array}{r} 6 \\ + \quad \square \\ \hline 11 \end{array}$$

43)
$$\begin{array}{r} \square \\ + \quad 0 \\ \hline 0 \end{array}$$

44)
$$\begin{array}{r} 4 \\ + \quad \square \\ \hline 10 \end{array}$$

45)
$$\begin{array}{r} \square \\ + \quad 2 \\ \hline 4 \end{array}$$

46)
$$\begin{array}{r} 10 \\ + \quad \square \\ \hline 13 \end{array}$$

47)
$$\begin{array}{r} \square \\ + \quad 5 \\ \hline 14 \end{array}$$

48)
$$\begin{array}{r} 9 \\ + \quad \square \\ \hline 11 \end{array}$$

49)
$$\begin{array}{r} \square \\ + \quad 7 \\ \hline 12 \end{array}$$

50)
$$\begin{array}{r} 7 \\ + \quad \square \\ \hline 17 \end{array}$$

51)
$$\begin{array}{r} \square \\ + \quad 10 \\ \hline 17 \end{array}$$

52)
$$\begin{array}{r} 6 \\ + \quad \square \\ \hline 6 \end{array}$$

53)
$$\begin{array}{r} \square \\ + \quad 0 \\ \hline 8 \end{array}$$

54)
$$\begin{array}{r} 3 \\ + \quad \square \\ \hline 4 \end{array}$$

55)
$$\begin{array}{r} \square \\ + \quad 2 \\ \hline 3 \end{array}$$

56)
$$\begin{array}{r} 3 \\ + \quad \square \\ \hline 12 \end{array}$$

57)
$$\begin{array}{r} \square \\ + \quad 10 \\ \hline 10 \end{array}$$

58)
$$\begin{array}{r} 6 \\ + \quad \square \\ \hline 16 \end{array}$$

59)
$$\begin{array}{r} \square \\ + \quad 8 \\ \hline 16 \end{array}$$

60)
$$\begin{array}{r} 2 \\ + \quad \square \\ \hline 10 \end{array}$$

Score:

/60

Name:

time   :

1)
$$\begin{array}{r} \square \\ + \ 4 \\ \hline 11 \end{array}$$

2)
$$\begin{array}{r} 3 \\ + \ \square \\ \hline 3 \end{array}$$

3)
$$\begin{array}{r} \square \\ + \ 0 \\ \hline 8 \end{array}$$

4)
$$\begin{array}{r} 4 \\ + \ \square \\ \hline 10 \end{array}$$

5)
$$\begin{array}{r} \square \\ + \ 2 \\ \hline 9 \end{array}$$

6)
$$\begin{array}{r} 2 \\ + \ \square \\ \hline 3 \end{array}$$

7)
$$\begin{array}{r} \square \\ + \ 5 \\ \hline 9 \end{array}$$

8)
$$\begin{array}{r} 8 \\ + \ \square \\ \hline 8 \end{array}$$

9)
$$\begin{array}{r} \square \\ + \ 9 \\ \hline 11 \end{array}$$

10)
$$\begin{array}{r} 2 \\ + \ \square \\ \hline 10 \end{array}$$

11)
$$\begin{array}{r} \square \\ + \ 8 \\ \hline 16 \end{array}$$

12)
$$\begin{array}{r} 1 \\ + \ \square \\ \hline 2 \end{array}$$

13)
$$\begin{array}{r} \square \\ + \ 5 \\ \hline 8 \end{array}$$

14)
$$\begin{array}{r} 3 \\ + \ \square \\ \hline 8 \end{array}$$

15)
$$\begin{array}{r} \square \\ + \ 0 \\ \hline 4 \end{array}$$

16)
$$\begin{array}{r} 7 \\ + \ \square \\ \hline 12 \end{array}$$

17)
$$\begin{array}{r} \square \\ + \ 9 \\ \hline 15 \end{array}$$

18)
$$\begin{array}{r} 2 \\ + \ \square \\ \hline 8 \end{array}$$

19)
$$\begin{array}{r} \square \\ + \ 4 \\ \hline 13 \end{array}$$

20)
$$\begin{array}{r} 8 \\ + \ \square \\ \hline 17 \end{array}$$

21)
$$\begin{array}{r} \square \\ + \ 7 \\ \hline 8 \end{array}$$

22)
$$\begin{array}{r} 9 \\ + \ \square \\ \hline 16 \end{array}$$

23)
$$\begin{array}{r} \square \\ + \ 6 \\ \hline 7 \end{array}$$

24)
$$\begin{array}{r} 1 \\ + \ \square \\ \hline 7 \end{array}$$

25)
$$\begin{array}{r} \square \\ + \ 4 \\ \hline 8 \end{array}$$

26)
$$\begin{array}{r} 10 \\ + \ \square \\ \hline 18 \end{array}$$

27)
$$\begin{array}{r} \square \\ + \ 2 \\ \hline 7 \end{array}$$

28)
$$\begin{array}{r} 5 \\ + \ \square \\ \hline 13 \end{array}$$

29)
$$\begin{array}{r} \square \\ + \ 1 \\ \hline 11 \end{array}$$

30)
$$\begin{array}{r} 5 \\ + \ \square \\ \hline 5 \end{array}$$

31)
$$\begin{array}{r} \square \\ + \ 2 \\ \hline 2 \end{array}$$

32)
$$\begin{array}{r} 7 \\ + \ \square \\ \hline 14 \end{array}$$

33)
$$\begin{array}{r} \square \\ + \ 9 \\ \hline 9 \end{array}$$

34)
$$\begin{array}{r} 10 \\ + \ \square \\ \hline 11 \end{array}$$

35)
$$\begin{array}{r} \square \\ + \ 2 \\ \hline 4 \end{array}$$

36)
$$\begin{array}{r} 5 \\ + \ \square \\ \hline 7 \end{array}$$

37)
$$\begin{array}{r} \square \\ + \ 3 \\ \hline 4 \end{array}$$

38)
$$\begin{array}{r} 5 \\ + \ \square \\ \hline 9 \end{array}$$

39)
$$\begin{array}{r} \square \\ + \ 10 \\ \hline 11 \end{array}$$

40)
$$\begin{array}{r} 8 \\ + \ \square \\ \hline 18 \end{array}$$

41)
$$\begin{array}{r} \square \\ + \ 4 \\ \hline 8 \end{array}$$

42)
$$\begin{array}{r} 5 \\ + \ \square \\ \hline 13 \end{array}$$

43)
$$\begin{array}{r} \square \\ + \ 3 \\ \hline 3 \end{array}$$

44)
$$\begin{array}{r} 3 \\ + \ \square \\ \hline 3 \end{array}$$

45)
$$\begin{array}{r} \square \\ + \ 0 \\ \hline 10 \end{array}$$

46)
$$\begin{array}{r} 4 \\ + \ \square \\ \hline 5 \end{array}$$

47)
$$\begin{array}{r} \square \\ + \ 2 \\ \hline 2 \end{array}$$

48)
$$\begin{array}{r} 8 \\ + \ \square \\ \hline 10 \end{array}$$

49)
$$\begin{array}{r} \square \\ + \ 9 \\ \hline 11 \end{array}$$

50)
$$\begin{array}{r} 2 \\ + \ \square \\ \hline 2 \end{array}$$

51)
$$\begin{array}{r} \square \\ + \ 2 \\ \hline 12 \end{array}$$

52)
$$\begin{array}{r} 5 \\ + \ \square \\ \hline 8 \end{array}$$

53)
$$\begin{array}{r} \square \\ + \ 2 \\ \hline 6 \end{array}$$

54)
$$\begin{array}{r} 0 \\ + \ \square \\ \hline 10 \end{array}$$

55)
$$\begin{array}{r} \square \\ + \ 2 \\ \hline 2 \end{array}$$

56)
$$\begin{array}{r} 10 \\ + \ \square \\ \hline 14 \end{array}$$

57)
$$\begin{array}{r} \square \\ + \ 8 \\ \hline 18 \end{array}$$

58)
$$\begin{array}{r} 8 \\ + \ \square \\ \hline 17 \end{array}$$

59)
$$\begin{array}{r} \square \\ + \ 1 \\ \hline 3 \end{array}$$

60)
$$\begin{array}{r} 4 \\ + \ \square \\ \hline 5 \end{array}$$

Score:

/60

Name:

time   :

1)
```
  □
+  3
―――
 11
```

2)
```
  10
+  □
―――
 15
```

3)
```
  □
+  2
―――
  4
```

4)
```
  3
+  □
―――
  7
```

5)
```
  □
+  5
―――
 13
```

6)
```
  10
+  □
―――
 12
```

7)
```
  □
+  4
―――
 10
```

8)
```
  2
+  □
―――
 11
```

9)
```
  □
+  2
―――
  4
```

10)
```
  3
+  □
―――
  8
```

11)
```
  □
+  0
―――
  0
```

12)
```
  4
+  □
―――
 13
```

13)
```
  □
+  7
―――
 14
```

14)
```
  2
+  □
―――
  3
```

15)
```
  □
+  3
―――
 12
```

16)
```
  6
+  □
―――
 12
```

17)
```
  □
+  4
―――
 14
```

18)
```
   7
+  □
―――
 17
```

19)
```
  □
+  1
―――
  4
```

20)
```
  6
+  □
―――
  8
```

21)
```
  □
+  8
―――
 12
```

22)
```
  0
+  □
―――
  5
```

23)
```
  □
+  9
―――
 19
```

24)
```
  6
+  □
―――
  8
```

25)
```
  □
+  0
―――
  4
```

26)
```
  2
+  □
―――
  9
```

27)
```
  □
+  4
―――
  7
```

28)
```
   3
+ □
―――
 13
```

29)
```
  □
+  9
―――
 10
```

30)
```
  2
+  □
―――
  9
```

31)
```
  □
+  5
―――
 10
```

32)
```
  9
+  □
―――
 18
```

33)
```
  □
+  3
―――
  8
```

34)
```
  6
+  □
―――
  8
```

35)
```
  □
+  3
―――
  7
```

36)
```
  8
+  □
―――
  9
```

37)
```
  □
+  7
―――
 12
```

38)
```
  4
+  □
―――
 13
```

39)
```
  □
+  4
―――
  7
```

40)
```
  4
+  □
―――
  7
```

41)
```
  □
+  3
―――
  7
```

42)
```
   8
+ □
―――
 18
```

43)
```
  □
+  1
―――
 10
```

44)
```
  2
+  □
―――
  8
```

45)
```
  □
+  1
―――
  6
```

46)
```
  3
+  □
―――
  3
```

47)
```
  □
+  0
―――
  6
```

48)
```
  5
+  □
―――
 12
```

49)
```
  □
+  7
―――
  7
```

50)
```
  2
+  □
―――
  8
```

51)
```
  □
+  6
―――
 12
```

52)
```
  0
+  □
―――
  6
```

53)
```
  □
+  5
―――
 12
```

54)
```
  8
+  □
―――
 14
```

55)
```
  □
+  6
―――
  8
```

56)
```
  5
+  □
―――
 11
```

57)
```
  □
+  9
―――
 15
```

58)
```
  1
+  □
―――
  5
```

59)
```
  □
+  4
―――
 11
```

60)
```
  7
+  □
―――
 12
```

Page 57

Score:

/60

Name:

Time   :

1)
```
   □
+  4
─────
  13
```

2)
```
   5
+  □
─────
  13
```

3)
```
   □
+  2
─────
   9
```

4)
```
   8
+  □
─────
  18
```

5)
```
   □
+  5
─────
   9
```

6)
```
   1
+  □
─────
   4
```

7)
```
   □
+  8
─────
  15
```

8)
```
   0
+  □
─────
   7
```

9)
```
   □
+  0
─────
   7
```

10)
```
  10
+  □
─────
  19
```

11)
```
   □
+  4
─────
  13
```

12)
```
   0
+  □
─────
   9
```

13)
```
   □
+  7
─────
   9
```

14)
```
   2
+  □
─────
   3
```

15)
```
   □
+  6
─────
  13
```

16)
```
   8
+  □
─────
   8
```

17)
```
   □
+  1
─────
  10
```

18)
```
   3
+  □
─────
  13
```

19)
```
   □
+  7
─────
  13
```

20)
```
   1
+  □
─────
   6
```

21)
```
   □
+  7
─────
  16
```

22)
```
   9
+  □
─────
  18
```

23)
```
   □
+  3
─────
  10
```

24)
```
   0
+  □
─────
   1
```

25)
```
   □
+ 10
─────
  12
```

26)
```
  10
+  □
─────
  10
```

27)
```
   □
+  5
─────
  13
```

28)
```
   2
+  □
─────
   2
```

29)
```
   □
+  5
─────
   5
```

30)
```
   4
+  □
─────
  12
```

31)
```
   □
+ 10
─────
  12
```

32)
```
   7
+  □
─────
  17
```

33)
```
   □
+  1
─────
   5
```

34)
```
   0
+  □
─────
  10
```

35)
```
   □
+  2
─────
   8
```

36)
```
   4
+  □
─────
  10
```

37)
```
   □
+  0
─────
   5
```

38)
```
   5
+  □
─────
   8
```

39)
```
   □
+  4
─────
   6
```

40)
```
   8
+  □
─────
  13
```

41)
```
   □
+  8
─────
  16
```

42)
```
   9
+  □
─────
  12
```

43)
```
   □
+ 10
─────
  16
```

44)
```
   1
+  □
─────
   4
```

45)
```
   □
+ 10
─────
  11
```

46)
```
   8
+  □
─────
  11
```

47)
```
   □
+  5
─────
  15
```

48)
```
   4
+  □
─────
   7
```

49)
```
   □
+  2
─────
   3
```

50)
```
   1
+  □
─────
   4
```

51)
```
   □
+  7
─────
   8
```

52)
```
   3
+  □
─────
   8
```

53)
```
   □
+ 10
─────
  14
```

54)
```
  10
+  □
─────
  19
```

55)
```
   □
+  0
─────
   2
```

56)
```
   3
+  □
─────
   5
```

57)
```
   □
+ 10
─────
  15
```

58)
```
   5
+  □
─────
   8
```

59)
```
   □
+  2
─────
   2
```

60)
```
   3
+  □
─────
  12
```

Score:

/60

Name:

time   :

1)
$$\begin{array}{r} \square \\ +\ 1 \\ \hline 9 \end{array}$$

2)
$$\begin{array}{r} 5 \\ +\ \square \\ \hline 6 \end{array}$$

3)
$$\begin{array}{r} \square \\ +\ 8 \\ \hline 17 \end{array}$$

4)
$$\begin{array}{r} 4 \\ +\ \square \\ \hline 4 \end{array}$$

5)
$$\begin{array}{r} \square \\ +\ 2 \\ \hline 3 \end{array}$$

6)
$$\begin{array}{r} 5 \\ +\ \square \\ \hline 13 \end{array}$$

7)
$$\begin{array}{r} \square \\ +\ 10 \\ \hline 18 \end{array}$$

8)
$$\begin{array}{r} 0 \\ +\ \square \\ \hline 3 \end{array}$$

9)
$$\begin{array}{r} \square \\ +\ 5 \\ \hline 7 \end{array}$$

10)
$$\begin{array}{r} 7 \\ +\ \square \\ \hline 12 \end{array}$$

11)
$$\begin{array}{r} \square \\ +\ 3 \\ \hline 9 \end{array}$$

12)
$$\begin{array}{r} 6 \\ +\ \square \\ \hline 15 \end{array}$$

13)
$$\begin{array}{r} \square \\ +\ 8 \\ \hline 8 \end{array}$$

14)
$$\begin{array}{r} 10 \\ +\ \square \\ \hline 17 \end{array}$$

15)
$$\begin{array}{r} \square \\ +\ 2 \\ \hline 3 \end{array}$$

16)
$$\begin{array}{r} 5 \\ +\ \square \\ \hline 13 \end{array}$$

17)
$$\begin{array}{r} \square \\ +\ 0 \\ \hline 10 \end{array}$$

18)
$$\begin{array}{r} 2 \\ +\ \square \\ \hline 5 \end{array}$$

19)
$$\begin{array}{r} \square \\ +\ 3 \\ \hline 3 \end{array}$$

20)
$$\begin{array}{r} 6 \\ +\ \square \\ \hline 12 \end{array}$$

21)
$$\begin{array}{r} \square \\ +\ 3 \\ \hline 5 \end{array}$$

22)
$$\begin{array}{r} 9 \\ +\ \square \\ \hline 10 \end{array}$$

23)
$$\begin{array}{r} \square \\ +\ 0 \\ \hline 5 \end{array}$$

24)
$$\begin{array}{r} 9 \\ +\ \square \\ \hline 14 \end{array}$$

25)
$$\begin{array}{r} \square \\ +\ 10 \\ \hline 10 \end{array}$$

26)
$$\begin{array}{r} 0 \\ +\ \square \\ \hline 4 \end{array}$$

27)
$$\begin{array}{r} \square \\ +\ 6 \\ \hline 9 \end{array}$$

28)
$$\begin{array}{r} 5 \\ +\ \square \\ \hline 15 \end{array}$$

29)
$$\begin{array}{r} \square \\ +\ 7 \\ \hline 8 \end{array}$$

30)
$$\begin{array}{r} 4 \\ +\ \square \\ \hline 9 \end{array}$$

31)
$$\begin{array}{r} \square \\ +\ 4 \\ \hline 7 \end{array}$$

32)
$$\begin{array}{r} 4 \\ +\ \square \\ \hline 11 \end{array}$$

33)
$$\begin{array}{r} \square \\ +\ 10 \\ \hline 16 \end{array}$$

34)
$$\begin{array}{r} 10 \\ +\ \square \\ \hline 15 \end{array}$$

35)
$$\begin{array}{r} \square \\ +\ 7 \\ \hline 11 \end{array}$$

36)
$$\begin{array}{r} 0 \\ +\ \square \\ \hline 8 \end{array}$$

37)
$$\begin{array}{r} \square \\ +\ 3 \\ \hline 6 \end{array}$$

38)
$$\begin{array}{r} 7 \\ +\ \square \\ \hline 7 \end{array}$$

39)
$$\begin{array}{r} \square \\ +\ 6 \\ \hline 8 \end{array}$$

40)
$$\begin{array}{r} 5 \\ +\ \square \\ \hline 7 \end{array}$$

41)
$$\begin{array}{r} \square \\ +\ 0 \\ \hline 10 \end{array}$$

42)
$$\begin{array}{r} 6 \\ +\ \square \\ \hline 14 \end{array}$$

43)
$$\begin{array}{r} \square \\ +\ 8 \\ \hline 16 \end{array}$$

44)
$$\begin{array}{r} 9 \\ +\ \square \\ \hline 19 \end{array}$$

45)
$$\begin{array}{r} \square \\ +\ 4 \\ \hline 5 \end{array}$$

46)
$$\begin{array}{r} 3 \\ +\ \square \\ \hline 3 \end{array}$$

47)
$$\begin{array}{r} \square \\ +\ 6 \\ \hline 9 \end{array}$$

48)
$$\begin{array}{r} 4 \\ +\ \square \\ \hline 11 \end{array}$$

49)
$$\begin{array}{r} \square \\ +\ 3 \\ \hline 12 \end{array}$$

50)
$$\begin{array}{r} 0 \\ +\ \square \\ \hline 9 \end{array}$$

51)
$$\begin{array}{r} \square \\ +\ 5 \\ \hline 15 \end{array}$$

52)
$$\begin{array}{r} 9 \\ +\ \square \\ \hline 19 \end{array}$$

53)
$$\begin{array}{r} \square \\ +\ 3 \\ \hline 3 \end{array}$$

54)
$$\begin{array}{r} 2 \\ +\ \square \\ \hline 3 \end{array}$$

55)
$$\begin{array}{r} \square \\ +\ 7 \\ \hline 8 \end{array}$$

56)
$$\begin{array}{r} 5 \\ +\ \square \\ \hline 10 \end{array}$$

57)
$$\begin{array}{r} \square \\ +\ 6 \\ \hline 16 \end{array}$$

58)
$$\begin{array}{r} 10 \\ +\ \square \\ \hline 14 \end{array}$$

59)
$$\begin{array}{r} \square \\ +\ 3 \\ \hline 12 \end{array}$$

60)
$$\begin{array}{r} 6 \\ +\ \square \\ \hline 13 \end{array}$$

Score: /60

Name:

time :

1)
```
     □
+    8
─────
     9
```

2)
```
     1
+    □
─────
     6
```

3)
```
     □
+    2
─────
     4
```

4)
```
    10
+    □
─────
    19
```

5)
```
     □
+    0
─────
     4
```

6)
```
     4
+    □
─────
    13
```

7)
```
     □
+   10
─────
    14
```

8)
```
     2
+    □
─────
     7
```

9)
```
     □
+   10
─────
    16
```

10)
```
     1
+    □
─────
     3
```

11)
```
     □
+    7
─────
    14
```

12)
```
     0
+    □
─────
     9
```

13)
```
     □
+    0
─────
     6
```

14)
```
     5
+    □
─────
    10
```

15)
```
     □
+    3
─────
    11
```

16)
```
     4
+    □
─────
    12
```

17)
```
     □
+    3
─────
     9
```

18)
```
     6
+    □
─────
    10
```

19)
```
     □
+    8
─────
    16
```

20)
```
     3
+    □
─────
    13
```

21)
```
     □
+    3
─────
    13
```

22)
```
     1
+    □
─────
     4
```

23)
```
     □
+    4
─────
     5
```

24)
```
     2
+    □
─────
    10
```

25)
```
     □
+   10
─────
    11
```

26)
```
     5
+    □
─────
     5
```

27)
```
     □
+    7
─────
    11
```

28)
```
     9
+    □
─────
    12
```

29)
```
     □
+    1
─────
     3
```

30)
```
     5
+    □
─────
    13
```

31)
```
     □
+    6
─────
    13
```

32)
```
     2
+    □
─────
     2
```

33)
```
     □
+   10
─────
    14
```

34)
```
    10
+    □
─────
    15
```

35)
```
     □
+    5
─────
    13
```

36)
```
    10
+    □
─────
    10
```

37)
```
     □
+    8
─────
    15
```

38)
```
     4
+    □
─────
    12
```

39)
```
     □
+    5
─────
    13
```

40)
```
     7
+    □
─────
    11
```

41)
```
     □
+    3
─────
    11
```

42)
```
     0
+    □
─────
     1
```

43)
```
     □
+    6
─────
     7
```

44)
```
     3
+    □
─────
     6
```

45)
```
     □
+    5
─────
     9
```

46)
```
     9
+    □
─────
    18
```

47)
```
     □
+    1
─────
     5
```

48)
```
     6
+    □
─────
     9
```

49)
```
     □
+    2
─────
     4
```

50)
```
     6
+    □
─────
    15
```

51)
```
     □
+    3
─────
     3
```

52)
```
     6
+    □
─────
    15
```

53)
```
     □
+    5
─────
    10
```

54)
```
     4
+    □
─────
    14
```

55)
```
     □
+    6
─────
    14
```

56)
```
     9
+    □
─────
    19
```

57)
```
     □
+   10
─────
    18
```

58)
```
    10
+    □
─────
    17
```

59)
```
     □
+    7
─────
     8
```

60)
```
     6
+    □
─────
    16
```

Name:

Score:

/60

time   :

1)   16
   + 19

2)   15
   + 19

3)   15
   + 18

4)   11
   + 13

5)   19
   + 20

6)   13
   + 10

7)   15
   + 12

8)   12
   + 20

9)   13
   + 15

10)   19
   + 12

11)   18
   + 13

12)   18
   + 19

13)   11
   + 17

14)   15
   + 10

15)   11
   + 19

16)   13
   + 10

17)   11
   + 12

18)   11
   + 10

19)   16
   + 17

20)   14
   + 14

21)   13
   + 16

22)   20
   + 20

23)   16
   + 11

24)   17
   + 20

25)   13
   + 20

26)   18
   + 15

27)   13
   + 11

28)   20
   + 19

29)   10
   + 12

30)   15
   + 14

31)   18
   + 11

32)   10
   + 11

33)   15
   + 12

34)   17
   + 10

35)   14
   + 16

36)   11
   + 18

37)   12
   + 15

38)   10
   + 11

39)   10
   + 14

40)   20
   + 11

41)   13
   + 15

42)   18
   + 19

43)   17
   + 13

44)   13
   + 12

45)   16
   + 11

46)   17
   + 15

47)   13
   + 11

48)   14
   + 12

49)   16
   + 17

50)   20
   + 19

51)   20
   + 12

52)   10
   + 14

53)   19
   + 20

54)   11
   + 17

55)   15
   + 20

56)   14
   + 18

57)   12
   + 16

58)   14
   + 18

59)   15
   + 15

60)   14
   + 18

Name:

Score:

/60

time   :

1)   12
   + 16

2)   17
   + 20

3)   18
   + 15

4)   18
   + 15

5)   14
   + 18

6)   20
   + 19

7)   14
   + 12

8)   17
   + 17

9)   16
   + 17

10)   19
    + 16

11)   14
    + 10

12)   12
    + 10

13)   11
    + 16

14)   19
    + 17

15)   16
    + 13

16)   19
    + 11

17)   17
    + 20

18)   19
    + 17

19)   10
    + 14

20)   11
    + 13

21)   13
    + 10

22)   12
    + 19

23)   17
    + 18

24)   14
    + 10

25)   11
    + 18

26)   11
    + 18

27)   14
    + 19

28)   12
    + 12

29)   18
    + 19

30)   16
    + 15

31)   18
    + 18

32)   14
    + 13

33)   14
    + 12

34)   18
    + 10

35)   13
    + 14

36)   16
    + 16

37)   18
    + 13

38)   17
    + 19

39)   18
    + 18

40)   16
    + 18

41)   18
    + 17

42)   16
    + 19

43)   14
    + 18

44)   10
    + 18

45)   16
    + 15

46)   13
    + 19

47)   16
    + 14

48)   20
    + 17

49)   11
    + 12

50)   15
    + 20

51)   14
    + 20

52)   17
    + 13

53)   14
    + 10

54)   12
    + 15

55)   12
    + 10

56)   12
    + 16

57)   15
    + 12

58)   15
    + 19

59)   14
    + 11

60)   11
    + 14

Name:

Score:

/60

time   :

1)   20
  + 14

2)   13
  + 15

3)   18
  + 12

4)   14
  + 19

5)   18
  + 10

6)   20
  + 20

7)   12
  + 19

8)   13
  + 11

9)   12
  + 14

10)   14
  + 11

11)   19
  + 14

12)   19
  + 13

13)   10
  + 10

14)   18
  + 14

15)   15
  + 17

16)   15
  + 18

17)   17
  + 16

18)   18
  + 14

19)   17
  + 20

20)   14
  + 13

21)   13
  + 15

22)   13
  + 20

23)   14
  + 20

24)   10
  + 20

25)   14
  + 19

26)   11
  + 12

27)   15
  + 18

28)   13
  + 14

29)   20
  + 13

30)   19
  + 16

31)   12
  + 18

32)   14
  + 15

33)   18
  + 16

34)   11
  + 16

35)   11
  + 14

36)   19
  + 14

37)   20
  + 20

38)   12
  + 17

39)   17
  + 20

40)   14
  + 11

41)   18
  + 12

42)   19
  + 15

43)   17
  + 17

44)   17
  + 16

45)   14
  + 13

46)   11
  + 20

47)   10
  + 12

48)   20
  + 13

49)   13
  + 16

50)   15
  + 13

51)   14
  + 18

52)   13
  + 13

53)   19
  + 13

54)   17
  + 10

55)   16
  + 10

56)   15
  + 17

57)   17
  + 19

58)   17
  + 14

59)   20
  + 20

60)   10
  + 20

Name:

Score:

/60

Time   :

1)
$$10$$
$$+ 11$$

2)
$$14$$
$$+ 11$$

3)
$$15$$
$$+ 13$$

4)
$$15$$
$$+ 15$$

5)
$$12$$
$$+ 13$$

6)
$$13$$
$$+ 11$$

7)
$$10$$
$$+ 15$$

8)
$$13$$
$$+ 15$$

9)
$$15$$
$$+ 11$$

10)
$$10$$
$$+ 19$$

11)
$$17$$
$$+ 20$$

12)
$$14$$
$$+ 13$$

13)
$$17$$
$$+ 11$$

14)
$$17$$
$$+ 19$$

15)
$$15$$
$$+ 14$$

16)
$$19$$
$$+ 15$$

17)
$$13$$
$$+ 12$$

18)
$$12$$
$$+ 15$$

19)
$$19$$
$$+ 11$$

20)
$$17$$
$$+ 15$$

21)
$$13$$
$$+ 12$$

22)
$$17$$
$$+ 11$$

23)
$$11$$
$$+ 17$$

24)
$$19$$
$$+ 17$$

25)
$$12$$
$$+ 17$$

26)
$$18$$
$$+ 19$$

27)
$$11$$
$$+ 20$$

28)
$$11$$
$$+ 16$$

29)
$$13$$
$$+ 18$$

30)
$$14$$
$$+ 14$$

31)
$$17$$
$$+ 15$$

32)
$$10$$
$$+ 11$$

33)
$$20$$
$$+ 11$$

34)
$$13$$
$$+ 13$$

35)
$$14$$
$$+ 18$$

36)
$$10$$
$$+ 16$$

37)
$$14$$
$$+ 15$$

38)
$$20$$
$$+ 11$$

39)
$$13$$
$$+ 10$$

40)
$$17$$
$$+ 18$$

41)
$$20$$
$$+ 18$$

42)
$$16$$
$$+ 16$$

43)
$$13$$
$$+ 19$$

44)
$$16$$
$$+ 12$$

45)
$$10$$
$$+ 18$$

46)
$$14$$
$$+ 11$$

47)
$$18$$
$$+ 16$$

48)
$$18$$
$$+ 17$$

49)
$$18$$
$$+ 17$$

50)
$$19$$
$$+ 20$$

51)
$$14$$
$$+ 18$$

52)
$$17$$
$$+ 14$$

53)
$$20$$
$$+ 12$$

54)
$$14$$
$$+ 12$$

55)
$$18$$
$$+ 15$$

56)
$$18$$
$$+ 14$$

57)
$$14$$
$$+ 10$$

58)
$$16$$
$$+ 16$$

59)
$$16$$
$$+ 19$$

60)
$$13$$
$$+ 20$$

Score:

/60

Name:

time   :

1) 10
  + 19

2) 14
  + 12

3) 12
  + 12

4) 17
  + 16

5) 11
  + 14

6) 18
  + 16

7) 14
  + 12

8) 14
  + 11

9) 14
  + 13

10) 14
   + 14

11) 18
   + 11

12) 19
   + 10

13) 18
   + 11

14) 13
   + 11

15) 11
   + 17

16) 12
   + 20

17) 12
   + 15

18) 12
   + 14

19) 10
   + 16

20) 13
   + 10

21) 10
   + 18

22) 12
   + 19

23) 16
   + 19

24) 17
   + 20

25) 20
   + 12

26) 20
   + 18

27) 19
   + 12

28) 17
   + 14

29) 16
   + 16

30) 11
   + 18

31) 11
   + 14

32) 16
   + 14

33) 15
   + 12

34) 18
   + 20

35) 18
   + 17

36) 14
   + 11

37) 14
   + 20

38) 14
   + 13

39) 19
   + 13

40) 16
   + 16

41) 17
   + 13

42) 17
   + 10

43) 16
   + 16

44) 18
   + 18

45) 14
   + 13

46) 13
   + 13

47) 10
   + 20

48) 20
   + 20

49) 16
   + 13

50) 19
   + 15

51) 15
   + 19

52) 18
   + 11

53) 11
   + 19

54) 10
   + 16

55) 18
   + 18

56) 12
   + 14

57) 10
   + 10

58) 16
   + 17

59) 19
   + 16

60) 13
   + 12

Name:

Score: /60

time :

1) 15 + 16

2) 11 + 13

3) 18 + 17

4) 14 + 15

5) 20 + 17

6) 20 + 11

7) 18 + 15

8) 10 + 16

9) 12 + 15

10) 15 + 18

11) 12 + 12

12) 19 + 17

13) 17 + 13

14) 16 + 10

15) 17 + 17

16) 14 + 19

17) 12 + 16

18) 19 + 11

19) 12 + 18

20) 13 + 17

21) 18 + 17

22) 16 + 18

23) 19 + 12

24) 13 + 19

25) 14 + 17

26) 10 + 19

27) 17 + 14

28) 11 + 15

29) 12 + 16

30) 20 + 18

31) 12 + 14

32) 13 + 18

33) 19 + 17

34) 16 + 12

35) 11 + 10

36) 16 + 12

37) 20 + 10

38) 13 + 12

39) 14 + 11

40) 15 + 19

41) 13 + 19

42) 19 + 20

43) 14 + 18

44) 20 + 14

45) 11 + 17

46) 12 + 13

47) 18 + 11

48) 14 + 20

49) 20 + 15

50) 20 + 19

51) 10 + 15

52) 10 + 18

53) 19 + 20

54) 15 + 18

55) 15 + 18

56) 20 + 14

57) 16 + 14

58) 13 + 19

59) 19 + 13

60) 11 + 12

Name: [   ]

Score:

/60

time   :

1) 19
  + 15

2) 17
  + 12

3) 17
  + 12

4) 13
  + 14

5) 14
  + 11

6) 12
  + 17

7) 11
  + 17

8) 18
  + 13

9) 12
  + 12

10) 17
   + 20

11) 19
   + 18

12) 10
   + 19

13) 10
   + 15

14) 14
   + 19

15) 16
   + 18

16) 13
   + 13

17) 15
   + 11

18) 20
   + 10

19) 17
   + 13

20) 19
   + 12

21) 10
   + 18

22) 13
   + 10

23) 19
   + 10

24) 14
   + 11

25) 20
   + 17

26) 14
   + 16

27) 17
   + 10

28) 18
   + 11

29) 13
   + 16

30) 15
   + 12

31) 19
   + 19

32) 17
   + 14

33) 15
   + 12

34) 16
   + 11

35) 20
   + 17

36) 18
   + 14

37) 18
   + 16

38) 20
   + 15

39) 19
   + 14

40) 11
   + 13

41) 14
   + 14

42) 18
   + 20

43) 18
   + 20

44) 11
   + 15

45) 15
   + 11

46) 19
   + 16

47) 11
   + 16

48) 19
   + 18

49) 15
   + 14

50) 11
   + 17

51) 11
   + 12

52) 15
   + 18

53) 12
   + 10

54) 10
   + 20

55) 11
   + 18

56) 16
   + 16

57) 11
   + 10

58) 16
   + 11

59) 10
   + 13

60) 11
   + 13

Name:

Score:

/60

time   :

1) 15
  + 11

2) 19
  + 18

3) 14
  + 11

4) 11
  + 16

5) 12
  + 15

6) 11
  + 12

7) 17
  + 11

8) 18
  + 15

9) 20
  + 17

10) 17
   + 20

11) 14
   + 16

12) 17
   + 17

13) 11
   + 15

14) 10
   + 17

15) 20
   + 14

16) 13
   + 12

17) 18
   + 11

18) 13
   + 12

19) 20
   + 15

20) 14
   + 20

21) 10
   + 12

22) 18
   + 12

23) 14
   + 18

24) 14
   + 13

25) 14
   + 16

26) 12
   + 15

27) 11
   + 18

28) 12
   + 10

29) 19
   + 13

30) 19
   + 13

31) 17
   + 19

32) 13
   + 18

33) 11
   + 15

34) 10
   + 19

35) 13
   + 14

36) 13
   + 19

37) 10
   + 15

38) 20
   + 18

39) 12
   + 14

40) 11
   + 15

41) 16
   + 13

42) 10
   + 10

43) 20
   + 20

44) 19
   + 18

45) 20
   + 18

46) 14
   + 10

47) 11
   + 15

48) 11
   + 10

49) 10
   + 15

50) 12
   + 18

51) 15
   + 20

52) 13
   + 20

53) 19
   + 13

54) 13
   + 13

55) 11
   + 11

56) 20
   + 12

57) 14
   + 11

58) 10
   + 15

59) 12
   + 14

60) 19
   + 18

Name:

Score:

/60

time   :

1) 10
  + 16

2) 13
  + 15

3) 17
  + 18

4) 13
  + 12

5) 13
  + 19

6) 18
  + 19

7) 12
  + 10

8) 18
  + 15

9) 10
  + 16

10) 15
   + 15

11) 14
   + 17

12) 11
   + 17

13) 10
   + 14

14) 13
   + 15

15) 14
   + 20

16) 11
   + 18

17) 11
   + 17

18) 20
   + 13

19) 16
   + 17

20) 17
   + 13

21) 10
   + 12

22) 11
   + 19

23) 18
   + 20

24) 11
   + 19

25) 18
   + 18

26) 10
   + 16

27) 11
   + 20

28) 15
   + 11

29) 12
   + 20

30) 16
   + 16

31) 15
   + 10

32) 16
   + 10

33) 19
   + 11

34) 12
   + 12

35) 16
   + 13

36) 16
   + 11

37) 19
   + 10

38) 12
   + 12

39) 15
   + 10

40) 20
   + 12

41) 14
   + 19

42) 12
   + 18

43) 20
   + 19

44) 13
   + 19

45) 16
   + 13

46) 16
   + 13

47) 11
   + 19

48) 14
   + 10

49) 17
   + 19

50) 19
   + 14

51) 14
   + 16

52) 16
   + 14

53) 18
   + 17

54) 11
   + 10

55) 18
   + 16

56) 15
   + 16

57) 13
   + 17

58) 15
   + 20

59) 20
   + 19

60) 11
   + 18

Name:

Score:

/60

Time :

1) 17
+ 20

2) 10
+ 10

3) 16
+ 20

4) 10
+ 20

5) 18
+ 18

6) 10
+ 20

7) 19
+ 18

8) 20
+ 12

9) 10
+ 13

10) 19
+ 14

11) 16
+ 14

12) 15
+ 16

13) 20
+ 14

14) 17
+ 16

15) 18
+ 14

16) 13
+ 18

17) 11
+ 14

18) 12
+ 18

19) 18
+ 18

20) 14
+ 20

21) 19
+ 12

22) 15
+ 19

23) 13
+ 16

24) 14
+ 17

25) 11
+ 15

26) 19
+ 20

27) 15
+ 12

28) 18
+ 16

29) 13
+ 18

30) 16
+ 20

31) 16
+ 15

32) 20
+ 13

33) 16
+ 11

34) 19
+ 19

35) 17
+ 14

36) 12
+ 12

37) 12
+ 20

38) 15
+ 18

39) 10
+ 19

40) 20
+ 19

41) 18
+ 11

42) 17
+ 17

43) 14
+ 14

44) 15
+ 17

45) 20
+ 10

46) 15
+ 17

47) 15
+ 11

48) 15
+ 14

49) 11
+ 20

50) 10
+ 13

51) 13
+ 11

52) 13
+ 12

53) 16
+ 16

54) 19
+ 13

55) 11
+ 16

56) 11
+ 19

57) 18
+ 17

58) 11
+ 13

59) 11
+ 20

60) 19
+ 19

Score:

/60

Name:

time   :

1)
```
   [ ]
 + 19
   37
```

2)
```
   20
 +[  ]
   31
```

3)
```
   [ ]
 + 15
   31
```

4)
```
   15
 +[  ]
   30
```

5)
```
   [ ]
 + 15
   35
```

6)
```
   12
 +[  ]
   27
```

7)
```
   [ ]
 + 13
   32
```

8)
```
   11
 +[  ]
   22
```

9)
```
   [ ]
 + 16
   27
```

10)
```
   16
 +[  ]
   27
```

11)
```
   [ ]
 + 18
   32
```

12)
```
   15
 +[  ]
   33
```

13)
```
   [ ]
 + 12
   23
```

14)
```
   14
 +[  ]
   33
```

15)
```
   [ ]
 + 17
   35
```

16)
```
   13
 +[  ]
   30
```

17)
```
   [ ]
 + 19
   32
```

18)
```
   14
 +[  ]
   31
```

19)
```
   [ ]
 + 15
   27
```

20)
```
   13
 +[  ]
   29
```

21)
```
   [ ]
 + 18
   33
```

22)
```
   11
 +[  ]
   27
```

23)
```
   [ ]
 + 10
   28
```

24)
```
   11
 +[  ]
   25
```

25)
```
   [ ]
 + 12
   27
```

26)
```
   18
 +[  ]
   28
```

27)
```
   [ ]
 + 18
   29
```

28)
```
   18
 +[  ]
   35
```

29)
```
   [ ]
 + 17
   31
```

30)
```
   10
 +[  ]
   30
```

31)
```
   [ ]
 + 12
   25
```

32)
```
   14
 +[  ]
   26
```

33)
```
   [ ]
 + 11
   29
```

34)
```
   15
 +[  ]
   25
```

35)
```
   [ ]
 + 15
   32
```

36)
```
   13
 +[  ]
   24
```

37)
```
   [ ]
 + 18
   37
```

38)
```
   11
 +[  ]
   23
```

39)
```
   [ ]
 + 11
   21
```

40)
```
   20
 +[  ]
   36
```

41)
```
   [ ]
 + 11
   22
```

42)
```
   16
 +[  ]
   32
```

43)
```
   [ ]
 + 16
   36
```

44)
```
   15
 +[  ]
   26
```

45)
```
   [ ]
 + 18
   36
```

46)
```
   20
 +[  ]
   40
```

47)
```
   [ ]
 + 12
   24
```

48)
```
   13
 +[  ]
   24
```

49)
```
   [ ]
 + 14
   32
```

50)
```
   18
 +[  ]
   32
```

51)
```
   [ ]
 + 18
   37
```

52)
```
   11
 +[  ]
   21
```

53)
```
   [ ]
 + 17
   30
```

54)
```
   20
 +[  ]
   40
```

55)
```
   [ ]
 + 20
   34
```

56)
```
   20
 +[  ]
   35
```

57)
```
   [ ]
 + 11
   30
```

58)
```
   18
 +[  ]
   30
```

59)
```
   [ ]
 + 20
   34
```

60)
```
   14
 +[  ]
   30
```

Score:

/60

Name:

Time   :

1)
```
  [  ]
+ 16
  29
```

2)
```
   14
+ [  ]
  33
```

3)
```
  [  ]
+ 16
  27
```

4)
```
   10
+ [  ]
  26
```

5)
```
  [  ]
+ 12
  27
```

6)
```
   19
+ [  ]
  39
```

7)
```
  [  ]
+ 13
  27
```

8)
```
   17
+ [  ]
  28
```

9)
```
  [  ]
+ 20
  39
```

10)
```
   15
+ [  ]
  32
```

11)
```
  [  ]
+ 16
  28
```

12)
```
   17
+ [  ]
  36
```

13)
```
  [  ]
+ 10
  28
```

14)
```
   10
+ [  ]
  30
```

15)
```
  [  ]
+ 16
  32
```

16)
```
   15
+ [  ]
  35
```

17)
```
  [  ]
+ 11
  30
```

18)
```
   11
+ [  ]
  26
```

19)
```
  [  ]
+ 18
  37
```

20)
```
   13
+ [  ]
  26
```

21)
```
  [  ]
+ 17
  34
```

22)
```
   15
+ [  ]
  31
```

23)
```
  [  ]
+ 15
  26
```

24)
```
   13
+ [  ]
  32
```

25)
```
  [  ]
+ 18
  30
```

26)
```
   15
+ [  ]
  31
```

27)
```
  [  ]
+ 19
  39
```

28)
```
   12
+ [  ]
  22
```

29)
```
  [  ]
+ 18
  30
```

30)
```
   18
+ [  ]
  37
```

31)
```
  [  ]
+ 14
  24
```

32)
```
   15
+ [  ]
  26
```

33)
```
  [  ]
+ 10
  30
```

34)
```
   18
+ [  ]
  32
```

35)
```
  [  ]
+ 13
  24
```

36)
```
   19
+ [  ]
  30
```

37)
```
  [  ]
+ 14
  24
```

38)
```
   17
+ [  ]
  35
```

39)
```
  [  ]
+ 16
  32
```

40)
```
   16
+ [  ]
  34
```

41)
```
  [  ]
+ 11
  21
```

42)
```
   20
+ [  ]
  37
```

43)
```
  [  ]
+ 19
  36
```

44)
```
   11
+ [  ]
  29
```

45)
```
  [  ]
+ 10
  21
```

46)
```
   14
+ [  ]
  31
```

47)
```
  [  ]
+ 11
  22
```

48)
```
   19
+ [  ]
  36
```

49)
```
  [  ]
+ 20
  35
```

50)
```
   19
+ [  ]
  36
```

51)
```
  [  ]
+ 12
  31
```

52)
```
   16
+ [  ]
  33
```

53)
```
  [  ]
+ 20
  37
```

54)
```
   15
+ [  ]
  35
```

55)
```
  [  ]
+ 19
  31
```

56)
```
   18
+ [  ]
  37
```

57)
```
  [  ]
+ 18
  32
```

58)
```
   17
+ [  ]
  29
```

59)
```
  [  ]
+ 18
  31
```

60)
```
   15
+ [  ]
  25
```

Score: /60

Name:

Time :

1)
$$\begin{array}{r} \boxed{} \\ +\ 14 \\ \hline 31 \end{array}$$

2)
$$\begin{array}{r} 16 \\ +\ \boxed{} \\ \hline 33 \end{array}$$

3)
$$\begin{array}{r} \boxed{} \\ +\ 18 \\ \hline 38 \end{array}$$

4)
$$\begin{array}{r} 16 \\ +\ \boxed{} \\ \hline 26 \end{array}$$

5)
$$\begin{array}{r} \boxed{} \\ +\ 19 \\ \hline 31 \end{array}$$

6)
$$\begin{array}{r} 16 \\ +\ \boxed{} \\ \hline 29 \end{array}$$

7)
$$\begin{array}{r} \boxed{} \\ +\ 18 \\ \hline 37 \end{array}$$

8)
$$\begin{array}{r} 13 \\ +\ \boxed{} \\ \hline 27 \end{array}$$

9)
$$\begin{array}{r} \boxed{} \\ +\ 16 \\ \hline 32 \end{array}$$

10)
$$\begin{array}{r} 12 \\ +\ \boxed{} \\ \hline 26 \end{array}$$

11)
$$\begin{array}{r} \boxed{} \\ +\ 12 \\ \hline 29 \end{array}$$

12)
$$\begin{array}{r} 17 \\ +\ \boxed{} \\ \hline 29 \end{array}$$

13)
$$\begin{array}{r} \boxed{} \\ +\ 17 \\ \hline 33 \end{array}$$

14)
$$\begin{array}{r} 14 \\ +\ \boxed{} \\ \hline 28 \end{array}$$

15)
$$\begin{array}{r} \boxed{} \\ +\ 11 \\ \hline 28 \end{array}$$

16)
$$\begin{array}{r} 16 \\ +\ \boxed{} \\ \hline 32 \end{array}$$

17)
$$\begin{array}{r} \boxed{} \\ +\ 19 \\ \hline 31 \end{array}$$

18)
$$\begin{array}{r} 16 \\ +\ \boxed{} \\ \hline 34 \end{array}$$

19)
$$\begin{array}{r} \boxed{} \\ +\ 16 \\ \hline 30 \end{array}$$

20)
$$\begin{array}{r} 15 \\ +\ \boxed{} \\ \hline 33 \end{array}$$

21)
$$\begin{array}{r} \boxed{} \\ +\ 15 \\ \hline 28 \end{array}$$

22)
$$\begin{array}{r} 17 \\ +\ \boxed{} \\ \hline 36 \end{array}$$

23)
$$\begin{array}{r} \boxed{} \\ +\ 12 \\ \hline 28 \end{array}$$

24)
$$\begin{array}{r} 10 \\ +\ \boxed{} \\ \hline 21 \end{array}$$

25)
$$\begin{array}{r} \boxed{} \\ +\ 10 \\ \hline 30 \end{array}$$

26)
$$\begin{array}{r} 13 \\ +\ \boxed{} \\ \hline 32 \end{array}$$

27)
$$\begin{array}{r} \boxed{} \\ +\ 16 \\ \hline 27 \end{array}$$

28)
$$\begin{array}{r} 15 \\ +\ \boxed{} \\ \hline 25 \end{array}$$

29)
$$\begin{array}{r} \boxed{} \\ +\ 13 \\ \hline 24 \end{array}$$

30)
$$\begin{array}{r} 10 \\ +\ \boxed{} \\ \hline 24 \end{array}$$

31)
$$\begin{array}{r} \boxed{} \\ +\ 11 \\ \hline 28 \end{array}$$

32)
$$\begin{array}{r} 10 \\ +\ \boxed{} \\ \hline 30 \end{array}$$

33)
$$\begin{array}{r} \boxed{} \\ +\ 14 \\ \hline 31 \end{array}$$

34)
$$\begin{array}{r} 20 \\ +\ \boxed{} \\ \hline 39 \end{array}$$

35)
$$\begin{array}{r} \boxed{} \\ +\ 20 \\ \hline 40 \end{array}$$

36)
$$\begin{array}{r} 12 \\ +\ \boxed{} \\ \hline 29 \end{array}$$

37)
$$\begin{array}{r} \boxed{} \\ +\ 14 \\ \hline 25 \end{array}$$

38)
$$\begin{array}{r} 11 \\ +\ \boxed{} \\ \hline 24 \end{array}$$

39)
$$\begin{array}{r} \boxed{} \\ +\ 12 \\ \hline 28 \end{array}$$

40)
$$\begin{array}{r} 12 \\ +\ \boxed{} \\ \hline 24 \end{array}$$

41)
$$\begin{array}{r} \boxed{} \\ +\ 13 \\ \hline 27 \end{array}$$

42)
$$\begin{array}{r} 14 \\ +\ \boxed{} \\ \hline 29 \end{array}$$

43)
$$\begin{array}{r} \boxed{} \\ +\ 19 \\ \hline 30 \end{array}$$

44)
$$\begin{array}{r} 17 \\ +\ \boxed{} \\ \hline 28 \end{array}$$

45)
$$\begin{array}{r} \boxed{} \\ +\ 18 \\ \hline 28 \end{array}$$

46)
$$\begin{array}{r} 17 \\ +\ \boxed{} \\ \hline 37 \end{array}$$

47)
$$\begin{array}{r} \boxed{} \\ +\ 16 \\ \hline 33 \end{array}$$

48)
$$\begin{array}{r} 12 \\ +\ \boxed{} \\ \hline 24 \end{array}$$

49)
$$\begin{array}{r} \boxed{} \\ +\ 14 \\ \hline 29 \end{array}$$

50)
$$\begin{array}{r} 10 \\ +\ \boxed{} \\ \hline 28 \end{array}$$

51)
$$\begin{array}{r} \boxed{} \\ +\ 15 \\ \hline 25 \end{array}$$

52)
$$\begin{array}{r} 18 \\ +\ \boxed{} \\ \hline 38 \end{array}$$

53)
$$\begin{array}{r} \boxed{} \\ +\ 14 \\ \hline 25 \end{array}$$

54)
$$\begin{array}{r} 16 \\ +\ \boxed{} \\ \hline 30 \end{array}$$

55)
$$\begin{array}{r} \boxed{} \\ +\ 18 \\ \hline 30 \end{array}$$

56)
$$\begin{array}{r} 14 \\ +\ \boxed{} \\ \hline 33 \end{array}$$

57)
$$\begin{array}{r} \boxed{} \\ +\ 15 \\ \hline 28 \end{array}$$

58)
$$\begin{array}{r} 12 \\ +\ \boxed{} \\ \hline 32 \end{array}$$

59)
$$\begin{array}{r} \boxed{} \\ +\ 13 \\ \hline 33 \end{array}$$

60)
$$\begin{array}{r} 14 \\ +\ \boxed{} \\ \hline 24 \end{array}$$

Score:

/60

Name:

Time   :

1) ☐
    + 10
    28

2) 20
    +☐
    32

3) ☐
    + 11
    30

4) 20
    +☐
    37

5) ☐
    + 15
    27

6) 11
    +☐
    21

7) ☐
    + 15
    34

8) 18
    +☐
    32

9) ☐
    + 16
    34

10) 19
    +☐
    31

11) ☐
    + 18
    34

12) 12
    +☐
    24

13) ☐
    + 17
    32

14) 18
    +☐
    35

15) ☐
    + 18
    33

16) 10
    +☐
    23

17) ☐
    + 14
    28

18) 20
    +☐
    31

19) ☐
    + 11
    22

20) 19
    +☐
    33

21) ☐
    + 14
    31

22) 14
    +☐
    32

23) ☐
    + 20
    35

24) 16
    +☐
    29

25) ☐
    + 12
    24

26) 11
    +☐
    26

27) ☐
    + 17
    29

28) 15
    +☐
    29

29) ☐
    + 11
    24

30) 20
    +☐
    31

31) ☐
    + 17
    27

32) 15
    +☐
    28

33) ☐
    + 10
    28

34) 12
    +☐
    30

35) ☐
    + 16
    35

36) 11
    +☐
    31

37) ☐
    + 11
    24

38) 17
    +☐
    28

39) ☐
    + 13
    28

40) 20
    +☐
    34

41) ☐
    + 11
    21

42) 10
    +☐
    23

43) ☐
    + 11
    25

44) 10
    +☐
    21

45) ☐
    + 12
    26

46) 14
    +☐
    28

47) ☐
    + 13
    23

48) 17
    +☐
    32

49) ☐
    + 10
    21

50) 14
    +☐
    30

51) ☐
    + 12
    32

52) 15
    +☐
    35

53) ☐
    + 19
    38

54) 18
    +☐
    38

55) ☐
    + 16
    36

56) 16
    +☐
    29

57) ☐
    + 14
    32

58) 13
    +☐
    26

59) ☐
    + 17
    37

60) 20
    +☐
    38

Score: /60

Name:

time :

1)
$\square$
+ 18
38

2)
18
+ $\square$
30

3)
$\square$
+ 19
33

4)
19
+ $\square$
36

5)
$\square$
+ 18
31

6)
17
+ $\square$
32

7)
$\square$
+ 10
29

8)
10
+ $\square$
28

9)
$\square$
+ 16
30

10)
11
+ $\square$
22

11)
$\square$
+ 12
22

12)
14
+ $\square$
26

13)
$\square$
+ 11
29

14)
10
+ $\square$
21

15)
$\square$
+ 19
35

16)
16
+ $\square$
36

17)
$\square$
+ 13
23

18)
12
+ $\square$
23

19)
$\square$
+ 15
27

20)
11
+ $\square$
24

21)
$\square$
+ 13
29

22)
11
+ $\square$
25

23)
$\square$
+ 19
29

24)
15
+ $\square$
27

25)
$\square$
+ 17
27

26)
17
+ $\square$
35

27)
$\square$
+ 20
30

28)
13
+ $\square$
24

29)
$\square$
+ 13
27

30)
12
+ $\square$
32

31)
$\square$
+ 20
40

32)
20
+ $\square$
37

33)
$\square$
+ 12
30

34)
16
+ $\square$
34

35)
$\square$
+ 14
27

36)
17
+ $\square$
33

37)
$\square$
+ 19
38

38)
14
+ $\square$
31

39)
$\square$
+ 13
30

40)
16
+ $\square$
36

41)
$\square$
+ 16
27

42)
10
+ $\square$
30

43)
$\square$
+ 20
40

44)
17
+ $\square$
35

45)
$\square$
+ 20
34

46)
12
+ $\square$
22

47)
$\square$
+ 14
29

48)
20
+ $\square$
38

49)
$\square$
+ 19
38

50)
18
+ $\square$
38

51)
$\square$
+ 15
31

52)
13
+ $\square$
33

53)
$\square$
+ 11
23

54)
15
+ $\square$
33

55)
$\square$
+ 11
24

56)
14
+ $\square$
26

57)
$\square$
+ 19
35

58)
16
+ $\square$
27

59)
$\square$
+ 20
37

60)
19
+ $\square$
35

Score:

160

Name:

time   :

1)
$$\boxed{} + 12 = 31$$

2)
$$12 + \boxed{} = 22$$

3)
$$\boxed{} + 17 = 37$$

4)
$$17 + \boxed{} = 29$$

5)
$$\boxed{} + 10 = 20$$

6)
$$20 + \boxed{} = 37$$

7)
$$\boxed{} + 16 = 26$$

8)
$$18 + \boxed{} = 30$$

9)
$$\boxed{} + 20 = 30$$

10)
$$13 + \boxed{} = 23$$

11)
$$\boxed{} + 11 = 22$$

12)
$$14 + \boxed{} = 28$$

13)
$$\boxed{} + 16 = 32$$

14)
$$11 + \boxed{} = 27$$

15)
$$\boxed{} + 17 = 34$$

16)
$$12 + \boxed{} = 25$$

17)
$$\boxed{} + 14 = 29$$

18)
$$13 + \boxed{} = 30$$

19)
$$\boxed{} + 18 = 30$$

20)
$$13 + \boxed{} = 31$$

21)
$$\boxed{} + 17 = 36$$

22)
$$12 + \boxed{} = 24$$

23)
$$\boxed{} + 17 = 27$$

24)
$$20 + \boxed{} = 31$$

25)
$$\boxed{} + 15 = 35$$

26)
$$15 + \boxed{} = 29$$

27)
$$\boxed{} + 11 = 24$$

28)
$$16 + \boxed{} = 27$$

29)
$$\boxed{} + 11 = 26$$

30)
$$10 + \boxed{} = 22$$

31)
$$\boxed{} + 19 = 36$$

32)
$$16 + \boxed{} = 26$$

33)
$$\boxed{} + 10 = 20$$

34)
$$19 + \boxed{} = 29$$

35)
$$\boxed{} + 16 = 28$$

36)
$$16 + \boxed{} = 27$$

37)
$$\boxed{} + 10 = 26$$

38)
$$12 + \boxed{} = 26$$

39)
$$\boxed{} + 18 = 29$$

40)
$$19 + \boxed{} = 32$$

41)
$$\boxed{} + 10 = 21$$

42)
$$13 + \boxed{} = 28$$

43)
$$\boxed{} + 19 = 32$$

44)
$$14 + \boxed{} = 33$$

45)
$$\boxed{} + 20 = 34$$

46)
$$10 + \boxed{} = 21$$

47)
$$\boxed{} + 18 = 32$$

48)
$$19 + \boxed{} = 29$$

49)
$$\boxed{} + 19 = 38$$

50)
$$10 + \boxed{} = 30$$

51)
$$\boxed{} + 14 = 26$$

52)
$$10 + \boxed{} = 20$$

53)
$$\boxed{} + 14 = 34$$

54)
$$10 + \boxed{} = 29$$

55)
$$\boxed{} + 10 = 25$$

56)
$$16 + \boxed{} = 33$$

57)
$$\boxed{} + 15 = 30$$

58)
$$19 + \boxed{} = 34$$

59)
$$\boxed{} + 15 = 33$$

60)
$$18 + \boxed{} = 28$$

Score:

Name:

/60

time   :

1) □
   + 10
    23

2) 10
   +□
    25

3) □
   + 17
    30

4) 11
   +□
    24

5) □
   + 18
    33

6) 17
   +□
    29

7) □
   + 18
    29

8) 17
   +□
    28

9) □
   + 11
    25

10) 17
   +□
    27

11) □
   + 18
    33

12) 14
   +□
    33

13) □
   + 13
    28

14) 10
   +□
    29

15) □
   + 17
    28

16) 10
   +□
    23

17) □
   + 20
    34

18) 12
   +□
    23

19) □
   + 11
    21

20) 18
   +□
    32

21) □
   + 11
    25

22) 17
   +□
    32

23) □
   + 12
    31

24) 20
   +□
    31

25) □
   + 14
    32

26) 14
   +□
    28

27) □
   + 19
    37

28) 10
   +□
    22

29) □
   + 13
    24

30) 19
   +□
    31

31) □
   + 10
    27

32) 15
   +□
    28

33) □
   + 14
    33

34) 18
   +□
    34

35) □
   + 18
    29

36) 14
   +□
    28

37) □
   + 19
    35

38) 20
   +□
    36

39) □
   + 20
    33

40) 16
   +□
    28

41) □
   + 13
    27

42) 15
   +□
    33

43) □
   + 14
    30

44) 10
   +□
    20

45) □
   + 12
    30

46) 15
   +□
    35

47) □
   + 19
    32

48) 14
   +□
    30

49) □
   + 17
    36

50) 12
   +□
    27

51) □
   + 11
    24

52) 15
   +□
    28

53) □
   + 15
    31

54) 16
   +□
    27

55) □
   + 19
    39

56) 10
   +□
    30

57) □
   + 17
    32

58) 13
   +□
    33

59) □
   + 12
    23

60) 15
   +□
    28

Page 77

Score:

/60

Name:

Time   :

1)
```
   [  ]
 + 16
   28
```

2)
```
   16
 +[  ]
   29
```

3)
```
   [  ]
 + 20
   35
```

4)
```
   12
 +[  ]
   28
```

5)
```
   [  ]
 + 15
   35
```

6)
```
   18
 +[  ]
   28
```

7)
```
   [  ]
 + 19
   30
```

8)
```
   13
 +[  ]
   33
```

9)
```
   [  ]
 + 18
   33
```

10)
```
   17
 +[  ]
   29
```

11)
```
   [  ]
 + 11
   29
```

12)
```
   15
 +[  ]
   25
```

13)
```
   [  ]
 + 16
   29
```

14)
```
   18
 +[  ]
   32
```

15)
```
   [  ]
 + 19
   31
```

16)
```
   20
 +[  ]
   31
```

17)
```
   [  ]
 + 12
   30
```

18)
```
   19
 +[  ]
   36
```

19)
```
   [  ]
 + 17
   31
```

20)
```
   15
 +[  ]
   26
```

21)
```
   [  ]
 + 17
   32
```

22)
```
   13
 +[  ]
   29
```

23)
```
   [  ]
 + 14
   33
```

24)
```
   19
 +[  ]
   30
```

25)
```
   [  ]
 + 20
   33
```

26)
```
   16
 +[  ]
   33
```

27)
```
   [  ]
 + 20
   38
```

28)
```
   10
 +[  ]
   20
```

29)
```
   [  ]
 + 10
   30
```

30)
```
   15
 +[  ]
   27
```

31)
```
   [  ]
 + 11
   26
```

32)
```
   12
 +[  ]
   28
```

33)
```
   [  ]
 + 12
   22
```

34)
```
   17
 +[  ]
   28
```

35)
```
   [  ]
 + 15
   27
```

36)
```
   16
 +[  ]
   35
```

37)
```
   [  ]
 + 12
   26
```

38)
```
   12
 +[  ]
   29
```

39)
```
   [  ]
 + 13
   33
```

40)
```
   17
 +[  ]
   37
```

41)
```
   [  ]
 + 10
   28
```

42)
```
   17
 +[  ]
   35
```

43)
```
   [  ]
 + 18
   37
```

44)
```
   16
 +[  ]
   26
```

45)
```
   [  ]
 + 10
   28
```

46)
```
   11
 +[  ]
   25
```

47)
```
   [  ]
 + 11
   25
```

48)
```
   13
 +[  ]
   31
```

49)
```
   [  ]
 + 10
   22
```

50)
```
   14
 +[  ]
   24
```

51)
```
   [  ]
 + 15
   29
```

52)
```
   14
 +[  ]
   31
```

53)
```
   [  ]
 + 11
   29
```

54)
```
   14
 +[  ]
   34
```

55)
```
   [  ]
 + 11
   24
```

56)
```
   15
 +[  ]
   31
```

57)
```
   [  ]
 + 17
   29
```

58)
```
   13
 +[  ]
   27
```

59)
```
   [  ]
 + 16
   31
```

60)
```
   15
 +[  ]
   35
```

Score:

/60

Name:

time   :

1)
```
  □
+ 11
  31
```

2)
```
  15
+ □
  30
```

3)
```
  □
+ 11
  27
```

4)
```
  15
+ □
  25
```

5)
```
  □
+ 16
  30
```

6)
```
  13
+ □
  26
```

7)
```
  □
+ 11
  28
```

8)
```
  13
+ □
  32
```

9)
```
  □
+ 10
  27
```

10)
```
  20
+ □
  36
```

11)
```
  □
+ 18
  36
```

12)
```
  13
+ □
  33
```

13)
```
  □
+ 14
  27
```

14)
```
  10
+ □
  27
```

15)
```
  □
+ 16
  34
```

16)
```
  10
+ □
  28
```

17)
```
  □
+ 19
  37
```

18)
```
  12
+ □
  23
```

19)
```
  □
+ 16
  26
```

20)
```
  17
+ □
  36
```

21)
```
  □
+ 14
  33
```

22)
```
  14
+ □
  32
```

23)
```
  □
+ 10
  23
```

24)
```
  16
+ □
  29
```

25)
```
  □
+ 10
  26
```

26)
```
  14
+ □
  24
```

27)
```
  □
+ 15
  34
```

28)
```
  12
+ □
  28
```

29)
```
  □
+ 16
  35
```

30)
```
  12
+ □
  22
```

31)
```
  □
+ 20
  33
```

32)
```
  13
+ □
  32
```

33)
```
  □
+ 15
  31
```

34)
```
  13
+ □
  31
```

35)
```
  □
+ 16
  29
```

36)
```
  18
+ □
  29
```

37)
```
  □
+ 19
  33
```

38)
```
  10
+ □
  23
```

39)
```
  □
+ 20
  32
```

40)
```
  18
+ □
  33
```

41)
```
  □
+ 16
  33
```

42)
```
  14
+ □
  25
```

43)
```
  □
+ 10
  23
```

44)
```
  17
+ □
  31
```

45)
```
  □
+ 19
  35
```

46)
```
  13
+ □
  33
```

47)
```
  □
+ 18
  37
```

48)
```
  19
+ □
  33
```

49)
```
  □
+ 13
  32
```

50)
```
  10
+ □
  23
```

51)
```
  □
+ 20
  40
```

52)
```
  19
+ □
  32
```

53)
```
  □
+ 19
  33
```

54)
```
  11
+ □
  30
```

55)
```
  □
+ 20
  31
```

56)
```
  13
+ □
  28
```

57)
```
  □
+ 10
  22
```

58)
```
  20
+ □
  32
```

59)
```
  □
+ 19
  33
```

60)
```
  20
+ □
  37
```

Page 79

Score:

/60

Name:

time   :

1)
```
   [  ]
 + 16
 ----
  35
```

2)
```
   16
 +[  ]
 ----
  34
```

3)
```
   [  ]
 + 10
 ----
  26
```

4)
```
   19
 +[  ]
 ----
  35
```

5)
```
   [  ]
 + 14
 ----
  25
```

6)
```
   11
 +[  ]
 ----
  31
```

7)
```
   [  ]
 + 13
 ----
  29
```

8)
```
   17
 +[  ]
 ----
  31
```

9)
```
   [  ]
 + 11
 ----
  29
```

10)
```
   19
 +[  ]
 ----
  30
```

11)
```
   [  ]
 + 10
 ----
  30
```

12)
```
   17
 +[  ]
 ----
  31
```

13)
```
   [  ]
 + 20
 ----
  31
```

14)
```
   20
 +[  ]
 ----
  34
```

15)
```
   [  ]
 + 19
 ----
  39
```

16)
```
   16
 +[  ]
 ----
  31
```

17)
```
   [  ]
 + 16
 ----
  27
```

18)
```
   14
 +[  ]
 ----
  29
```

19)
```
   [  ]
 + 12
 ----
  23
```

20)
```
   13
 +[  ]
 ----
  32
```

21)
```
   [  ]
 + 16
 ----
  33
```

22)
```
   18
 +[  ]
 ----
  32
```

23)
```
   [  ]
 + 12
 ----
  28
```

24)
```
   10
 +[  ]
 ----
  21
```

25)
```
   [  ]
 + 17
 ----
  28
```

26)
```
   20
 +[  ]
 ----
  35
```

27)
```
   [  ]
 + 12
 ----
  23
```

28)
```
   10
 +[  ]
 ----
  21
```

29)
```
   [  ]
 + 18
 ----
  29
```

30)
```
   16
 +[  ]
 ----
  30
```

31)
```
   [  ]
 + 11
 ----
  22
```

32)
```
   17
 +[  ]
 ----
  30
```

33)
```
   [  ]
 + 11
 ----
  31
```

34)
```
   18
 +[  ]
 ----
  34
```

35)
```
   [  ]
 + 15
 ----
  35
```

36)
```
   12
 +[  ]
 ----
  32
```

37)
```
   [  ]
 + 15
 ----
  27
```

38)
```
   19
 +[  ]
 ----
  32
```

39)
```
   [  ]
 + 17
 ----
  37
```

40)
```
   19
 +[  ]
 ----
  37
```

41)
```
   [  ]
 + 18
 ----
  28
```

42)
```
   10
 +[  ]
 ----
  23
```

43)
```
   [  ]
 + 18
 ----
  31
```

44)
```
   12
 +[  ]
 ----
  22
```

45)
```
   [  ]
 + 20
 ----
  36
```

46)
```
   19
 +[  ]
 ----
  39
```

47)
```
   [  ]
 + 12
 ----
  31
```

48)
```
   17
 +[  ]
 ----
  30
```

49)
```
   [  ]
 + 13
 ----
  30
```

50)
```
   17
 +[  ]
 ----
  36
```

51)
```
   [  ]
 + 18
 ----
  34
```

52)
```
   15
 +[  ]
 ----
  31
```

53)
```
   [  ]
 + 13
 ----
  31
```

54)
```
   17
 +[  ]
 ----
  33
```

55)
```
   [  ]
 + 14
 ----
  32
```

56)
```
   13
 +[  ]
 ----
  23
```

57)
```
   [  ]
 + 14
 ----
  25
```

58)
```
   15
 +[  ]
 ----
  32
```

59)
```
   [  ]
 + 12
 ----
  22
```

60)
```
   15
 +[  ]
 ----
  28
```

Name:

Score:

/60

Time   :

1) 3
   - 1

2) 4
   - 0

3) 3
   - 0

4) 5
   - 5

5) 4
   - 3

6) 5
   - 4

7) 4
   - 3

8) 2
   - 2

9) 5
   - 3

10) 5
   - 2

11) 5
   - 0

12) 4
   - 1

13) 1
   - 1

14) 2
   - 2

15) 5
   - 4

16) 2
   - 0

17) 5
   - 5

18) 5
   - 1

19) 4
   - 2

20) 5
   - 5

21) 1
   - 0

22) 3
   - 0

23) 4
   - 0

24) 0
   - 0

25) 3
   - 0

26) 4
   - 1

27) 2
   - 1

28) 1
   - 1

29) 4
   - 2

30) 5
   - 0

31) 5
   - 2

32) 0
   - 0

33) 5
   - 1

34) 1
   - 0

35) 4
   - 0

36) 5
   - 4

37) 2
   - 0

38) 3
   - 1

39) 5
   - 0

40) 2
   - 2

41) 5
   - 2

42) 4
   - 4

43) 4
   - 0

44) 4
   - 0

45) 2
   - 0

46) 5
   - 1

47) 2
   - 0

48) 4
   - 0

49) 3
   - 3

50) 5
   - 1

51) 4
   - 2

52) 4
   - 3

53) 5
   - 5

54) 5
   - 0

55) 4
   - 0

56) 3
   - 0

57) 3
   - 3

58) 5
   - 4

59) 5
   - 4

60) 5
   - 2

Score:

/60

Name:

Time   :

1) 2
  - 2

2) 4
  - 2

3) 3
  - 3

4) 5
  - 5

5) 3
  - 1

6) 3
  - 0

7) 5
  - 5

8) 3
  - 3

9) 1
  - 0

10) 3
  - 1

11) 3
  - 3

12) 5
  - 0

13) 5
  - 3

14) 4
  - 3

15) 5
  - 5

16) 5
  - 3

17) 2
  - 0

18) 3
  - 1

19) 5
  - 4

20) 5
  - 4

21) 2
  - 2

22) 1
  - 1

23) 4
  - 3

24) 4
  - 1

25) 4
  - 1

26) 1
  - 1

27) 1
  - 1

28) 4
  - 3

29) 3
  - 0

30) 5
  - 3

31) 0
  - 0

32) 5
  - 2

33) 1
  - 0

34) 5
  - 1

35) 3
  - 2

36) 5
  - 4

37) 5
  - 5

38) 3
  - 0

39) 0
  - 0

40) 4
  - 0

41) 2
  - 2

42) 3
  - 3

43) 4
  - 2

44) 2
  - 1

45) 4
  - 3

46) 5
  - 5

47) 3
  - 2

48) 2
  - 0

49) 3
  - 3

50) 5
  - 0

51) 2
  - 0

52) 1
  - 1

53) 2
  - 1

54) 5
  - 1

55) 2
  - 2

56) 3
  - 0

57) 4
  - 3

58) 4
  - 3

59) 5
  - 4

60) 2
  - 0

Name:

Score: /60

Time :

1) 3 − 0

2) 4 − 1

3) 4 − 0

4) 4 − 1

5) 5 − 3

6) 5 − 1

7) 4 − 3

8) 5 − 1

9) 4 − 4

10) 4 − 4

11) 1 − 0

12) 5 − 4

13) 4 − 4

14) 3 − 0

15) 3 − 3

16) 3 − 1

17) 3 − 2

18) 4 − 0

19) 4 − 4

20) 5 − 3

21) 5 − 4

22) 4 − 1

23) 4 − 0

24) 5 − 2

25) 5 − 4

26) 4 − 1

27) 5 − 4

28) 4 − 1

29) 4 − 4

30) 3 − 3

31) 5 − 3

32) 1 − 0

33) 5 − 3

34) 2 − 2

35) 5 − 0

36) 5 − 0

37) 4 − 2

38) 3 − 2

39) 5 − 1

40) 4 − 3

41) 4 − 1

42) 1 − 0

43) 2 − 0

44) 5 − 0

45) 2 − 2

46) 2 − 1

47) 4 − 2

48) 3 − 0

49) 5 − 0

50) 1 − 0

51) 4 − 4

52) 5 − 0

53) 2 − 2

54) 5 − 4

55) 4 − 1

56) 4 − 1

57) 0 − 0

58) 5 − 4

59) 4 − 0

60) 5 − 5

Name:

Score:

/60

time   :

1)
$$\begin{array}{r} 3 \\ -\ 3 \\ \hline \end{array}$$

2)
$$\begin{array}{r} 5 \\ -\ 0 \\ \hline \end{array}$$

3)
$$\begin{array}{r} 3 \\ -\ 0 \\ \hline \end{array}$$

4)
$$\begin{array}{r} 0 \\ -\ 0 \\ \hline \end{array}$$

5)
$$\begin{array}{r} 2 \\ -\ 1 \\ \hline \end{array}$$

6)
$$\begin{array}{r} 5 \\ -\ 2 \\ \hline \end{array}$$

7)
$$\begin{array}{r} 0 \\ -\ 0 \\ \hline \end{array}$$

8)
$$\begin{array}{r} 3 \\ -\ 1 \\ \hline \end{array}$$

9)
$$\begin{array}{r} 1 \\ -\ 1 \\ \hline \end{array}$$

10)
$$\begin{array}{r} 5 \\ -\ 4 \\ \hline \end{array}$$

11)
$$\begin{array}{r} 5 \\ -\ 5 \\ \hline \end{array}$$

12)
$$\begin{array}{r} 5 \\ -\ 5 \\ \hline \end{array}$$

13)
$$\begin{array}{r} 5 \\ -\ 4 \\ \hline \end{array}$$

14)
$$\begin{array}{r} 4 \\ -\ 0 \\ \hline \end{array}$$

15)
$$\begin{array}{r} 5 \\ -\ 1 \\ \hline \end{array}$$

16)
$$\begin{array}{r} 0 \\ -\ 0 \\ \hline \end{array}$$

17)
$$\begin{array}{r} 3 \\ -\ 2 \\ \hline \end{array}$$

18)
$$\begin{array}{r} 0 \\ -\ 0 \\ \hline \end{array}$$

19)
$$\begin{array}{r} 4 \\ -\ 0 \\ \hline \end{array}$$

20)
$$\begin{array}{r} 4 \\ -\ 4 \\ \hline \end{array}$$

21)
$$\begin{array}{r} 0 \\ -\ 0 \\ \hline \end{array}$$

22)
$$\begin{array}{r} 4 \\ -\ 3 \\ \hline \end{array}$$

23)
$$\begin{array}{r} 4 \\ -\ 0 \\ \hline \end{array}$$

24)
$$\begin{array}{r} 1 \\ -\ 1 \\ \hline \end{array}$$

25)
$$\begin{array}{r} 3 \\ -\ 3 \\ \hline \end{array}$$

26)
$$\begin{array}{r} 4 \\ -\ 2 \\ \hline \end{array}$$

27)
$$\begin{array}{r} 3 \\ -\ 2 \\ \hline \end{array}$$

28)
$$\begin{array}{r} 2 \\ -\ 0 \\ \hline \end{array}$$

29)
$$\begin{array}{r} 3 \\ -\ 3 \\ \hline \end{array}$$

30)
$$\begin{array}{r} 1 \\ -\ 1 \\ \hline \end{array}$$

31)
$$\begin{array}{r} 4 \\ -\ 0 \\ \hline \end{array}$$

32)
$$\begin{array}{r} 3 \\ -\ 0 \\ \hline \end{array}$$

33)
$$\begin{array}{r} 4 \\ -\ 2 \\ \hline \end{array}$$

34)
$$\begin{array}{r} 3 \\ -\ 2 \\ \hline \end{array}$$

35)
$$\begin{array}{r} 5 \\ -\ 4 \\ \hline \end{array}$$

36)
$$\begin{array}{r} 2 \\ -\ 1 \\ \hline \end{array}$$

37)
$$\begin{array}{r} 0 \\ -\ 0 \\ \hline \end{array}$$

38)
$$\begin{array}{r} 0 \\ -\ 0 \\ \hline \end{array}$$

39)
$$\begin{array}{r} 3 \\ -\ 0 \\ \hline \end{array}$$

40)
$$\begin{array}{r} 4 \\ -\ 3 \\ \hline \end{array}$$

41)
$$\begin{array}{r} 2 \\ -\ 1 \\ \hline \end{array}$$

42)
$$\begin{array}{r} 3 \\ -\ 1 \\ \hline \end{array}$$

43)
$$\begin{array}{r} 5 \\ -\ 3 \\ \hline \end{array}$$

44)
$$\begin{array}{r} 3 \\ -\ 2 \\ \hline \end{array}$$

45)
$$\begin{array}{r} 3 \\ -\ 3 \\ \hline \end{array}$$

46)
$$\begin{array}{r} 5 \\ -\ 5 \\ \hline \end{array}$$

47)
$$\begin{array}{r} 0 \\ -\ 0 \\ \hline \end{array}$$

48)
$$\begin{array}{r} 4 \\ -\ 0 \\ \hline \end{array}$$

49)
$$\begin{array}{r} 5 \\ -\ 2 \\ \hline \end{array}$$

50)
$$\begin{array}{r} 4 \\ -\ 4 \\ \hline \end{array}$$

51)
$$\begin{array}{r} 3 \\ -\ 3 \\ \hline \end{array}$$

52)
$$\begin{array}{r} 3 \\ -\ 2 \\ \hline \end{array}$$

53)
$$\begin{array}{r} 5 \\ -\ 3 \\ \hline \end{array}$$

54)
$$\begin{array}{r} 4 \\ -\ 3 \\ \hline \end{array}$$

55)
$$\begin{array}{r} 2 \\ -\ 1 \\ \hline \end{array}$$

56)
$$\begin{array}{r} 3 \\ -\ 0 \\ \hline \end{array}$$

57)
$$\begin{array}{r} 4 \\ -\ 0 \\ \hline \end{array}$$

58)
$$\begin{array}{r} 5 \\ -\ 2 \\ \hline \end{array}$$

59)
$$\begin{array}{r} 4 \\ -\ 4 \\ \hline \end{array}$$

60)
$$\begin{array}{r} 2 \\ -\ 2 \\ \hline \end{array}$$

Name:

Score: /60

time   :

1) 5
 - 1

2) 5
 - 2

3) 4
 - 0

4) 5
 - 0

5) 0
 - 0

6) 5
 - 5

7) 5
 - 1

8) 3
 - 2

9) 5
 - 3

10) 4
 - 0

11) 3
 - 1

12) 2
 - 2

13) 3
 - 3

14) 2
 - 0

15) 5
 - 3

16) 5
 - 1

17) 3
 - 2

18) 2
 - 0

19) 3
 - 2

20) 2
 - 2

21) 3
 - 3

22) 3
 - 0

23) 5
 - 0

24) 3
 - 0

25) 4
 - 1

26) 4
 - 0

27) 5
 - 4

28) 5
 - 4

29) 5
 - 0

30) 4
 - 2

31) 5
 - 2

32) 1
 - 0

33) 1
 - 0

34) 5
 - 2

35) 2
 - 0

36) 5
 - 0

37) 4
 - 3

38) 3
 - 2

39) 4
 - 1

40) 5
 - 2

41) 5
 - 3

42) 3
 - 1

43) 0
 - 0

44) 3
 - 2

45) 3
 - 3

46) 4
 - 4

47) 1
 - 0

48) 5
 - 2

49) 5
 - 3

50) 5
 - 2

51) 2
 - 2

52) 3
 - 3

53) 4
 - 4

54) 0
 - 0

55) 4
 - 2

56) 2
 - 0

57) 5
 - 4

58) 4
 - 1

59) 5
 - 5

60) 5
 - 3

Name:

Score:

/60

time   :

1) $\begin{array}{r} 1 \\ -1 \\ \hline \end{array}$
2) $\begin{array}{r} 5 \\ -4 \\ \hline \end{array}$
3) $\begin{array}{r} 1 \\ -1 \\ \hline \end{array}$
4) $\begin{array}{r} 3 \\ -3 \\ \hline \end{array}$
5) $\begin{array}{r} 3 \\ -2 \\ \hline \end{array}$
6) $\begin{array}{r} 5 \\ -1 \\ \hline \end{array}$

7) $\begin{array}{r} 3 \\ -1 \\ \hline \end{array}$
8) $\begin{array}{r} 5 \\ -2 \\ \hline \end{array}$
9) $\begin{array}{r} 1 \\ -1 \\ \hline \end{array}$
10) $\begin{array}{r} 3 \\ -2 \\ \hline \end{array}$
11) $\begin{array}{r} 2 \\ -1 \\ \hline \end{array}$
12) $\begin{array}{r} 2 \\ -1 \\ \hline \end{array}$

13) $\begin{array}{r} 4 \\ -0 \\ \hline \end{array}$
14) $\begin{array}{r} 2 \\ -2 \\ \hline \end{array}$
15) $\begin{array}{r} 4 \\ -3 \\ \hline \end{array}$
16) $\begin{array}{r} 5 \\ -0 \\ \hline \end{array}$
17) $\begin{array}{r} 4 \\ -2 \\ \hline \end{array}$
18) $\begin{array}{r} 3 \\ -1 \\ \hline \end{array}$

19) $\begin{array}{r} 0 \\ -0 \\ \hline \end{array}$
20) $\begin{array}{r} 4 \\ -4 \\ \hline \end{array}$
21) $\begin{array}{r} 5 \\ -5 \\ \hline \end{array}$
22) $\begin{array}{r} 2 \\ -1 \\ \hline \end{array}$
23) $\begin{array}{r} 1 \\ -0 \\ \hline \end{array}$
24) $\begin{array}{r} 0 \\ -0 \\ \hline \end{array}$

25) $\begin{array}{r} 2 \\ -0 \\ \hline \end{array}$
26) $\begin{array}{r} 2 \\ -2 \\ \hline \end{array}$
27) $\begin{array}{r} 4 \\ -1 \\ \hline \end{array}$
28) $\begin{array}{r} 4 \\ -1 \\ \hline \end{array}$
29) $\begin{array}{r} 3 \\ -3 \\ \hline \end{array}$
30) $\begin{array}{r} 4 \\ -3 \\ \hline \end{array}$

31) $\begin{array}{r} 5 \\ -5 \\ \hline \end{array}$
32) $\begin{array}{r} 4 \\ -0 \\ \hline \end{array}$
33) $\begin{array}{r} 3 \\ -0 \\ \hline \end{array}$
34) $\begin{array}{r} 2 \\ -0 \\ \hline \end{array}$
35) $\begin{array}{r} 2 \\ -0 \\ \hline \end{array}$
36) $\begin{array}{r} 5 \\ -1 \\ \hline \end{array}$

37) $\begin{array}{r} 4 \\ -2 \\ \hline \end{array}$
38) $\begin{array}{r} 5 \\ -0 \\ \hline \end{array}$
39) $\begin{array}{r} 4 \\ -3 \\ \hline \end{array}$
40) $\begin{array}{r} 3 \\ -2 \\ \hline \end{array}$
41) $\begin{array}{r} 5 \\ -1 \\ \hline \end{array}$
42) $\begin{array}{r} 3 \\ -3 \\ \hline \end{array}$

43) $\begin{array}{r} 4 \\ -3 \\ \hline \end{array}$
44) $\begin{array}{r} 2 \\ -2 \\ \hline \end{array}$
45) $\begin{array}{r} 5 \\ -0 \\ \hline \end{array}$
46) $\begin{array}{r} 2 \\ -2 \\ \hline \end{array}$
47) $\begin{array}{r} 0 \\ -0 \\ \hline \end{array}$
48) $\begin{array}{r} 3 \\ -3 \\ \hline \end{array}$

49) $\begin{array}{r} 5 \\ -2 \\ \hline \end{array}$
50) $\begin{array}{r} 2 \\ -1 \\ \hline \end{array}$
51) $\begin{array}{r} 4 \\ -1 \\ \hline \end{array}$
52) $\begin{array}{r} 4 \\ -1 \\ \hline \end{array}$
53) $\begin{array}{r} 2 \\ -1 \\ \hline \end{array}$
54) $\begin{array}{r} 4 \\ -0 \\ \hline \end{array}$

55) $\begin{array}{r} 4 \\ -0 \\ \hline \end{array}$
56) $\begin{array}{r} 3 \\ -1 \\ \hline \end{array}$
57) $\begin{array}{r} 4 \\ -3 \\ \hline \end{array}$
58) $\begin{array}{r} 4 \\ -1 \\ \hline \end{array}$
59) $\begin{array}{r} 5 \\ -1 \\ \hline \end{array}$
60) $\begin{array}{r} 1 \\ -1 \\ \hline \end{array}$

Name:

Score:

/60

time   :

1)
$$\begin{array}{r} 3 \\ -\ 2 \\ \hline \end{array}$$

2)
$$\begin{array}{r} 2 \\ -\ 1 \\ \hline \end{array}$$

3)
$$\begin{array}{r} 3 \\ -\ 0 \\ \hline \end{array}$$

4)
$$\begin{array}{r} 2 \\ -\ 2 \\ \hline \end{array}$$

5)
$$\begin{array}{r} 4 \\ -\ 1 \\ \hline \end{array}$$

6)
$$\begin{array}{r} 5 \\ -\ 3 \\ \hline \end{array}$$

7)
$$\begin{array}{r} 5 \\ -\ 0 \\ \hline \end{array}$$

8)
$$\begin{array}{r} 5 \\ -\ 4 \\ \hline \end{array}$$

9)
$$\begin{array}{r} 4 \\ -\ 3 \\ \hline \end{array}$$

10)
$$\begin{array}{r} 1 \\ -\ 0 \\ \hline \end{array}$$

11)
$$\begin{array}{r} 3 \\ -\ 2 \\ \hline \end{array}$$

12)
$$\begin{array}{r} 2 \\ -\ 0 \\ \hline \end{array}$$

13)
$$\begin{array}{r} 2 \\ -\ 0 \\ \hline \end{array}$$

14)
$$\begin{array}{r} 3 \\ -\ 3 \\ \hline \end{array}$$

15)
$$\begin{array}{r} 4 \\ -\ 1 \\ \hline \end{array}$$

16)
$$\begin{array}{r} 4 \\ -\ 0 \\ \hline \end{array}$$

17)
$$\begin{array}{r} 2 \\ -\ 0 \\ \hline \end{array}$$

18)
$$\begin{array}{r} 4 \\ -\ 1 \\ \hline \end{array}$$

19)
$$\begin{array}{r} 5 \\ -\ 2 \\ \hline \end{array}$$

20)
$$\begin{array}{r} 0 \\ -\ 0 \\ \hline \end{array}$$

21)
$$\begin{array}{r} 3 \\ -\ 0 \\ \hline \end{array}$$

22)
$$\begin{array}{r} 4 \\ -\ 4 \\ \hline \end{array}$$

23)
$$\begin{array}{r} 5 \\ -\ 5 \\ \hline \end{array}$$

24)
$$\begin{array}{r} 2 \\ -\ 1 \\ \hline \end{array}$$

25)
$$\begin{array}{r} 3 \\ -\ 1 \\ \hline \end{array}$$

26)
$$\begin{array}{r} 4 \\ -\ 2 \\ \hline \end{array}$$

27)
$$\begin{array}{r} 5 \\ -\ 5 \\ \hline \end{array}$$

28)
$$\begin{array}{r} 0 \\ -\ 0 \\ \hline \end{array}$$

29)
$$\begin{array}{r} 5 \\ -\ 3 \\ \hline \end{array}$$

30)
$$\begin{array}{r} 3 \\ -\ 1 \\ \hline \end{array}$$

31)
$$\begin{array}{r} 1 \\ -\ 0 \\ \hline \end{array}$$

32)
$$\begin{array}{r} 5 \\ -\ 3 \\ \hline \end{array}$$

33)
$$\begin{array}{r} 5 \\ -\ 0 \\ \hline \end{array}$$

34)
$$\begin{array}{r} 5 \\ -\ 2 \\ \hline \end{array}$$

35)
$$\begin{array}{r} 5 \\ -\ 5 \\ \hline \end{array}$$

36)
$$\begin{array}{r} 2 \\ -\ 0 \\ \hline \end{array}$$

37)
$$\begin{array}{r} 1 \\ -\ 1 \\ \hline \end{array}$$

38)
$$\begin{array}{r} 4 \\ -\ 4 \\ \hline \end{array}$$

39)
$$\begin{array}{r} 5 \\ -\ 4 \\ \hline \end{array}$$

40)
$$\begin{array}{r} 3 \\ -\ 2 \\ \hline \end{array}$$

41)
$$\begin{array}{r} 5 \\ -\ 5 \\ \hline \end{array}$$

42)
$$\begin{array}{r} 2 \\ -\ 1 \\ \hline \end{array}$$

43)
$$\begin{array}{r} 4 \\ -\ 1 \\ \hline \end{array}$$

44)
$$\begin{array}{r} 3 \\ -\ 3 \\ \hline \end{array}$$

45)
$$\begin{array}{r} 5 \\ -\ 5 \\ \hline \end{array}$$

46)
$$\begin{array}{r} 3 \\ -\ 2 \\ \hline \end{array}$$

47)
$$\begin{array}{r} 4 \\ -\ 1 \\ \hline \end{array}$$

48)
$$\begin{array}{r} 2 \\ -\ 2 \\ \hline \end{array}$$

49)
$$\begin{array}{r} 3 \\ -\ 3 \\ \hline \end{array}$$

50)
$$\begin{array}{r} 2 \\ -\ 2 \\ \hline \end{array}$$

51)
$$\begin{array}{r} 2 \\ -\ 0 \\ \hline \end{array}$$

52)
$$\begin{array}{r} 4 \\ -\ 3 \\ \hline \end{array}$$

53)
$$\begin{array}{r} 1 \\ -\ 0 \\ \hline \end{array}$$

54)
$$\begin{array}{r} 5 \\ -\ 2 \\ \hline \end{array}$$

55)
$$\begin{array}{r} 4 \\ -\ 3 \\ \hline \end{array}$$

56)
$$\begin{array}{r} 5 \\ -\ 1 \\ \hline \end{array}$$

57)
$$\begin{array}{r} 4 \\ -\ 4 \\ \hline \end{array}$$

58)
$$\begin{array}{r} 3 \\ -\ 2 \\ \hline \end{array}$$

59)
$$\begin{array}{r} 5 \\ -\ 3 \\ \hline \end{array}$$

60)
$$\begin{array}{r} 5 \\ -\ 0 \\ \hline \end{array}$$

Name:

Score: /60

Time   :

1) 4
  - 3

2) 5
  - 4

3) 4
  - 4

4) 4
  - 0

5) 4
  - 3

6) 4
  - 1

7) 4
  - 1

8) 3
  - 2

9) 5
  - 1

10) 3
   - 2

11) 5
   - 3

12) 5
   - 5

13) 5
   - 2

14) 5
   - 0

15) 4
   - 4

16) 2
   - 2

17) 3
   - 1

18) 2
   - 2

19) 3
   - 0

20) 2
   - 2

21) 3
   - 3

22) 1
   - 0

23) 5
   - 0

24) 0
   - 0

25) 2
   - 2

26) 5
   - 4

27) 4
   - 3

28) 5
   - 5

29) 4
   - 4

30) 5
   - 2

31) 5
   - 3

32) 4
   - 0

33) 3
   - 1

34) 2
   - 1

35) 2
   - 2

36) 3
   - 0

37) 4
   - 2

38) 4
   - 3

39) 3
   - 2

40) 0
   - 0

41) 1
   - 1

42) 5
   - 5

43) 3
   - 0

44) 4
   - 2

45) 1
   - 0

46) 5
   - 4

47) 3
   - 0

48) 3
   - 1

49) 4
   - 4

50) 4
   - 1

51) 5
   - 5

52) 2
   - 0

53) 3
   - 0

54) 5
   - 0

55) 5
   - 2

56) 4
   - 3

57) 4
   - 4

58) 4
   - 0

59) 4
   - 4

60) 5
   - 4

Page 88

Name:

Score:

/60

Time   :

1) 4
  − 4

2) 3
  − 2

3) 4
  − 0

4) 4
  − 1

5) 1
  − 1

6) 5
  − 1

7) 1
  − 1

8) 3
  − 0

9) 5
  − 0

10) 5
   − 4

11) 4
   − 0

12) 5
   − 1

13) 5
   − 1

14) 5
   − 0

15) 3
   − 3

16) 5
   − 4

17) 4
   − 2

18) 4
   − 2

19) 5
   − 5

20) 4
   − 2

21) 1
   − 1

22) 5
   − 4

23) 4
   − 4

24) 1
   − 0

25) 3
   − 0

26) 1
   − 1

27) 4
   − 3

28) 5
   − 4

29) 5
   − 5

30) 5
   − 3

31) 0
   − 0

32) 5
   − 2

33) 1
   − 1

34) 1
   − 1

35) 1
   − 1

36) 5
   − 2

37) 2
   − 1

38) 3
   − 0

39) 4
   − 0

40) 3
   − 2

41) 3
   − 2

42) 4
   − 3

43) 5
   − 2

44) 4
   − 4

45) 5
   − 0

46) 2
   − 0

47) 5
   − 2

48) 2
   − 2

49) 4
   − 2

50) 5
   − 3

51) 5
   − 2

52) 5
   − 4

53) 5
   − 5

54) 5
   − 0

55) 3
   − 1

56) 5
   − 1

57) 5
   − 4

58) 2
   − 2

59) 2
   − 2

60) 5
   − 2

Name:

Score: /60

Time :

1) 2 − 0

2) 1 − 0

3) 3 − 1

4) 3 − 0

5) 4 − 1

6) 3 − 0

7) 5 − 2

8) 1 − 0

9) 1 − 1

10) 3 − 0

11) 5 − 2

12) 3 − 1

13) 3 − 3

14) 5 − 0

15) 2 − 0

16) 3 − 2

17) 5 − 4

18) 3 − 1

19) 3 − 0

20) 5 − 0

21) 3 − 3

22) 3 − 0

23) 5 − 4

24) 3 − 1

25) 4 − 2

26) 0 − 0

27) 1 − 0

28) 4 − 0

29) 4 − 3

30) 1 − 0

31) 1 − 0

32) 3 − 2

33) 4 − 4

34) 2 − 1

35) 1 − 1

36) 5 − 4

37) 0 − 0

38) 5 − 1

39) 2 − 0

40) 2 − 1

41) 3 − 3

42) 4 − 1

43) 4 − 2

44) 3 − 0

45) 1 − 1

46) 4 − 0

47) 1 − 0

48) 5 − 5

49) 3 − 0

50) 3 − 2

51) 0 − 0

52) 5 − 1

53) 2 − 2

54) 3 − 3

55) 3 − 2

56) 3 − 0

57) 1 − 1

58) 1 − 0

59) 4 − 0

60) 5 − 0

Name:

Score:

/60

time   :

1) □
  − 0
    5

2)   5
  − □
    2

3) □
  − 1
    4

4)   5
  − □
    4

5) □
  − 1
    4

6)   5
  − □
    5

7) □
  − 0
    0

8)   5
  − □
    1

9) □
  − 4
    1

10)   0
  − □
    0

11) □
  − 0
    5

12)   4
  − □
    2

13) □
  − 3
    0

14)   5
  − □
    4

15) □
  − 0
    2

16)   4
  − □
    4

17) □
  − 3
    0

18)   1
  − □
    0

19) □
  − 1
    3

20)   5
  − □
    2

21) □
  − 2
    3

22)   2
  − □
    2

23) □
  − 4
    1

24)   3
  − □
    2

25) □
  − 0
    2

26)   3
  − □
    1

27) □
  − 2
    0

28)   4
  − □
    4

29) □
  − 0
    4

30)   4
  − □
    1

31) □
  − 5
    0

32)   2
  − □
    1

33) □
  − 5
    0

34)   2
  − □
    1

35) □
  − 4
    1

36)   5
  − □
    1

37) □
  − 4
    0

38)   4
  − □
    3

39) □
  − 2
    2

40)   4
  − □
    4

41) □
  − 0
    0

42)   4
  − □
    1

43) □
  − 4
    1

44)   4
  − □
    3

45) □
  − 3
    0

46)   4
  − □
    2

47) □
  − 2
    1

48)   4
  − □
    4

49) □
  − 1
    2

50)   0
  − □
    0

51) □
  − 4
    1

52)   3
  − □
    0

53) □
  − 4
    1

54)   5
  − □
    0

55) □
  − 1
    3

56)   2
  − □
    2

57) □
  − 1
    3

58)   4
  − □
    3

59) □
  − 0
    2

60)   2
  − □
    2

Score:

/60

Name:

time   :

1)
```
  □
- 1
---
  2
```

2)
```
  5
- □
---
  5
```

3)
```
  □
- 2
---
  2
```

4)
```
  5
- □
---
  4
```

5)
```
  □
- 1
---
  2
```

6)
```
  5
- □
---
  1
```

7)
```
  □
- 0
---
  1
```

8)
```
  4
- □
---
  3
```

9)
```
  □
- 1
---
  4
```

10)
```
  4
- □
---
  2
```

11)
```
  □
- 0
---
  3
```

12)
```
  5
- □
---
  5
```

13)
```
  □
- 0
---
  4
```

14)
```
  5
- □
---
  5
```

15)
```
  □
- 3
---
  2
```

16)
```
  1
- □
---
  0
```

17)
```
  □
- 1
---
  4
```

18)
```
  5
- □
---
  0
```

19)
```
  □
- 0
---
  5
```

20)
```
  3
- □
---
  2
```

21)
```
  □
- 3
---
  1
```

22)
```
  3
- □
---
  1
```

23)
```
  □
- 1
---
  3
```

24)
```
  2
- □
---
  1
```

25)
```
  □
- 2
---
  1
```

26)
```
  3
- □
---
  1
```

27)
```
  □
- 3
---
  1
```

28)
```
  3
- □
---
  1
```

29)
```
  □
- 1
---
  1
```

30)
```
  4
- □
---
  2
```

31)
```
  □
- 0
---
  4
```

32)
```
  1
- □
---
  1
```

33)
```
  □
- 1
---
  1
```

34)
```
  0
- □
---
  0
```

35)
```
  □
- 0
---
  3
```

36)
```
  2
- □
---
  2
```

37)
```
  □
- 0
---
  5
```

38)
```
  4
- □
---
  1
```

39)
```
  □
- 2
---
  2
```

40)
```
  4
- □
---
  2
```

41)
```
  □
- 5
---
  0
```

42)
```
  5
- □
---
  5
```

43)
```
  □
- 4
---
  0
```

44)
```
  3
- □
---
  2
```

45)
```
  □
- 0
---
  4
```

46)
```
  3
- □
---
  3
```

47)
```
  □
- 5
---
  0
```

48)
```
  4
- □
---
  4
```

49)
```
  □
- 0
---
  4
```

50)
```
  5
- □
---
  4
```

51)
```
  □
- 1
---
  1
```

52)
```
  4
- □
---
  3
```

53)
```
  □
- 2
---
  3
```

54)
```
  3
- □
---
  3
```

55)
```
  □
- 1
---
  4
```

56)
```
  3
- □
---
  3
```

57)
```
  □
- 3
---
  2
```

58)
```
  3
- □
---
  2
```

59)
```
  □
- 1
---
  0
```

60)
```
  4
- □
---
  0
```

Page 92

Score:

/60

Name:

time   :

1) ☐
  − 1
   4

2)   5
  − ☐
   0

3) ☐
  − 2
   2

4)   4
  − ☐
   4

5) ☐
  − 0
   5

6)   3
  − ☐
   2

7) ☐
  − 5
   0

8)   5
  − ☐
   0

9) ☐
  − 3
   1

10)   3
  − ☐
   1

11) ☐
  − 0
   4

12)   2
  − ☐
   1

13) ☐
  − 4
   0

14)   0
  − ☐
   0

15) ☐
  − 5
   0

16)   4
  − ☐
   3

17) ☐
  − 1
   3

18)   4
  − ☐
   1

19) ☐
  − 4
   1

20)   5
  − ☐
   5

21) ☐
  − 4
   1

22)   5
  − ☐
   5

23) ☐
  − 2
   0

24)   4
  − ☐
   4

25) ☐
  − 3
   1

26)   5
  − ☐
   2

27) ☐
  − 0
   1

28)   5
  − ☐
   3

29) ☐
  − 1
   3

30)   3
  − ☐
   3

31) ☐
  − 5
   0

32)   4
  − ☐
   4

33) ☐
  − 0
   2

34)   4
  − ☐
   2

35) ☐
  − 0
   3

36)   3
  − ☐
   1

37) ☐
  − 0
   4

38)   2
  − ☐
   2

39) ☐
  − 2
   3

40)   2
  − ☐
   1

41) ☐
  − 1
   4

42)   3
  − ☐
   2

43) ☐
  − 0
   4

44)   5
  − ☐
   3

45) ☐
  − 0
   4

46)   4
  − ☐
   0

47) ☐
  − 4
   1

48)   4
  − ☐
   3

49) ☐
  − 0
   3

50)   4
  − ☐
   3

51) ☐
  − 3
   1

52)   5
  − ☐
   1

53) ☐
  − 0
   1

54)   5
  − ☐
   1

55) ☐
  − 0
   2

56)   4
  − ☐
   3

57) ☐
  − 1
   2

58)   0
  − ☐
   0

59) ☐
  − 0
   4

60)   5
  − ☐
   5

Score:

/60

Name:

time   :

1) □
  − 0
  ───
    3

2)   4
  − □
  ───
    0

3) □
  − 0
  ───
    3

4)   2
  − □
  ───
    0

5) □
  − 2
  ───
    3

6)   1
  − □
  ───
    1

7) □
  − 0
  ───
    2

8)   1
  − □
  ───
    0

9) □
  − 4
  ───
    0

10)   4
  − □
  ───
    4

11) □
  − 0
  ───
    3

12)   2
  − □
  ───
    1

13) □
  − 0
  ───
    0

14)   5
  − □
  ───
    0

15) □
  − 0
  ───
    5

16)   5
  − □
  ───
    5

17) □
  − 0
  ───
    5

18)   5
  − □
  ───
    3

19) □
  − 2
  ───
    1

20)   4
  − □
  ───
    4

21) □
  − 0
  ───
    1

22)   4
  − □
  ───
    0

23) □
  − 1
  ───
    3

24)   5
  − □
  ───
    4

25) □
  − 3
  ───
    0

26)   2
  − □
  ───
    1

27) □
  − 4
  ───
    0

28)   2
  − □
  ───
    1

29) □
  − 0
  ───
    1

30)   2
  − □
  ───
    1

31) □
  − 0
  ───
    4

32)   5
  − □
  ───
    5

33) □
  − 2
  ───
    2

34)   3
  − □
  ───
    2

35) □
  − 2
  ───
    2

36)   4
  − □
  ───
    4

37) □
  − 3
  ───
    1

38)   5
  − □
  ───
    2

39) □
  − 0
  ───
    3

40)   2
  − □
  ───
    0

41) □
  − 1
  ───
    4

42)   2
  − □
  ───
    0

43) □
  − 1
  ───
    1

44)   3
  − □
  ───
    0

45) □
  − 0
  ───
    4

46)   2
  − □
  ───
    1

47) □
  − 0
  ───
    3

48)   2
  − □
  ───
    1

49) □
  − 0
  ───
    5

50)   0
  − □
  ───
    0

51) □
  − 4
  ───
    1

52)   5
  − □
  ───
    3

53) □
  − 0
  ───
    1

54)   5
  − □
  ───
    5

55) □
  − 2
  ───
    1

56)   0
  − □
  ───
    0

57) □
  − 4
  ───
    1

58)   2
  − □
  ───
    1

59) □
  − 3
  ───
    2

60)   0
  − □
  ───
    0

Page 94

Score:

Name:

/60

Time :

1) □
  − 3
    2

2)   2
  − □
    1

3) □
  − 3
    1

4)   4
  − □
    4

5) □
  − 3
    0

6)   3
  − □
    3

7) □
  − 1
    4

8)   4
  − □
    4

9) □
  − 5
    0

10)   4
  − □
    0

11) □
  − 0
    1

12)   1
  − □
    0

13) □
  − 1
    2

14)   3
  − □
    2

15) □
  − 5
    0

16)   5
  − □
    5

17) □
  − 1
    4

18)   5
  − □
    0

19) □
  − 0
    2

20)   4
  − □
    1

21) □
  − 1
    2

22)   3
  − □
    3

23) □
  − 1
    4

24)   2
  − □
    2

25) □
  − 1
    4

26)   5
  − □
    1

27) □
  − 4
    0

28)   2
  − □
    2

29) □
  − 1
    1

30)   4
  − □
    4

31) □
  − 3
    0

32)   3
  − □
    1

33) □
  − 2
    1

34)   2
  − □
    1

35) □
  − 4
    0

36)   5
  − □
    1

37) □
  − 3
    1

38)   3
  − □
    3

39) □
  − 2
    2

40)   3
  − □
    0

41) □
  − 1
    3

42)   3
  − □
    3

43) □
  − 3
    2

44)   4
  − □
    2

45) □
  − 2
    3

46)   5
  − □
    2

47) □
  − 2
    1

48)   5
  − □
    2

49) □
  − 2
    0

50)   4
  − □
    0

51) □
  − 0
    3

52)   2
  − □
    0

53) □
  − 5
    0

54)   4
  − □
    0

55) □
  − 0
    4

56)   4
  − □
    3

57) □
  − 2
    2

58)   4
  − □
    0

59) □
  − 3
    1

60)   4
  − □
    1

Score:

/60

Name:

Time   :

1)
```
  □
- 4
___
  0
```

2)
```
  4
- □
___
  3
```

3)
```
  □
- 5
___
  0
```

4)
```
  4
- □
___
  3
```

5)
```
  □
- 0
___
  5
```

6)
```
  3
- □
___
  0
```

7)
```
  □
- 3
___
  2
```

8)
```
  3
- □
___
  2
```

9)
```
  □
- 1
___
  1
```

10)
```
  3
- □
___
  2
```

11)
```
  □
- 2
___
  2
```

12)
```
  5
- □
___
  4
```

13)
```
  □
- 4
___
  1
```

14)
```
  4
- □
___
  1
```

15)
```
  □
- 0
___
  1
```

16)
```
  4
- □
___
  0
```

17)
```
  □
- 2
___
  0
```

18)
```
  4
- □
___
  3
```

19)
```
  □
- 4
___
  0
```

20)
```
  5
- □
___
  3
```

21)
```
  □
- 2
___
  2
```

22)
```
  1
- □
___
  0
```

23)
```
  □
- 0
___
  3
```

24)
```
  5
- □
___
  3
```

25)
```
  □
- 2
___
  0
```

26)
```
  4
- □
___
  1
```

27)
```
  □
- 2
___
  3
```

28)
```
  5
- □
___
  2
```

29)
```
  □
- 4
___
  1
```

30)
```
  4
- □
___
  0
```

31)
```
  □
- 3
___
  0
```

32)
```
  1
- □
___
  0
```

33)
```
  □
- 2
___
  3
```

34)
```
  3
- □
___
  2
```

35)
```
  □
- 0
___
  4
```

36)
```
  2
- □
___
  1
```

37)
```
  □
- 0
___
  5
```

38)
```
  5
- □
___
  0
```

39)
```
  □
- 0
___
  2
```

40)
```
  3
- □
___
  3
```

41)
```
  □
- 1
___
  1
```

42)
```
  1
- □
___
  0
```

43)
```
  □
- 0
___
  4
```

44)
```
  3
- □
___
  3
```

45)
```
  □
- 2
___
  3
```

46)
```
  1
- □
___
  0
```

47)
```
  □
- 3
___
  1
```

48)
```
  3
- □
___
  0
```

49)
```
  □
- 3
___
  2
```

50)
```
  1
- □
___
  1
```

51)
```
  □
- 0
___
  5
```

52)
```
  4
- □
___
  0
```

53)
```
  □
- 0
___
  2
```

54)
```
  4
- □
___
  2
```

55)
```
  □
- 0
___
  3
```

56)
```
  4
- □
___
  0
```

57)
```
  □
- 0
___
  0
```

58)
```
  5
- □
___
  2
```

59)
```
  □
- 1
___
  3
```

60)
```
  5
- □
___
  5
```

Score:

Name:

/60

Time   :

1)
```
  □
- 1
─────
  3
```

2)
```
  4
- □
─────
  0
```

3)
```
  □
- 1
─────
  1
```

4)
```
  5
- □
─────
  0
```

5)
```
  □
- 1
─────
  0
```

6)
```
  5
- □
─────
  1
```

7)
```
  □
- 4
─────
  0
```

8)
```
  2
- □
─────
  1
```

9)
```
  □
- 0
─────
  4
```

10)
```
  2
- □
─────
  1
```

11)
```
  □
- 0
─────
  1
```

12)
```
  5
- □
─────
  3
```

13)
```
  □
- 1
─────
  1
```

14)
```
  4
- □
─────
  4
```

15)
```
  □
- 1
─────
  2
```

16)
```
  4
- □
─────
  3
```

17)
```
  □
- 0
─────
  5
```

18)
```
  3
- □
─────
  3
```

19)
```
  □
- 2
─────
  1
```

20)
```
  5
- □
─────
  0
```

21)
```
  □
- 0
─────
  5
```

22)
```
  4
- □
─────
  2
```

23)
```
  □
- 2
─────
  2
```

24)
```
  4
- □
─────
  4
```

25)
```
  □
- 0
─────
  3
```

26)
```
  5
- □
─────
  4
```

27)
```
  □
- 0
─────
  4
```

28)
```
  4
- □
─────
  0
```

29)
```
  □
- 3
─────
  1
```

30)
```
  3
- □
─────
  0
```

31)
```
  □
- 1
─────
  1
```

32)
```
  5
- □
─────
  0
```

33)
```
  □
- 1
─────
  3
```

34)
```
  5
- □
─────
  5
```

35)
```
  □
- 1
─────
  4
```

36)
```
  5
- □
─────
  3
```

37)
```
  □
- 0
─────
  5
```

38)
```
  3
- □
─────
  1
```

39)
```
  □
- 0
─────
  1
```

40)
```
  2
- □
─────
  0
```

41)
```
  □
- 1
─────
  0
```

42)
```
  5
- □
─────
  5
```

43)
```
  □
- 0
─────
  0
```

44)
```
  4
- □
─────
  1
```

45)
```
  □
- 4
─────
  1
```

46)
```
  3
- □
─────
  2
```

47)
```
  □
- 2
─────
  2
```

48)
```
  3
- □
─────
  0
```

49)
```
  □
- 1
─────
  0
```

50)
```
  3
- □
─────
  3
```

51)
```
  □
- 1
─────
  1
```

52)
```
  5
- □
─────
  1
```

53)
```
  □
- 4
─────
  0
```

54)
```
  5
- □
─────
  0
```

55)
```
  □
- 4
─────
  0
```

56)
```
  5
- □
─────
  3
```

57)
```
  □
- 4
─────
  0
```

58)
```
  2
- □
─────
  0
```

59)
```
  □
- 1
─────
  2
```

60)
```
  4
- □
─────
  1
```

Score: /60

Name:

Time :

1)
$$\begin{array}{r} \square \\ -\ 4 \\ \hline 1 \end{array}$$

2)
$$\begin{array}{r} 4 \\ -\ \square \\ \hline 3 \end{array}$$

3)
$$\begin{array}{r} \square \\ -\ 0 \\ \hline 2 \end{array}$$

4)
$$\begin{array}{r} 5 \\ -\ \square \\ \hline 1 \end{array}$$

5)
$$\begin{array}{r} \square \\ -\ 0 \\ \hline 0 \end{array}$$

6)
$$\begin{array}{r} 5 \\ -\ \square \\ \hline 0 \end{array}$$

7)
$$\begin{array}{r} \square \\ -\ 3 \\ \hline 1 \end{array}$$

8)
$$\begin{array}{r} 5 \\ -\ \square \\ \hline 5 \end{array}$$

9)
$$\begin{array}{r} \square \\ -\ 0 \\ \hline 0 \end{array}$$

10)
$$\begin{array}{r} 2 \\ -\ \square \\ \hline 1 \end{array}$$

11)
$$\begin{array}{r} \square \\ -\ 1 \\ \hline 2 \end{array}$$

12)
$$\begin{array}{r} 5 \\ -\ \square \\ \hline 3 \end{array}$$

13)
$$\begin{array}{r} \square \\ -\ 2 \\ \hline 1 \end{array}$$

14)
$$\begin{array}{r} 5 \\ -\ \square \\ \hline 5 \end{array}$$

15)
$$\begin{array}{r} \square \\ -\ 0 \\ \hline 3 \end{array}$$

16)
$$\begin{array}{r} 2 \\ -\ \square \\ \hline 1 \end{array}$$

17)
$$\begin{array}{r} \square \\ -\ 1 \\ \hline 4 \end{array}$$

18)
$$\begin{array}{r} 2 \\ -\ \square \\ \hline 1 \end{array}$$

19)
$$\begin{array}{r} \square \\ -\ 4 \\ \hline 1 \end{array}$$

20)
$$\begin{array}{r} 3 \\ -\ \square \\ \hline 3 \end{array}$$

21)
$$\begin{array}{r} \square \\ -\ 1 \\ \hline 3 \end{array}$$

22)
$$\begin{array}{r} 0 \\ -\ \square \\ \hline 0 \end{array}$$

23)
$$\begin{array}{r} \square \\ -\ 4 \\ \hline 0 \end{array}$$

24)
$$\begin{array}{r} 5 \\ -\ \square \\ \hline 5 \end{array}$$

25)
$$\begin{array}{r} \square \\ -\ 0 \\ \hline 5 \end{array}$$

26)
$$\begin{array}{r} 4 \\ -\ \square \\ \hline 3 \end{array}$$

27)
$$\begin{array}{r} \square \\ -\ 2 \\ \hline 3 \end{array}$$

28)
$$\begin{array}{r} 3 \\ -\ \square \\ \hline 1 \end{array}$$

29)
$$\begin{array}{r} \square \\ -\ 4 \\ \hline 1 \end{array}$$

30)
$$\begin{array}{r} 2 \\ -\ \square \\ \hline 1 \end{array}$$

31)
$$\begin{array}{r} \square \\ -\ 0 \\ \hline 1 \end{array}$$

32)
$$\begin{array}{r} 2 \\ -\ \square \\ \hline 1 \end{array}$$

33)
$$\begin{array}{r} \square \\ -\ 0 \\ \hline 2 \end{array}$$

34)
$$\begin{array}{r} 1 \\ -\ \square \\ \hline 0 \end{array}$$

35)
$$\begin{array}{r} \square \\ -\ 3 \\ \hline 1 \end{array}$$

36)
$$\begin{array}{r} 5 \\ -\ \square \\ \hline 3 \end{array}$$

37)
$$\begin{array}{r} \square \\ -\ 0 \\ \hline 3 \end{array}$$

38)
$$\begin{array}{r} 5 \\ -\ \square \\ \hline 0 \end{array}$$

39)
$$\begin{array}{r} \square \\ -\ 2 \\ \hline 1 \end{array}$$

40)
$$\begin{array}{r} 0 \\ -\ \square \\ \hline 0 \end{array}$$

41)
$$\begin{array}{r} \square \\ -\ 0 \\ \hline 0 \end{array}$$

42)
$$\begin{array}{r} 4 \\ -\ \square \\ \hline 3 \end{array}$$

43)
$$\begin{array}{r} \square \\ -\ 1 \\ \hline 2 \end{array}$$

44)
$$\begin{array}{r} 5 \\ -\ \square \\ \hline 0 \end{array}$$

45)
$$\begin{array}{r} \square \\ -\ 3 \\ \hline 2 \end{array}$$

46)
$$\begin{array}{r} 1 \\ -\ \square \\ \hline 1 \end{array}$$

47)
$$\begin{array}{r} \square \\ -\ 4 \\ \hline 1 \end{array}$$

48)
$$\begin{array}{r} 2 \\ -\ \square \\ \hline 1 \end{array}$$

49)
$$\begin{array}{r} \square \\ -\ 3 \\ \hline 0 \end{array}$$

50)
$$\begin{array}{r} 2 \\ -\ \square \\ \hline 2 \end{array}$$

51)
$$\begin{array}{r} \square \\ -\ 4 \\ \hline 1 \end{array}$$

52)
$$\begin{array}{r} 4 \\ -\ \square \\ \hline 4 \end{array}$$

53)
$$\begin{array}{r} \square \\ -\ 5 \\ \hline 0 \end{array}$$

54)
$$\begin{array}{r} 3 \\ -\ \square \\ \hline 3 \end{array}$$

55)
$$\begin{array}{r} \square \\ -\ 1 \\ \hline 2 \end{array}$$

56)
$$\begin{array}{r} 1 \\ -\ \square \\ \hline 0 \end{array}$$

57)
$$\begin{array}{r} \square \\ -\ 1 \\ \hline 3 \end{array}$$

58)
$$\begin{array}{r} 4 \\ -\ \square \\ \hline 4 \end{array}$$

59)
$$\begin{array}{r} \square \\ -\ 2 \\ \hline 2 \end{array}$$

60)
$$\begin{array}{r} 5 \\ -\ \square \\ \hline 3 \end{array}$$

Score: /60

Name:

Time   :

1)
$$\begin{array}{r} \square \\ -\ 4 \\ \hline 1 \end{array}$$

2)
$$\begin{array}{r} 2 \\ -\ \square \\ \hline 2 \end{array}$$

3)
$$\begin{array}{r} \square \\ -\ 1 \\ \hline 3 \end{array}$$

4)
$$\begin{array}{r} 4 \\ -\ \square \\ \hline 1 \end{array}$$

5)
$$\begin{array}{r} \square \\ -\ 0 \\ \hline 1 \end{array}$$

6)
$$\begin{array}{r} 0 \\ -\ \square \\ \hline 0 \end{array}$$

7)
$$\begin{array}{r} \square \\ -\ 0 \\ \hline 5 \end{array}$$

8)
$$\begin{array}{r} 5 \\ -\ \square \\ \hline 2 \end{array}$$

9)
$$\begin{array}{r} \square \\ -\ 2 \\ \hline 1 \end{array}$$

10)
$$\begin{array}{r} 3 \\ -\ \square \\ \hline 2 \end{array}$$

11)
$$\begin{array}{r} \square \\ -\ 3 \\ \hline 1 \end{array}$$

12)
$$\begin{array}{r} 5 \\ -\ \square \\ \hline 1 \end{array}$$

13)
$$\begin{array}{r} \square \\ -\ 0 \\ \hline 4 \end{array}$$

14)
$$\begin{array}{r} 3 \\ -\ \square \\ \hline 0 \end{array}$$

15)
$$\begin{array}{r} \square \\ -\ 1 \\ \hline 4 \end{array}$$

16)
$$\begin{array}{r} 3 \\ -\ \square \\ \hline 1 \end{array}$$

17)
$$\begin{array}{r} \square \\ -\ 0 \\ \hline 5 \end{array}$$

18)
$$\begin{array}{r} 0 \\ -\ \square \\ \hline 0 \end{array}$$

19)
$$\begin{array}{r} \square \\ -\ 1 \\ \hline 3 \end{array}$$

20)
$$\begin{array}{r} 4 \\ -\ \square \\ \hline 2 \end{array}$$

21)
$$\begin{array}{r} \square \\ -\ 0 \\ \hline 1 \end{array}$$

22)
$$\begin{array}{r} 0 \\ -\ \square \\ \hline 0 \end{array}$$

23)
$$\begin{array}{r} \square \\ -\ 5 \\ \hline 0 \end{array}$$

24)
$$\begin{array}{r} 5 \\ -\ \square \\ \hline 5 \end{array}$$

25)
$$\begin{array}{r} \square \\ -\ 1 \\ \hline 1 \end{array}$$

26)
$$\begin{array}{r} 5 \\ -\ \square \\ \hline 5 \end{array}$$

27)
$$\begin{array}{r} \square \\ -\ 0 \\ \hline 5 \end{array}$$

28)
$$\begin{array}{r} 2 \\ -\ \square \\ \hline 0 \end{array}$$

29)
$$\begin{array}{r} \square \\ -\ 0 \\ \hline 2 \end{array}$$

30)
$$\begin{array}{r} 3 \\ -\ \square \\ \hline 1 \end{array}$$

31)
$$\begin{array}{r} \square \\ -\ 1 \\ \hline 0 \end{array}$$

32)
$$\begin{array}{r} 3 \\ -\ \square \\ \hline 1 \end{array}$$

33)
$$\begin{array}{r} \square \\ -\ 4 \\ \hline 0 \end{array}$$

34)
$$\begin{array}{r} 2 \\ -\ \square \\ \hline 0 \end{array}$$

35)
$$\begin{array}{r} \square \\ -\ 3 \\ \hline 1 \end{array}$$

36)
$$\begin{array}{r} 5 \\ -\ \square \\ \hline 4 \end{array}$$

37)
$$\begin{array}{r} \square \\ -\ 0 \\ \hline 4 \end{array}$$

38)
$$\begin{array}{r} 2 \\ -\ \square \\ \hline 0 \end{array}$$

39)
$$\begin{array}{r} \square \\ -\ 3 \\ \hline 1 \end{array}$$

40)
$$\begin{array}{r} 5 \\ -\ \square \\ \hline 1 \end{array}$$

41)
$$\begin{array}{r} \square \\ -\ 3 \\ \hline 1 \end{array}$$

42)
$$\begin{array}{r} 5 \\ -\ \square \\ \hline 5 \end{array}$$

43)
$$\begin{array}{r} \square \\ -\ 0 \\ \hline 0 \end{array}$$

44)
$$\begin{array}{r} 4 \\ -\ \square \\ \hline 3 \end{array}$$

45)
$$\begin{array}{r} \square \\ -\ 2 \\ \hline 1 \end{array}$$

46)
$$\begin{array}{r} 3 \\ -\ \square \\ \hline 1 \end{array}$$

47)
$$\begin{array}{r} \square \\ -\ 0 \\ \hline 0 \end{array}$$

48)
$$\begin{array}{r} 3 \\ -\ \square \\ \hline 3 \end{array}$$

49)
$$\begin{array}{r} \square \\ -\ 3 \\ \hline 0 \end{array}$$

50)
$$\begin{array}{r} 5 \\ -\ \square \\ \hline 4 \end{array}$$

51)
$$\begin{array}{r} \square \\ -\ 4 \\ \hline 1 \end{array}$$

52)
$$\begin{array}{r} 4 \\ -\ \square \\ \hline 0 \end{array}$$

53)
$$\begin{array}{r} \square \\ -\ 2 \\ \hline 0 \end{array}$$

54)
$$\begin{array}{r} 5 \\ -\ \square \\ \hline 0 \end{array}$$

55)
$$\begin{array}{r} \square \\ -\ 2 \\ \hline 2 \end{array}$$

56)
$$\begin{array}{r} 4 \\ -\ \square \\ \hline 4 \end{array}$$

57)
$$\begin{array}{r} \square \\ -\ 0 \\ \hline 2 \end{array}$$

58)
$$\begin{array}{r} 4 \\ -\ \square \\ \hline 0 \end{array}$$

59)
$$\begin{array}{r} \square \\ -\ 4 \\ \hline 0 \end{array}$$

60)
$$\begin{array}{r} 1 \\ -\ \square \\ \hline 0 \end{array}$$

Score: /60

Name:

Time :

1)
```
  □
- 3
---
  2
```

2)
```
  3
- □
---
  0
```

3)
```
  □
- 0
---
  3
```

4)
```
  2
- □
---
  2
```

5)
```
  □
- 0
---
  2
```

6)
```
  0
- □
---
  0
```

7)
```
  □
- 1
---
  2
```

8)
```
  4
- □
---
  2
```

9)
```
  □
- 1
---
  4
```

10)
```
  5
- □
---
  5
```

11)
```
  □
- 0
---
  0
```

12)
```
  5
- □
---
  5
```

13)
```
  □
- 2
---
  1
```

14)
```
  4
- □
---
  2
```

15)
```
  □
- 0
---
  5
```

16)
```
  5
- □
---
  0
```

17)
```
  □
- 1
---
  2
```

18)
```
  5
- □
---
  0
```

19)
```
  □
- 2
---
  3
```

20)
```
  5
- □
---
  4
```

21)
```
  □
- 1
---
  4
```

22)
```
  3
- □
---
  2
```

23)
```
  □
- 4
---
  1
```

24)
```
  4
- □
---
  0
```

25)
```
  □
- 1
---
  1
```

26)
```
  4
- □
---
  3
```

27)
```
  □
- 0
---
  0
```

28)
```
  5
- □
---
  5
```

29)
```
  □
- 1
---
  4
```

30)
```
  5
- □
---
  0
```

31)
```
  □
- 1
---
  1
```

32)
```
  5
- □
---
  2
```

33)
```
  □
- 1
---
  3
```

34)
```
  5
- □
---
  3
```

35)
```
  □
- 3
---
  2
```

36)
```
  2
- □
---
  1
```

37)
```
  □
- 0
---
  5
```

38)
```
  2
- □
---
  0
```

39)
```
  □
- 1
---
  4
```

40)
```
  4
- □
---
  2
```

41)
```
  □
- 1
---
  2
```

42)
```
  3
- □
---
  3
```

43)
```
  □
- 5
---
  0
```

44)
```
  2
- □
---
  2
```

45)
```
  □
- 0
---
  4
```

46)
```
  4
- □
---
  3
```

47)
```
  □
- 0
---
  0
```

48)
```
  4
- □
---
  0
```

49)
```
  □
- 0
---
  5
```

50)
```
  3
- □
---
  2
```

51)
```
  □
- 2
---
  3
```

52)
```
  5
- □
---
  3
```

53)
```
  □
- 2
---
  2
```

54)
```
  4
- □
---
  3
```

55)
```
  □
- 0
---
  2
```

56)
```
  2
- □
---
  0
```

57)
```
  □
- 1
---
  2
```

58)
```
  3
- □
---
  1
```

59)
```
  □
- 1
---
  0
```

60)
```
  2
- □
---
  2
```

Name:

Score:

/60

Time   :

1) 6
 - 5

2) 7
 - 2

3) 6
 - 0

4) 7
 - 0

5) 4
 - 3

6) 7
 - 1

7) 5
 - 2

8) 4
 - 4

9) 2
 - 1

10) 6
 - 6

11) 7
 - 0

12) 6
 - 2

13) 7
 - 1

14) 1
 - 0

15) 6
 - 4

16) 2
 - 0

17) 7
 - 0

18) 7
 - 3

19) 5
 - 4

20) 2
 - 2

21) 5
 - 0

22) 5
 - 0

23) 0
 - 0

24) 4
 - 1

25) 7
 - 7

26) 1
 - 1

27) 7
 - 6

28) 5
 - 0

29) 5
 - 4

30) 4
 - 4

31) 7
 - 3

32) 3
 - 1

33) 0
 - 0

34) 0
 - 0

35) 5
 - 0

36) 5
 - 1

37) 7
 - 6

38) 7
 - 3

39) 3
 - 1

40) 3
 - 0

41) 7
 - 4

42) 7
 - 1

43) 5
 - 0

44) 5
 - 0

45) 6
 - 1

46) 6
 - 0

47) 6
 - 1

48) 5
 - 4

49) 7
 - 5

50) 4
 - 4

51) 7
 - 1

52) 4
 - 4

53) 5
 - 4

54) 5
 - 5

55) 3
 - 3

56) 7
 - 1

57) 5
 - 2

58) 6
 - 2

59) 2
 - 1

60) 7
 - 1

Name:

Score:

/60

time   :

1)
$$\begin{array}{r} 7 \\ -6 \\ \hline \end{array}$$

2)
$$\begin{array}{r} 4 \\ -3 \\ \hline \end{array}$$

3)
$$\begin{array}{r} 3 \\ -0 \\ \hline \end{array}$$

4)
$$\begin{array}{r} 7 \\ -1 \\ \hline \end{array}$$

5)
$$\begin{array}{r} 5 \\ -3 \\ \hline \end{array}$$

6)
$$\begin{array}{r} 4 \\ -4 \\ \hline \end{array}$$

7)
$$\begin{array}{r} 4 \\ -4 \\ \hline \end{array}$$

8)
$$\begin{array}{r} 6 \\ -6 \\ \hline \end{array}$$

9)
$$\begin{array}{r} 4 \\ -0 \\ \hline \end{array}$$

10)
$$\begin{array}{r} 6 \\ -0 \\ \hline \end{array}$$

11)
$$\begin{array}{r} 7 \\ -1 \\ \hline \end{array}$$

12)
$$\begin{array}{r} 6 \\ -1 \\ \hline \end{array}$$

13)
$$\begin{array}{r} 6 \\ -0 \\ \hline \end{array}$$

14)
$$\begin{array}{r} 2 \\ -1 \\ \hline \end{array}$$

15)
$$\begin{array}{r} 4 \\ -2 \\ \hline \end{array}$$

16)
$$\begin{array}{r} 2 \\ -2 \\ \hline \end{array}$$

17)
$$\begin{array}{r} 5 \\ -5 \\ \hline \end{array}$$

18)
$$\begin{array}{r} 5 \\ -4 \\ \hline \end{array}$$

19)
$$\begin{array}{r} 6 \\ -1 \\ \hline \end{array}$$

20)
$$\begin{array}{r} 7 \\ -5 \\ \hline \end{array}$$

21)
$$\begin{array}{r} 7 \\ -3 \\ \hline \end{array}$$

22)
$$\begin{array}{r} 4 \\ -2 \\ \hline \end{array}$$

23)
$$\begin{array}{r} 6 \\ -0 \\ \hline \end{array}$$

24)
$$\begin{array}{r} 0 \\ -0 \\ \hline \end{array}$$

25)
$$\begin{array}{r} 6 \\ -1 \\ \hline \end{array}$$

26)
$$\begin{array}{r} 7 \\ -7 \\ \hline \end{array}$$

27)
$$\begin{array}{r} 5 \\ -2 \\ \hline \end{array}$$

28)
$$\begin{array}{r} 6 \\ -3 \\ \hline \end{array}$$

29)
$$\begin{array}{r} 3 \\ -2 \\ \hline \end{array}$$

30)
$$\begin{array}{r} 6 \\ -3 \\ \hline \end{array}$$

31)
$$\begin{array}{r} 3 \\ -1 \\ \hline \end{array}$$

32)
$$\begin{array}{r} 6 \\ -1 \\ \hline \end{array}$$

33)
$$\begin{array}{r} 2 \\ -0 \\ \hline \end{array}$$

34)
$$\begin{array}{r} 6 \\ -6 \\ \hline \end{array}$$

35)
$$\begin{array}{r} 7 \\ -3 \\ \hline \end{array}$$

36)
$$\begin{array}{r} 4 \\ -0 \\ \hline \end{array}$$

37)
$$\begin{array}{r} 6 \\ -1 \\ \hline \end{array}$$

38)
$$\begin{array}{r} 3 \\ -2 \\ \hline \end{array}$$

39)
$$\begin{array}{r} 7 \\ -2 \\ \hline \end{array}$$

40)
$$\begin{array}{r} 1 \\ -0 \\ \hline \end{array}$$

41)
$$\begin{array}{r} 0 \\ -0 \\ \hline \end{array}$$

42)
$$\begin{array}{r} 7 \\ -1 \\ \hline \end{array}$$

43)
$$\begin{array}{r} 0 \\ -0 \\ \hline \end{array}$$

44)
$$\begin{array}{r} 3 \\ -2 \\ \hline \end{array}$$

45)
$$\begin{array}{r} 0 \\ -0 \\ \hline \end{array}$$

46)
$$\begin{array}{r} 7 \\ -1 \\ \hline \end{array}$$

47)
$$\begin{array}{r} 2 \\ -2 \\ \hline \end{array}$$

48)
$$\begin{array}{r} 5 \\ -2 \\ \hline \end{array}$$

49)
$$\begin{array}{r} 0 \\ -0 \\ \hline \end{array}$$

50)
$$\begin{array}{r} 5 \\ -2 \\ \hline \end{array}$$

51)
$$\begin{array}{r} 3 \\ -0 \\ \hline \end{array}$$

52)
$$\begin{array}{r} 5 \\ -1 \\ \hline \end{array}$$

53)
$$\begin{array}{r} 3 \\ -3 \\ \hline \end{array}$$

54)
$$\begin{array}{r} 7 \\ -2 \\ \hline \end{array}$$

55)
$$\begin{array}{r} 4 \\ -2 \\ \hline \end{array}$$

56)
$$\begin{array}{r} 1 \\ -0 \\ \hline \end{array}$$

57)
$$\begin{array}{r} 7 \\ -3 \\ \hline \end{array}$$

58)
$$\begin{array}{r} 2 \\ -0 \\ \hline \end{array}$$

59)
$$\begin{array}{r} 3 \\ -1 \\ \hline \end{array}$$

60)
$$\begin{array}{r} 4 \\ -1 \\ \hline \end{array}$$

Name:

Score:

/60

Time   :

1) $3 - 3$

2) $6 - 4$

3) $7 - 3$

4) $7 - 6$

5) $6 - 2$

6) $0 - 0$

7) $4 - 1$

8) $4 - 4$

9) $4 - 3$

10) $7 - 2$

11) $7 - 6$

12) $1 - 1$

13) $3 - 2$

14) $7 - 7$

15) $4 - 1$

16) $7 - 5$

17) $4 - 1$

18) $6 - 6$

19) $1 - 0$

20) $5 - 5$

21) $4 - 3$

22) $6 - 2$

23) $3 - 3$

24) $2 - 1$

25) $7 - 1$

26) $7 - 4$

27) $4 - 0$

28) $5 - 0$

29) $3 - 1$

30) $6 - 1$

31) $5 - 3$

32) $2 - 1$

33) $4 - 1$

34) $7 - 5$

35) $6 - 1$

36) $7 - 6$

37) $3 - 2$

38) $4 - 0$

39) $6 - 5$

40) $5 - 2$

41) $7 - 1$

42) $3 - 1$

43) $6 - 0$

44) $5 - 4$

45) $3 - 2$

46) $3 - 3$

47) $1 - 1$

48) $5 - 4$

49) $5 - 1$

50) $2 - 2$

51) $4 - 3$

52) $6 - 1$

53) $3 - 0$

54) $3 - 0$

55) $6 - 1$

56) $3 - 1$

57) $4 - 0$

58) $4 - 2$

59) $3 - 2$

60) $6 - 5$

Name:

Score:

/60

time   :

1) 3
  − 0

2) 7
  − 2

3) 7
  − 2

4) 0
  − 0

5) 4
  − 0

6) 1
  − 1

7) 7
  − 4

8) 6
  − 5

9) 7
  − 2

10) 2
  − 1

11) 0
  − 0

12) 0
  − 0

13) 4
  − 4

14) 3
  − 0

15) 4
  − 2

16) 1
  − 0

17) 7
  − 4

18) 2
  − 2

19) 0
  − 0

20) 3
  − 2

21) 1
  − 0

22) 5
  − 5

23) 5
  − 2

24) 6
  − 3

25) 5
  − 3

26) 4
  − 2

27) 3
  − 0

28) 2
  − 0

29) 1
  − 0

30) 3
  − 0

31) 6
  − 4

32) 6
  − 6

33) 6
  − 6

34) 1
  − 1

35) 2
  − 1

36) 3
  − 3

37) 1
  − 0

38) 6
  − 6

39) 6
  − 1

40) 3
  − 3

41) 4
  − 3

42) 7
  − 5

43) 6
  − 3

44) 3
  − 1

45) 4
  − 2

46) 2
  − 1

47) 5
  − 1

48) 3
  − 3

49) 5
  − 0

50) 4
  − 0

51) 5
  − 2

52) 5
  − 1

53) 4
  − 0

54) 2
  − 0

55) 6
  − 0

56) 5
  − 2

57) 4
  − 1

58) 0
  − 0

59) 5
  − 2

60) 6
  − 3

Name:

Score:

/60

time   :

1)
$$\begin{array}{r} 0 \\ -\ 0 \\ \hline \end{array}$$

2)
$$\begin{array}{r} 6 \\ -\ 5 \\ \hline \end{array}$$

3)
$$\begin{array}{r} 6 \\ -\ 4 \\ \hline \end{array}$$

4)
$$\begin{array}{r} 7 \\ -\ 0 \\ \hline \end{array}$$

5)
$$\begin{array}{r} 3 \\ -\ 0 \\ \hline \end{array}$$

6)
$$\begin{array}{r} 5 \\ -\ 3 \\ \hline \end{array}$$

7)
$$\begin{array}{r} 7 \\ -\ 5 \\ \hline \end{array}$$

8)
$$\begin{array}{r} 5 \\ -\ 2 \\ \hline \end{array}$$

9)
$$\begin{array}{r} 2 \\ -\ 0 \\ \hline \end{array}$$

10)
$$\begin{array}{r} 2 \\ -\ 2 \\ \hline \end{array}$$

11)
$$\begin{array}{r} 5 \\ -\ 4 \\ \hline \end{array}$$

12)
$$\begin{array}{r} 7 \\ -\ 3 \\ \hline \end{array}$$

13)
$$\begin{array}{r} 4 \\ -\ 2 \\ \hline \end{array}$$

14)
$$\begin{array}{r} 6 \\ -\ 6 \\ \hline \end{array}$$

15)
$$\begin{array}{r} 4 \\ -\ 0 \\ \hline \end{array}$$

16)
$$\begin{array}{r} 7 \\ -\ 6 \\ \hline \end{array}$$

17)
$$\begin{array}{r} 6 \\ -\ 1 \\ \hline \end{array}$$

18)
$$\begin{array}{r} 3 \\ -\ 0 \\ \hline \end{array}$$

19)
$$\begin{array}{r} 3 \\ -\ 1 \\ \hline \end{array}$$

20)
$$\begin{array}{r} 7 \\ -\ 1 \\ \hline \end{array}$$

21)
$$\begin{array}{r} 7 \\ -\ 4 \\ \hline \end{array}$$

22)
$$\begin{array}{r} 6 \\ -\ 1 \\ \hline \end{array}$$

23)
$$\begin{array}{r} 3 \\ -\ 3 \\ \hline \end{array}$$

24)
$$\begin{array}{r} 4 \\ -\ 0 \\ \hline \end{array}$$

25)
$$\begin{array}{r} 4 \\ -\ 1 \\ \hline \end{array}$$

26)
$$\begin{array}{r} 6 \\ -\ 6 \\ \hline \end{array}$$

27)
$$\begin{array}{r} 5 \\ -\ 5 \\ \hline \end{array}$$

28)
$$\begin{array}{r} 4 \\ -\ 1 \\ \hline \end{array}$$

29)
$$\begin{array}{r} 4 \\ -\ 2 \\ \hline \end{array}$$

30)
$$\begin{array}{r} 5 \\ -\ 5 \\ \hline \end{array}$$

31)
$$\begin{array}{r} 4 \\ -\ 1 \\ \hline \end{array}$$

32)
$$\begin{array}{r} 7 \\ -\ 1 \\ \hline \end{array}$$

33)
$$\begin{array}{r} 5 \\ -\ 5 \\ \hline \end{array}$$

34)
$$\begin{array}{r} 7 \\ -\ 4 \\ \hline \end{array}$$

35)
$$\begin{array}{r} 7 \\ -\ 0 \\ \hline \end{array}$$

36)
$$\begin{array}{r} 5 \\ -\ 4 \\ \hline \end{array}$$

37)
$$\begin{array}{r} 5 \\ -\ 1 \\ \hline \end{array}$$

38)
$$\begin{array}{r} 7 \\ -\ 5 \\ \hline \end{array}$$

39)
$$\begin{array}{r} 4 \\ -\ 3 \\ \hline \end{array}$$

40)
$$\begin{array}{r} 4 \\ -\ 2 \\ \hline \end{array}$$

41)
$$\begin{array}{r} 3 \\ -\ 3 \\ \hline \end{array}$$

42)
$$\begin{array}{r} 4 \\ -\ 2 \\ \hline \end{array}$$

43)
$$\begin{array}{r} 5 \\ -\ 0 \\ \hline \end{array}$$

44)
$$\begin{array}{r} 3 \\ -\ 3 \\ \hline \end{array}$$

45)
$$\begin{array}{r} 5 \\ -\ 4 \\ \hline \end{array}$$

46)
$$\begin{array}{r} 4 \\ -\ 4 \\ \hline \end{array}$$

47)
$$\begin{array}{r} 1 \\ -\ 0 \\ \hline \end{array}$$

48)
$$\begin{array}{r} 7 \\ -\ 7 \\ \hline \end{array}$$

49)
$$\begin{array}{r} 4 \\ -\ 0 \\ \hline \end{array}$$

50)
$$\begin{array}{r} 2 \\ -\ 2 \\ \hline \end{array}$$

51)
$$\begin{array}{r} 7 \\ -\ 0 \\ \hline \end{array}$$

52)
$$\begin{array}{r} 3 \\ -\ 1 \\ \hline \end{array}$$

53)
$$\begin{array}{r} 6 \\ -\ 5 \\ \hline \end{array}$$

54)
$$\begin{array}{r} 6 \\ -\ 0 \\ \hline \end{array}$$

55)
$$\begin{array}{r} 7 \\ -\ 0 \\ \hline \end{array}$$

56)
$$\begin{array}{r} 3 \\ -\ 1 \\ \hline \end{array}$$

57)
$$\begin{array}{r} 5 \\ -\ 0 \\ \hline \end{array}$$

58)
$$\begin{array}{r} 0 \\ -\ 0 \\ \hline \end{array}$$

59)
$$\begin{array}{r} 5 \\ -\ 3 \\ \hline \end{array}$$

60)
$$\begin{array}{r} 4 \\ -\ 2 \\ \hline \end{array}$$

Name:

Score:

/60

Time   :

1) 3
   - 1

2) 2
   - 0

3) 4
   - 4

4) 3
   - 0

5) 5
   - 5

6) 5
   - 5

7) 6
   - 4

8) 6
   - 3

9) 5
   - 4

10) 6
   - 4

11) 6
   - 2

12) 6
   - 0

13) 6
   - 2

14) 5
   - 2

15) 4
   - 0

16) 4
   - 3

17) 7
   - 6

18) 4
   - 0

19) 6
   - 4

20) 4
   - 1

21) 6
   - 2

22) 3
   - 3

23) 6
   - 5

24) 1
   - 1

25) 0
   - 0

26) 6
   - 1

27) 5
   - 2

28) 6
   - 1

29) 7
   - 7

30) 6
   - 4

31) 6
   - 0

32) 6
   - 3

33) 6
   - 0

34) 2
   - 2

35) 7
   - 0

36) 3
   - 3

37) 5
   - 2

38) 7
   - 5

39) 6
   - 5

40) 2
   - 0

41) 6
   - 5

42) 6
   - 0

43) 7
   - 6

44) 1
   - 1

45) 4
   - 2

46) 6
   - 0

47) 5
   - 1

48) 1
   - 0

49) 7
   - 5

50) 6
   - 6

51) 1
   - 1

52) 6
   - 2

53) 7
   - 3

54) 3
   - 0

55) 7
   - 2

56) 5
   - 4

57) 7
   - 3

58) 7
   - 6

59) 5
   - 5

60) 5
   - 1

Name:

Score: /60

Time :

1)
$$\begin{array}{r} 6 \\ -1 \end{array}$$

2)
$$\begin{array}{r} 0 \\ -0 \end{array}$$

3)
$$\begin{array}{r} 4 \\ -3 \end{array}$$

4)
$$\begin{array}{r} 3 \\ -1 \end{array}$$

5)
$$\begin{array}{r} 5 \\ -1 \end{array}$$

6)
$$\begin{array}{r} 3 \\ -2 \end{array}$$

7)
$$\begin{array}{r} 3 \\ -3 \end{array}$$

8)
$$\begin{array}{r} 7 \\ -7 \end{array}$$

9)
$$\begin{array}{r} 4 \\ -3 \end{array}$$

10)
$$\begin{array}{r} 5 \\ -0 \end{array}$$

11)
$$\begin{array}{r} 1 \\ -0 \end{array}$$

12)
$$\begin{array}{r} 1 \\ -0 \end{array}$$

13)
$$\begin{array}{r} 3 \\ -2 \end{array}$$

14)
$$\begin{array}{r} 5 \\ -2 \end{array}$$

15)
$$\begin{array}{r} 6 \\ -5 \end{array}$$

16)
$$\begin{array}{r} 2 \\ -2 \end{array}$$

17)
$$\begin{array}{r} 7 \\ -6 \end{array}$$

18)
$$\begin{array}{r} 4 \\ -4 \end{array}$$

19)
$$\begin{array}{r} 6 \\ -2 \end{array}$$

20)
$$\begin{array}{r} 7 \\ -1 \end{array}$$

21)
$$\begin{array}{r} 7 \\ -0 \end{array}$$

22)
$$\begin{array}{r} 2 \\ -1 \end{array}$$

23)
$$\begin{array}{r} 4 \\ -4 \end{array}$$

24)
$$\begin{array}{r} 5 \\ -5 \end{array}$$

25)
$$\begin{array}{r} 5 \\ -2 \end{array}$$

26)
$$\begin{array}{r} 5 \\ -5 \end{array}$$

27)
$$\begin{array}{r} 2 \\ -2 \end{array}$$

28)
$$\begin{array}{r} 7 \\ -3 \end{array}$$

29)
$$\begin{array}{r} 6 \\ -3 \end{array}$$

30)
$$\begin{array}{r} 7 \\ -4 \end{array}$$

31)
$$\begin{array}{r} 1 \\ -0 \end{array}$$

32)
$$\begin{array}{r} 7 \\ -6 \end{array}$$

33)
$$\begin{array}{r} 5 \\ -0 \end{array}$$

34)
$$\begin{array}{r} 7 \\ -1 \end{array}$$

35)
$$\begin{array}{r} 2 \\ -2 \end{array}$$

36)
$$\begin{array}{r} 3 \\ -3 \end{array}$$

37)
$$\begin{array}{r} 7 \\ -1 \end{array}$$

38)
$$\begin{array}{r} 4 \\ -0 \end{array}$$

39)
$$\begin{array}{r} 7 \\ -6 \end{array}$$

40)
$$\begin{array}{r} 1 \\ -0 \end{array}$$

41)
$$\begin{array}{r} 5 \\ -1 \end{array}$$

42)
$$\begin{array}{r} 3 \\ -3 \end{array}$$

43)
$$\begin{array}{r} 6 \\ -5 \end{array}$$

44)
$$\begin{array}{r} 0 \\ -0 \end{array}$$

45)
$$\begin{array}{r} 5 \\ -0 \end{array}$$

46)
$$\begin{array}{r} 2 \\ -1 \end{array}$$

47)
$$\begin{array}{r} 2 \\ -0 \end{array}$$

48)
$$\begin{array}{r} 6 \\ -6 \end{array}$$

49)
$$\begin{array}{r} 6 \\ -3 \end{array}$$

50)
$$\begin{array}{r} 6 \\ -3 \end{array}$$

51)
$$\begin{array}{r} 2 \\ -2 \end{array}$$

52)
$$\begin{array}{r} 6 \\ -0 \end{array}$$

53)
$$\begin{array}{r} 3 \\ -2 \end{array}$$

54)
$$\begin{array}{r} 3 \\ -0 \end{array}$$

55)
$$\begin{array}{r} 7 \\ -3 \end{array}$$

56)
$$\begin{array}{r} 7 \\ -1 \end{array}$$

57)
$$\begin{array}{r} 2 \\ -1 \end{array}$$

58)
$$\begin{array}{r} 4 \\ -3 \end{array}$$

59)
$$\begin{array}{r} 7 \\ -0 \end{array}$$

60)
$$\begin{array}{r} 6 \\ -6 \end{array}$$

Name:

Score:

/60

time   :

1) 5
  - 2

2) 1
  - 1

3) 7
  - 0

4) 7
  - 4

5) 6
  - 0

6) 2
  - 1

7) 6
  - 3

8) 3
  - 2

9) 5
  - 3

10) 6
   - 0

11) 6
   - 0

12) 4
   - 4

13) 3
   - 0

14) 4
   - 4

15) 6
   - 3

16) 7
   - 5

17) 7
   - 4

18) 5
   - 4

19) 5
   - 1

20) 7
   - 3

21) 5
   - 0

22) 5
   - 2

23) 5
   - 4

24) 6
   - 5

25) 4
   - 3

26) 7
   - 1

27) 3
   - 2

28) 0
   - 0

29) 7
   - 1

30) 6
   - 3

31) 2
   - 2

32) 7
   - 5

33) 6
   - 1

34) 5
   - 5

35) 4
   - 1

36) 5
   - 3

37) 4
   - 0

38) 0
   - 0

39) 4
   - 0

40) 3
   - 3

41) 5
   - 0

42) 5
   - 5

43) 4
   - 0

44) 2
   - 0

45) 7
   - 7

46) 2
   - 2

47) 1
   - 1

48) 6
   - 6

49) 5
   - 2

50) 6
   - 0

51) 6
   - 1

52) 6
   - 5

53) 7
   - 0

54) 7
   - 1

55) 2
   - 2

56) 4
   - 4

57) 7
   - 6

58) 4
   - 0

59) 3
   - 0

60) 4
   - 4

Score:

/60

Name:

time   :

1) 6
   - 1

2) 5
   - 1

3) 1
   - 0

4) 6
   - 0

5) 5
   - 0

6) 5
   - 5

7) 6
   - 6

8) 5
   - 1

9) 6
   - 5

10) 3
    - 3

11) 0
    - 0

12) 5
    - 3

13) 7
    - 7

14) 3
    - 1

15) 7
    - 2

16) 6
    - 6

17) 7
    - 7

18) 4
    - 0

19) 5
    - 3

20) 4
    - 3

21) 3
    - 2

22) 6
    - 1

23) 1
    - 0

24) 4
    - 2

25) 7
    - 2

26) 5
    - 0

27) 3
    - 2

28) 7
    - 7

29) 4
    - 2

30) 5
    - 5

31) 5
    - 4

32) 6
    - 5

33) 0
    - 0

34) 7
    - 5

35) 2
    - 2

36) 6
    - 1

37) 6
    - 6

38) 5
    - 5

39) 7
    - 3

40) 7
    - 5

41) 7
    - 7

42) 1
    - 1

43) 2
    - 0

44) 3
    - 2

45) 5
    - 0

46) 4
    - 1

47) 7
    - 7

48) 4
    - 4

49) 3
    - 3

50) 3
    - 0

51) 7
    - 1

52) 1
    - 1

53) 3
    - 3

54) 1
    - 0

55) 3
    - 2

56) 7
    - 3

57) 7
    - 0

58) 6
    - 2

59) 2
    - 2

60) 6
    - 0

Name:

Score:

/60

time   :

1) 3
  - 3

2) 0
  - 0

3) 4
  - 3

4) 3
  - 3

5) 6
  - 0

6) 6
  - 1

7) 6
  - 1

8) 3
  - 3

9) 6
  - 3

10) 6
   - 6

11) 7
   - 6

12) 1
   - 1

13) 1
   - 0

14) 3
   - 1

15) 4
   - 4

16) 7
   - 0

17) 5
   - 4

18) 5
   - 5

19) 3
   - 1

20) 3
   - 0

21) 4
   - 0

22) 3
   - 3

23) 7
   - 3

24) 5
   - 2

25) 7
   - 6

26) 2
   - 0

27) 3
   - 1

28) 5
   - 0

29) 6
   - 6

30) 7
   - 2

31) 3
   - 0

32) 7
   - 2

33) 3
   - 2

34) 0
   - 0

35) 6
   - 1

36) 1
   - 1

37) 4
   - 0

38) 6
   - 4

39) 5
   - 2

40) 5
   - 3

41) 7
   - 0

42) 7
   - 2

43) 5
   - 5

44) 6
   - 6

45) 5
   - 5

46) 7
   - 4

47) 7
   - 1

48) 2
   - 1

49) 5
   - 2

50) 6
   - 3

51) 5
   - 2

52) 7
   - 6

53) 2
   - 2

54) 4
   - 0

55) 6
   - 6

56) 4
   - 3

57) 6
   - 0

58) 5
   - 3

59) 3
   - 0

60) 7
   - 3

Name: _____   Score: /60   Time   : _____

1) □ − 3 = 2

2) 4 − □ = 0

3) □ − 0 = 4

4) 5 − □ = 3

5) □ − 0 = 3

6) 6 − □ = 6

7) □ − 3 = 1

8) 4 − □ = 0

9) □ − 1 = 0

10) 7 − □ = 5

11) □ − 2 = 0

12) 2 − □ = 0

13) □ − 4 = 3

14) 2 − □ = 0

15) □ − 0 = 2

16) 7 − □ = 6

17) □ − 0 = 4

18) 4 − □ = 3

19) □ − 7 = 0

20) 3 − □ = 0

21) □ − 0 = 5

22) 6 − □ = 0

23) □ − 0 = 2

24) 6 − □ = 5

25) □ − 4 = 1

26) 7 − □ = 2

27) □ − 0 = 2

28) 6 − □ = 0

29) □ − 0 = 3

30) 7 − □ = 5

31) □ − 6 = 0

32) 5 − □ = 1

33) □ − 1 = 2

34) 7 − □ = 4

35) □ − 3 = 0

36) 3 − □ = 0

37) □ − 1 = 0

38) 4 − □ = 2

39) □ − 6 = 0

40) 6 − □ = 2

41) □ − 1 = 4

42) 5 − □ = 0

43) □ − 1 = 0

44) 4 − □ = 4

45) □ − 3 = 4

46) 5 − □ = 3

47) □ − 3 = 1

48) 7 − □ = 7

49) □ − 3 = 2

50) 4 − □ = 1

51) □ − 0 = 1

52) 5 − □ = 5

53) □ − 6 = 0

54) 6 − □ = 0

55) □ − 2 = 4

56) 6 − □ = 0

57) □ − 2 = 4

58) 5 − □ = 2

59) □ − 0 = 5

60) 5 − □ = 1

1)
```
    □
  - 3
  ───
    4
```

2)
```
    1
  - □
  ───
    1
```

3)
```
    □
  - 2
  ───
    2
```

4)
```
    7
  - □
  ───
    0
```

5)
```
    □
  - 2
  ───
    4
```

6)
```
    6
  - □
  ───
    5
```

7)
```
    □
  - 4
  ───
    1
```

8)
```
    2
  - □
  ───
    2
```

9)
```
    □
  - 3
  ───
    3
```

10)
```
    7
  - □
  ───
    7
```

11)
```
    □
  - 5
  ───
    0
```

12)
```
    4
  - □
  ───
    0
```

13)
```
    □
  - 1
  ───
    5
```

14)
```
    2
  - □
  ───
    2
```

15)
```
    □
  - 1
  ───
    1
```

16)
```
    3
  - □
  ───
    2
```

17)
```
    □
  - 1
  ───
    6
```

18)
```
    3
  - □
  ───
    1
```

19)
```
    □
  - 1
  ───
    6
```

20)
```
    3
  - □
  ───
    0
```

21)
```
    □
  - 1
  ───
    4
```

22)
```
    3
  - □
  ───
    3
```

23)
```
    □
  - 5
  ───
    0
```

24)
```
    5
  - □
  ───
    4
```

25)
```
    □
  - 2
  ───
    2
```

26)
```
    3
  - □
  ───
    2
```

27)
```
    □
  - 1
  ───
    3
```

28)
```
    5
  - □
  ───
    4
```

29)
```
    □
  - 1
  ───
    5
```

30)
```
    4
  - □
  ───
    4
```

31)
```
    □
  - 2
  ───
    3
```

32)
```
    5
  - □
  ───
    3
```

33)
```
    □
  - 7
  ───
    0
```

34)
```
    3
  - □
  ───
    2
```

35)
```
    □
  - 4
  ───
    1
```

36)
```
    7
  - □
  ───
    1
```

37)
```
    □
  - 4
  ───
    2
```

38)
```
    3
  - □
  ───
    1
```

39)
```
    □
  - 0
  ───
    2
```

40)
```
    6
  - □
  ───
    1
```

41)
```
    □
  - 0
  ───
    5
```

42)
```
    6
  - □
  ───
    4
```

43)
```
    □
  - 1
  ───
    0
```

44)
```
    2
  - □
  ───
    1
```

45)
```
    □
  - 2
  ───
    1
```

46)
```
    7
  - □
  ───
    7
```

47)
```
    □
  - 5
  ───
    2
```

48)
```
    5
  - □
  ───
    0
```

49)
```
    □
  - 5
  ───
    2
```

50)
```
    2
  - □
  ───
    0
```

51)
```
    □
  - 1
  ───
    0
```

52)
```
    7
  - □
  ───
    2
```

53)
```
    □
  - 2
  ───
    0
```

54)
```
    1
  - □
  ───
    1
```

55)
```
    □
  - 5
  ───
    1
```

56)
```
    3
  - □
  ───
    2
```

57)
```
    □
  - 2
  ───
    4
```

58)
```
    3
  - □
  ───
    1
```

59)
```
    □
  - 0
  ───
    2
```

60)
```
    4
  - □
  ───
    0
```

Score:

/60

Name:

time   :

1)
```
  □
- 0
  3
```

2)
```
  2
- □
  0
```

3)
```
  □
- 1
  3
```

4)
```
  7
- □
  5
```

5)
```
  □
- 3
  2
```

6)
```
  4
- □
  2
```

7)
```
  □
- 2
  5
```

8)
```
  7
- □
  2
```

9)
```
  □
- 1
  5
```

10)
```
  7
- □
  1
```

11)
```
  □
- 4
  1
```

12)
```
  5
- □
  2
```

13)
```
  □
- 0
  3
```

14)
```
  4
- □
  3
```

15)
```
  □
- 2
  0
```

16)
```
  4
- □
  4
```

17)
```
  □
- 1
  2
```

18)
```
  0
- □
  0
```

19)
```
  □
- 0
  0
```

20)
```
  6
- □
  2
```

21)
```
  □
- 0
  0
```

22)
```
  6
- □
  4
```

23)
```
  □
- 4
  2
```

24)
```
  4
- □
  4
```

25)
```
  □
- 7
  0
```

26)
```
  3
- □
  1
```

27)
```
  □
- 2
  4
```

28)
```
  4
- □
  1
```

29)
```
  □
- 2
  4
```

30)
```
  5
- □
  4
```

31)
```
  □
- 0
  0
```

32)
```
  6
- □
  1
```

33)
```
  □
- 4
  2
```

34)
```
  1
- □
  0
```

35)
```
  □
- 2
  2
```

36)
```
  4
- □
  1
```

37)
```
  □
- 5
  0
```

38)
```
  6
- □
  0
```

39)
```
  □
- 4
  0
```

40)
```
  5
- □
  2
```

41)
```
  □
- 2
  4
```

42)
```
  7
- □
  5
```

43)
```
  □
- 1
  1
```

44)
```
  2
- □
  0
```

45)
```
  □
- 4
  1
```

46)
```
  5
- □
  0
```

47)
```
  □
- 3
  3
```

48)
```
  2
- □
  2
```

49)
```
  □
- 4
  1
```

50)
```
  6
- □
  6
```

51)
```
  □
- 2
  3
```

52)
```
  5
- □
  4
```

53)
```
  □
- 4
  3
```

54)
```
  3
- □
  2
```

55)
```
  □
- 1
  3
```

56)
```
  6
- □
  2
```

57)
```
  □
- 2
  3
```

58)
```
  4
- □
  0
```

59)
```
  □
- 4
  3
```

60)
```
  6
- □
  5
```

Page 113

Score:

/60

Name:

time   :

1) □ − 2 = 1

2) 3 − □ = 1

3) □ − 0 = 3

4) 7 − □ = 4

5) □ − 1 = 4

6) 0 − □ = 0

7) □ − 5 = 2

8) 3 − □ = 3

9) □ − 0 = 7

10) 7 − □ = 5

11) □ − 5 = 0

12) 5 − □ = 5

13) □ − 5 = 1

14) 7 − □ = 5

15) □ − 3 = 2

16) 7 − □ = 7

17) □ − 1 = 3

18) 3 − □ = 2

19) □ − 1 = 5

20) 4 − □ = 0

21) □ − 0 = 6

22) 4 − □ = 1

23) □ − 5 = 0

24) 3 − □ = 1

25) □ − 3 = 0

26) 3 − □ = 1

27) □ − 3 = 1

28) 4 − □ = 0

29) □ − 4 = 2

30) 3 − □ = 3

31) □ − 0 = 0

32) 7 − □ = 0

33) □ − 7 = 0

34) 5 − □ = 1

35) □ − 0 = 6

36) 2 − □ = 1

37) □ − 1 = 0

38) 7 − □ = 1

39) □ − 4 = 3

40) 5 − □ = 2

41) □ − 0 = 3

42) 3 − □ = 1

43) □ − 1 = 5

44) 2 − □ = 2

45) □ − 3 = 3

46) 1 − □ = 1

47) □ − 1 = 6

48) 2 − □ = 2

49) □ − 6 = 1

50) 3 − □ = 2

51) □ − 2 = 0

52) 7 − □ = 5

53) □ − 2 = 1

54) 5 − □ = 4

55) □ − 6 = 1

56) 4 − □ = 3

57) □ − 2 = 4

58) 7 − □ = 5

59) □ − 3 = 1

60) 7 − □ = 7

Page 114

Score:

/60

Name:

Time   :

1)
```
   □
 - 6
 ───
   1
```

2)
```
   7
 - □
 ───
   2
```

3)
```
   □
 - 0
 ───
   6
```

4)
```
   5
 - □
 ───
   5
```

5)
```
   □
 - 3
 ───
   2
```

6)
```
   1
 - □
 ───
   0
```

7)
```
   □
 - 7
 ───
   0
```

8)
```
   1
 - □
 ───
   0
```

9)
```
   □
 - 2
 ───
   5
```

10)
```
   7
 - □
 ───
   6
```

11)
```
   □
 - 1
 ───
   6
```

12)
```
   1
 - □
 ───
   1
```

13)
```
   □
 - 2
 ───
   0
```

14)
```
   3
 - □
 ───
   2
```

15)
```
   □
 - 0
 ───
   4
```

16)
```
   2
 - □
 ───
   2
```

17)
```
   □
 - 2
 ───
   1
```

18)
```
   3
 - □
 ───
   2
```

19)
```
   □
 - 3
 ───
   0
```

20)
```
   6
 - □
 ───
   5
```

21)
```
   □
 - 6
 ───
   1
```

22)
```
   2
 - □
 ───
   1
```

23)
```
   □
 - 4
 ───
   2
```

24)
```
   7
 - □
 ───
   3
```

25)
```
   □
 - 4
 ───
   2
```

26)
```
   5
 - □
 ───
   2
```

27)
```
   □
 - 4
 ───
   3
```

28)
```
   7
 - □
 ───
   4
```

29)
```
   □
 - 2
 ───
   5
```

30)
```
   2
 - □
 ───
   1
```

31)
```
   □
 - 5
 ───
   0
```

32)
```
   3
 - □
 ───
   1
```

33)
```
   □
 - 0
 ───
   7
```

34)
```
   5
 - □
 ───
   3
```

35)
```
   □
 - 0
 ───
   3
```

36)
```
   6
 - □
 ───
   0
```

37)
```
   □
 - 0
 ───
   0
```

38)
```
   7
 - □
 ───
   5
```

39)
```
   □
 - 2
 ───
   3
```

40)
```
   4
 - □
 ───
   4
```

41)
```
   □
 - 0
 ───
   3
```

42)
```
   5
 - □
 ───
   0
```

43)
```
   □
 - 0
 ───
   6
```

44)
```
   3
 - □
 ───
   3
```

45)
```
   □
 - 1
 ───
   3
```

46)
```
   6
 - □
 ───
   3
```

47)
```
   □
 - 5
 ───
   1
```

48)
```
   7
 - □
 ───
   3
```

49)
```
   □
 - 0
 ───
   7
```

50)
```
   3
 - □
 ───
   0
```

51)
```
   □
 - 3
 ───
   2
```

52)
```
   4
 - □
 ───
   2
```

53)
```
   □
 - 1
 ───
   3
```

54)
```
   5
 - □
 ───
   3
```

55)
```
   □
 - 4
 ───
   3
```

56)
```
   0
 - □
 ───
   0
```

57)
```
   □
 - 3
 ───
   0
```

58)
```
   7
 - □
 ───
   5
```

59)
```
   □
 - 6
 ───
   0
```

60)
```
   1
 - □
 ───
   0
```

Score:

/60

time   :

Name:

1)
```
   □
 - 0
 ___
   6
```

2)
```
   7
 - □
 ___
   6
```

3)
```
   □
 - 0
 ___
   4
```

4)
```
   6
 - □
 ___
   3
```

5)
```
   □
 - 1
 ___
   3
```

6)
```
   5
 - □
 ___
   5
```

7)
```
   □
 - 6
 ___
   0
```

8)
```
   4
 - □
 ___
   4
```

9)
```
   □
 - 0
 ___
   4
```

10)
```
   5
 - □
 ___
   3
```

11)
```
   □
 - 0
 ___
   3
```

12)
```
   6
 - □
 ___
   0
```

13)
```
   □
 - 2
 ___
   2
```

14)
```
   6
 - □
 ___
   1
```

15)
```
   □
 - 2
 ___
   0
```

16)
```
   6
 - □
 ___
   4
```

17)
```
   □
 - 2
 ___
   1
```

18)
```
   7
 - □
 ___
   0
```

19)
```
   □
 - 4
 ___
   2
```

20)
```
   6
 - □
 ___
   1
```

21)
```
   □
 - 2
 ___
   4
```

22)
```
   7
 - □
 ___
   3
```

23)
```
   □
 - 3
 ___
   2
```

24)
```
   2
 - □
 ___
   2
```

25)
```
   □
 - 1
 ___
   3
```

26)
```
   0
 - □
 ___
   0
```

27)
```
   □
 - 1
 ___
   5
```

28)
```
   7
 - □
 ___
   5
```

29)
```
   □
 - 2
 ___
   5
```

30)
```
   5
 - □
 ___
   4
```

31)
```
   □
 - 3
 ___
   3
```

32)
```
   2
 - □
 ___
   2
```

33)
```
   □
 - 3
 ___
   3
```

34)
```
   2
 - □
 ___
   2
```

35)
```
   □
 - 1
 ___
   5
```

36)
```
   4
 - □
 ___
   1
```

37)
```
   □
 - 1
 ___
   5
```

38)
```
   5
 - □
 ___
   0
```

39)
```
   □
 - 6
 ___
   1
```

40)
```
   1
 - □
 ___
   0
```

41)
```
   □
 - 0
 ___
   4
```

42)
```
   7
 - □
 ___
   2
```

43)
```
   □
 - 1
 ___
   0
```

44)
```
   3
 - □
 ___
   3
```

45)
```
   □
 - 0
 ___
   3
```

46)
```
   7
 - □
 ___
   0
```

47)
```
   □
 - 3
 ___
   2
```

48)
```
   4
 - □
 ___
   1
```

49)
```
   □
 - 4
 ___
   1
```

50)
```
   7
 - □
 ___
   2
```

51)
```
   □
 - 6
 ___
   1
```

52)
```
   6
 - □
 ___
   3
```

53)
```
   □
 - 6
 ___
   1
```

54)
```
   6
 - □
 ___
   0
```

55)
```
   □
 - 6
 ___
   0
```

56)
```
   5
 - □
 ___
   3
```

57)
```
   □
 - 0
 ___
   7
```

58)
```
   5
 - □
 ___
   3
```

59)
```
   □
 - 1
 ___
   2
```

60)
```
   6
 - □
 ___
   5
```

Name:

Score:

/60

time   :

1)
$$\square$$
$$- 1$$
$$4$$

2)
$$7$$
$$- \square$$
$$1$$

3)
$$\square$$
$$- 3$$
$$3$$

4)
$$7$$
$$- \square$$
$$7$$

5)
$$\square$$
$$- 1$$
$$4$$

6)
$$4$$
$$- \square$$
$$2$$

7)
$$\square$$
$$- 6$$
$$0$$

8)
$$2$$
$$- \square$$
$$2$$

9)
$$\square$$
$$- 1$$
$$5$$

10)
$$4$$
$$- \square$$
$$4$$

11)
$$\square$$
$$- 0$$
$$6$$

12)
$$3$$
$$- \square$$
$$2$$

13)
$$\square$$
$$- 2$$
$$0$$

14)
$$6$$
$$- \square$$
$$5$$

15)
$$\square$$
$$- 3$$
$$4$$

16)
$$6$$
$$- \square$$
$$4$$

17)
$$\square$$
$$- 3$$
$$1$$

18)
$$1$$
$$- \square$$
$$0$$

19)
$$\square$$
$$- 0$$
$$5$$

20)
$$6$$
$$- \square$$
$$6$$

21)
$$\square$$
$$- 5$$
$$2$$

22)
$$7$$
$$- \square$$
$$5$$

23)
$$\square$$
$$- 1$$
$$0$$

24)
$$6$$
$$- \square$$
$$2$$

25)
$$\square$$
$$- 1$$
$$0$$

26)
$$7$$
$$- \square$$
$$0$$

27)
$$\square$$
$$- 0$$
$$1$$

28)
$$6$$
$$- \square$$
$$5$$

29)
$$\square$$
$$- 5$$
$$0$$

30)
$$4$$
$$- \square$$
$$2$$

31)
$$\square$$
$$- 1$$
$$1$$

32)
$$5$$
$$- \square$$
$$4$$

33)
$$\square$$
$$- 7$$
$$0$$

34)
$$4$$
$$- \square$$
$$3$$

35)
$$\square$$
$$- 0$$
$$2$$

36)
$$4$$
$$- \square$$
$$3$$

37)
$$\square$$
$$- 1$$
$$5$$

38)
$$2$$
$$- \square$$
$$1$$

39)
$$\square$$
$$- 4$$
$$2$$

40)
$$1$$
$$- \square$$
$$1$$

41)
$$\square$$
$$- 4$$
$$2$$

42)
$$6$$
$$- \square$$
$$3$$

43)
$$\square$$
$$- 0$$
$$4$$

44)
$$6$$
$$- \square$$
$$0$$

45)
$$\square$$
$$- 6$$
$$0$$

46)
$$3$$
$$- \square$$
$$0$$

47)
$$\square$$
$$- 1$$
$$6$$

48)
$$5$$
$$- \square$$
$$0$$

49)
$$\square$$
$$- 6$$
$$1$$

50)
$$6$$
$$- \square$$
$$3$$

51)
$$\square$$
$$- 5$$
$$2$$

52)
$$7$$
$$- \square$$
$$6$$

53)
$$\square$$
$$- 2$$
$$1$$

54)
$$5$$
$$- \square$$
$$5$$

55)
$$\square$$
$$- 1$$
$$5$$

56)
$$7$$
$$- \square$$
$$3$$

57)
$$\square$$
$$- 5$$
$$2$$

58)
$$3$$
$$- \square$$
$$3$$

59)
$$\square$$
$$- 0$$
$$6$$

60)
$$7$$
$$- \square$$
$$5$$

Score:

/60

Name:

Time   :

1)
```
  □
-  6
-----
  1
```

2)
```
   4
-  □
-----
   0
```

3)
```
  □
-  2
-----
  0
```

4)
```
   0
-  □
-----
   0
```

5)
```
  □
-  2
-----
  0
```

6)
```
   6
-  □
-----
   2
```

7)
```
  □
-  1
-----
  4
```

8)
```
   4
-  □
-----
   2
```

9)
```
  □
-  3
-----
  3
```

10)
```
   5
-  □
-----
   0
```

11)
```
  □
-  6
-----
  1
```

12)
```
   6
-  □
-----
   2
```

13)
```
  □
-  1
-----
  1
```

14)
```
   2
-  □
-----
   0
```

15)
```
  □
-  1
-----
  3
```

16)
```
   5
-  □
-----
   1
```

17)
```
  □
-  2
-----
  4
```

18)
```
   6
-  □
-----
   0
```

19)
```
  □
-  5
-----
  0
```

20)
```
   7
-  □
-----
   1
```

21)
```
  □
-  2
-----
  4
```

22)
```
   4
-  □
-----
   0
```

23)
```
  □
-  1
-----
  0
```

24)
```
   5
-  □
-----
   2
```

25)
```
  □
-  1
-----
  4
```

26)
```
   0
-  □
-----
   0
```

27)
```
  □
-  5
-----
  2
```

28)
```
   6
-  □
-----
   1
```

29)
```
  □
-  4
-----
  1
```

30)
```
   3
-  □
-----
   3
```

31)
```
  □
-  3
-----
  3
```

32)
```
   6
-  □
-----
   2
```

33)
```
  □
-  2
-----
  3
```

34)
```
   3
-  □
-----
   3
```

35)
```
  □
-  2
-----
  1
```

36)
```
   3
-  □
-----
   1
```

37)
```
  □
-  3
-----
  4
```

38)
```
   6
-  □
-----
   1
```

39)
```
  □
-  3
-----
  0
```

40)
```
   4
-  □
-----
   1
```

41)
```
  □
-  3
-----
  4
```

42)
```
   5
-  □
-----
   1
```

43)
```
  □
-  3
-----
  0
```

44)
```
   2
-  □
-----
   2
```

45)
```
  □
-  1
-----
  0
```

46)
```
   5
-  □
-----
   5
```

47)
```
  □
-  7
-----
  0
```

48)
```
   4
-  □
-----
   3
```

49)
```
  □
-  0
-----
  2
```

50)
```
   4
-  □
-----
   0
```

51)
```
  □
-  2
-----
  4
```

52)
```
   7
-  □
-----
   4
```

53)
```
  □
-  0
-----
  0
```

54)
```
   2
-  □
-----
   2
```

55)
```
  □
-  3
-----
  0
```

56)
```
   4
-  □
-----
   0
```

57)
```
  □
-  6
-----
  0
```

58)
```
   5
-  □
-----
   2
```

59)
```
  □
-  1
-----
  6
```

60)
```
   4
-  □
-----
   0
```

Score: /60

Name:

Time   :

1) $\square - 0 = 1$

2) $6 - \square = 0$

3) $\square - 0 = 1$

4) $7 - \square = 5$

5) $\square - 1 = 4$

6) $3 - \square = 1$

7) $\square - 1 = 5$

8) $3 - \square = 0$

9) $\square - 4 = 0$

10) $5 - \square = 0$

11) $\square - 0 = 0$

12) $5 - \square = 3$

13) $\square - 0 = 4$

14) $4 - \square = 4$

15) $\square - 0 = 7$

16) $3 - \square = 3$

17) $\square - 3 = 3$

18) $5 - \square = 4$

19) $\square - 2 = 1$

20) $7 - \square = 6$

21) $\square - 4 = 0$

22) $2 - \square = 1$

23) $\square - 1 = 0$

24) $0 - \square = 0$

25) $\square - 3 = 2$

26) $7 - \square = 6$

27) $\square - 3 = 4$

28) $3 - \square = 2$

29) $\square - 4 = 0$

30) $5 - \square = 3$

31) $\square - 1 = 6$

32) $4 - \square = 0$

33) $\square - 0 = 0$

34) $6 - \square = 6$

35) $\square - 2 = 4$

36) $7 - \square = 0$

37) $\square - 3 = 2$

38) $2 - \square = 2$

39) $\square - 5 = 1$

40) $5 - \square = 5$

41) $\square - 3 = 1$

42) $1 - \square = 1$

43) $\square - 0 = 3$

44) $5 - \square = 1$

45) $\square - 3 = 4$

46) $4 - \square = 3$

47) $\square - 1 = 0$

48) $5 - \square = 0$

49) $\square - 4 = 1$

50) $1 - \square = 0$

51) $\square - 3 = 0$

52) $5 - \square = 5$

53) $\square - 4 = 0$

54) $5 - \square = 1$

55) $\square - 3 = 4$

56) $7 - \square = 4$

57) $\square - 2 = 2$

58) $2 - \square = 0$

59) $\square - 0 = 3$

60) $4 - \square = 2$

Score: /60

Name:

Time :

1)
$$\begin{array}{r} \square \\ -\ 5 \\ \hline 0 \end{array}$$

2)
$$\begin{array}{r} 3 \\ -\ \square \\ \hline 0 \end{array}$$

3)
$$\begin{array}{r} \square \\ -\ 0 \\ \hline 7 \end{array}$$

4)
$$\begin{array}{r} 7 \\ -\ \square \\ \hline 7 \end{array}$$

5)
$$\begin{array}{r} \square \\ -\ 1 \\ \hline 3 \end{array}$$

6)
$$\begin{array}{r} 7 \\ -\ \square \\ \hline 3 \end{array}$$

7)
$$\begin{array}{r} \square \\ -\ 1 \\ \hline 3 \end{array}$$

8)
$$\begin{array}{r} 7 \\ -\ \square \\ \hline 2 \end{array}$$

9)
$$\begin{array}{r} \square \\ -\ 3 \\ \hline 0 \end{array}$$

10)
$$\begin{array}{r} 7 \\ -\ \square \\ \hline 3 \end{array}$$

11)
$$\begin{array}{r} \square \\ -\ 2 \\ \hline 1 \end{array}$$

12)
$$\begin{array}{r} 6 \\ -\ \square \\ \hline 2 \end{array}$$

13)
$$\begin{array}{r} \square \\ -\ 6 \\ \hline 0 \end{array}$$

14)
$$\begin{array}{r} 6 \\ -\ \square \\ \hline 1 \end{array}$$

15)
$$\begin{array}{r} \square \\ -\ 0 \\ \hline 1 \end{array}$$

16)
$$\begin{array}{r} 7 \\ -\ \square \\ \hline 3 \end{array}$$

17)
$$\begin{array}{r} \square \\ -\ 4 \\ \hline 2 \end{array}$$

18)
$$\begin{array}{r} 7 \\ -\ \square \\ \hline 0 \end{array}$$

19)
$$\begin{array}{r} \square \\ -\ 6 \\ \hline 1 \end{array}$$

20)
$$\begin{array}{r} 6 \\ -\ \square \\ \hline 2 \end{array}$$

21)
$$\begin{array}{r} \square \\ -\ 3 \\ \hline 2 \end{array}$$

22)
$$\begin{array}{r} 4 \\ -\ \square \\ \hline 0 \end{array}$$

23)
$$\begin{array}{r} \square \\ -\ 4 \\ \hline 2 \end{array}$$

24)
$$\begin{array}{r} 1 \\ -\ \square \\ \hline 1 \end{array}$$

25)
$$\begin{array}{r} \square \\ -\ 1 \\ \hline 0 \end{array}$$

26)
$$\begin{array}{r} 7 \\ -\ \square \\ \hline 6 \end{array}$$

27)
$$\begin{array}{r} \square \\ -\ 2 \\ \hline 3 \end{array}$$

28)
$$\begin{array}{r} 7 \\ -\ \square \\ \hline 1 \end{array}$$

29)
$$\begin{array}{r} \square \\ -\ 1 \\ \hline 1 \end{array}$$

30)
$$\begin{array}{r} 7 \\ -\ \square \\ \hline 1 \end{array}$$

31)
$$\begin{array}{r} \square \\ -\ 2 \\ \hline 5 \end{array}$$

32)
$$\begin{array}{r} 7 \\ -\ \square \\ \hline 1 \end{array}$$

33)
$$\begin{array}{r} \square \\ -\ 1 \\ \hline 0 \end{array}$$

34)
$$\begin{array}{r} 5 \\ -\ \square \\ \hline 4 \end{array}$$

35)
$$\begin{array}{r} \square \\ -\ 3 \\ \hline 2 \end{array}$$

36)
$$\begin{array}{r} 7 \\ -\ \square \\ \hline 6 \end{array}$$

37)
$$\begin{array}{r} \square \\ -\ 0 \\ \hline 6 \end{array}$$

38)
$$\begin{array}{r} 7 \\ -\ \square \\ \hline 7 \end{array}$$

39)
$$\begin{array}{r} \square \\ -\ 5 \\ \hline 1 \end{array}$$

40)
$$\begin{array}{r} 6 \\ -\ \square \\ \hline 2 \end{array}$$

41)
$$\begin{array}{r} \square \\ -\ 1 \\ \hline 5 \end{array}$$

42)
$$\begin{array}{r} 0 \\ -\ \square \\ \hline 0 \end{array}$$

43)
$$\begin{array}{r} \square \\ -\ 2 \\ \hline 4 \end{array}$$

44)
$$\begin{array}{r} 6 \\ -\ \square \\ \hline 5 \end{array}$$

45)
$$\begin{array}{r} \square \\ -\ 5 \\ \hline 0 \end{array}$$

46)
$$\begin{array}{r} 5 \\ -\ \square \\ \hline 1 \end{array}$$

47)
$$\begin{array}{r} \square \\ -\ 5 \\ \hline 1 \end{array}$$

48)
$$\begin{array}{r} 5 \\ -\ \square \\ \hline 4 \end{array}$$

49)
$$\begin{array}{r} \square \\ -\ 2 \\ \hline 2 \end{array}$$

50)
$$\begin{array}{r} 7 \\ -\ \square \\ \hline 5 \end{array}$$

51)
$$\begin{array}{r} \square \\ -\ 4 \\ \hline 2 \end{array}$$

52)
$$\begin{array}{r} 5 \\ -\ \square \\ \hline 2 \end{array}$$

53)
$$\begin{array}{r} \square \\ -\ 0 \\ \hline 0 \end{array}$$

54)
$$\begin{array}{r} 3 \\ -\ \square \\ \hline 1 \end{array}$$

55)
$$\begin{array}{r} \square \\ -\ 3 \\ \hline 0 \end{array}$$

56)
$$\begin{array}{r} 5 \\ -\ \square \\ \hline 2 \end{array}$$

57)
$$\begin{array}{r} \square \\ -\ 0 \\ \hline 7 \end{array}$$

58)
$$\begin{array}{r} 4 \\ -\ \square \\ \hline 0 \end{array}$$

59)
$$\begin{array}{r} \square \\ -\ 2 \\ \hline 5 \end{array}$$

60)
$$\begin{array}{r} 7 \\ -\ \square \\ \hline 4 \end{array}$$

Name:

Score: /60

time :

1) 8 − 6

2) 9 − 2

3) 1 − 0

4) 4 − 2

5) 9 − 6

6) 1 − 1

7) 3 − 1

8) 10 − 7

9) 8 − 1

10) 10 − 2

11) 10 − 7

12) 8 − 2

13) 5 − 4

14) 10 − 2

15) 10 − 10

16) 7 − 5

17) 9 − 7

18) 8 − 4

19) 8 − 4

20) 10 − 9

21) 3 − 1

22) 9 − 8

23) 6 − 0

24) 8 − 6

25) 2 − 1

26) 10 − 4

27) 9 − 4

28) 3 − 2

29) 6 − 1

30) 3 − 1

31) 9 − 7

32) 8 − 8

33) 9 − 5

34) 10 − 10

35) 7 − 7

36) 5 − 3

37) 8 − 3

38) 5 − 2

39) 10 − 7

40) 5 − 4

41) 10 − 2

42) 8 − 8

43) 6 − 2

44) 10 − 4

45) 8 − 2

46) 9 − 2

47) 6 − 5

48) 4 − 2

49) 10 − 7

50) 1 − 1

51) 6 − 0

52) 9 − 7

53) 9 − 2

54) 8 − 0

55) 10 − 7

56) 4 − 3

57) 7 − 7

58) 10 − 1

59) 8 − 0

60) 8 − 6

Name:

Score:

/60

Time   :

1) 5
  − 5

2) 10
  − 0

3) 3
  − 0

4) 10
  − 10

5) 6
  − 5

6) 6
  − 0

7) 5
  − 2

8) 5
  − 1

9) 6
  − 1

10) 9
  − 7

11) 7
  − 2

12) 6
  − 6

13) 4
  − 2

14) 9
  − 1

15) 7
  − 7

16) 10
  − 0

17) 9
  − 8

18) 6
  − 3

19) 8
  − 0

20) 4
  − 0

21) 4
  − 0

22) 5
  − 5

23) 3
  − 3

24) 10
  − 4

25) 9
  − 3

26) 9
  − 4

27) 7
  − 3

28) 10
  − 6

29) 7
  − 2

30) 3
  − 3

31) 9
  − 5

32) 8
  − 6

33) 9
  − 3

34) 10
  − 7

35) 1
  − 1

36) 0
  − 0

37) 10
  − 1

38) 7
  − 7

39) 5
  − 3

40) 9
  − 8

41) 10
  − 2

42) 8
  − 8

43) 1
  − 1

44) 7
  − 2

45) 2
  − 0

46) 4
  − 0

47) 4
  − 2

48) 10
  − 7

49) 5
  − 2

50) 8
  − 1

51) 9
  − 3

52) 7
  − 0

53) 7
  − 5

54) 8
  − 3

55) 6
  − 0

56) 2
  − 2

57) 10
  − 8

58) 4
  − 2

59) 9
  − 6

60) 3
  − 3

Name:

Score:

/60

Time   :

1) $\begin{array}{r} 5 \\ - 2 \\ \hline \end{array}$

2) $\begin{array}{r} 9 \\ - 2 \\ \hline \end{array}$

3) $\begin{array}{r} 9 \\ - 8 \\ \hline \end{array}$

4) $\begin{array}{r} 9 \\ - 4 \\ \hline \end{array}$

5) $\begin{array}{r} 10 \\ - 1 \\ \hline \end{array}$

6) $\begin{array}{r} 8 \\ - 0 \\ \hline \end{array}$

7) $\begin{array}{r} 10 \\ - 5 \\ \hline \end{array}$

8) $\begin{array}{r} 9 \\ - 1 \\ \hline \end{array}$

9) $\begin{array}{r} 5 \\ - 0 \\ \hline \end{array}$

10) $\begin{array}{r} 9 \\ - 2 \\ \hline \end{array}$

11) $\begin{array}{r} 3 \\ - 3 \\ \hline \end{array}$

12) $\begin{array}{r} 9 \\ - 2 \\ \hline \end{array}$

13) $\begin{array}{r} 9 \\ - 4 \\ \hline \end{array}$

14) $\begin{array}{r} 9 \\ - 8 \\ \hline \end{array}$

15) $\begin{array}{r} 5 \\ - 4 \\ \hline \end{array}$

16) $\begin{array}{r} 9 \\ - 2 \\ \hline \end{array}$

17) $\begin{array}{r} 10 \\ - 8 \\ \hline \end{array}$

18) $\begin{array}{r} 4 \\ - 2 \\ \hline \end{array}$

19) $\begin{array}{r} 4 \\ - 2 \\ \hline \end{array}$

20) $\begin{array}{r} 4 \\ - 3 \\ \hline \end{array}$

21) $\begin{array}{r} 10 \\ - 5 \\ \hline \end{array}$

22) $\begin{array}{r} 7 \\ - 4 \\ \hline \end{array}$

23) $\begin{array}{r} 9 \\ - 1 \\ \hline \end{array}$

24) $\begin{array}{r} 5 \\ - 4 \\ \hline \end{array}$

25) $\begin{array}{r} 8 \\ - 3 \\ \hline \end{array}$

26) $\begin{array}{r} 6 \\ - 0 \\ \hline \end{array}$

27) $\begin{array}{r} 10 \\ - 10 \\ \hline \end{array}$

28) $\begin{array}{r} 8 \\ - 7 \\ \hline \end{array}$

29) $\begin{array}{r} 6 \\ - 5 \\ \hline \end{array}$

30) $\begin{array}{r} 10 \\ - 6 \\ \hline \end{array}$

31) $\begin{array}{r} 8 \\ - 3 \\ \hline \end{array}$

32) $\begin{array}{r} 3 \\ - 1 \\ \hline \end{array}$

33) $\begin{array}{r} 7 \\ - 3 \\ \hline \end{array}$

34) $\begin{array}{r} 3 \\ - 1 \\ \hline \end{array}$

35) $\begin{array}{r} 6 \\ - 6 \\ \hline \end{array}$

36) $\begin{array}{r} 10 \\ - 5 \\ \hline \end{array}$

37) $\begin{array}{r} 7 \\ - 1 \\ \hline \end{array}$

38) $\begin{array}{r} 10 \\ - 0 \\ \hline \end{array}$

39) $\begin{array}{r} 6 \\ - 2 \\ \hline \end{array}$

40) $\begin{array}{r} 2 \\ - 2 \\ \hline \end{array}$

41) $\begin{array}{r} 9 \\ - 9 \\ \hline \end{array}$

42) $\begin{array}{r} 9 \\ - 4 \\ \hline \end{array}$

43) $\begin{array}{r} 8 \\ - 1 \\ \hline \end{array}$

44) $\begin{array}{r} 7 \\ - 7 \\ \hline \end{array}$

45) $\begin{array}{r} 0 \\ - 0 \\ \hline \end{array}$

46) $\begin{array}{r} 4 \\ - 3 \\ \hline \end{array}$

47) $\begin{array}{r} 6 \\ - 5 \\ \hline \end{array}$

48) $\begin{array}{r} 9 \\ - 0 \\ \hline \end{array}$

49) $\begin{array}{r} 7 \\ - 5 \\ \hline \end{array}$

50) $\begin{array}{r} 5 \\ - 1 \\ \hline \end{array}$

51) $\begin{array}{r} 3 \\ - 0 \\ \hline \end{array}$

52) $\begin{array}{r} 9 \\ - 3 \\ \hline \end{array}$

53) $\begin{array}{r} 6 \\ - 3 \\ \hline \end{array}$

54) $\begin{array}{r} 7 \\ - 1 \\ \hline \end{array}$

55) $\begin{array}{r} 10 \\ - 10 \\ \hline \end{array}$

56) $\begin{array}{r} 5 \\ - 5 \\ \hline \end{array}$

57) $\begin{array}{r} 9 \\ - 0 \\ \hline \end{array}$

58) $\begin{array}{r} 9 \\ - 3 \\ \hline \end{array}$

59) $\begin{array}{r} 8 \\ - 8 \\ \hline \end{array}$

60) $\begin{array}{r} 4 \\ - 1 \\ \hline \end{array}$

Score: /60

Name:

Time :

1) 10 − 9

2) 3 − 3

3) 8 − 1

4) 8 − 3

5) 1 − 0

6) 8 − 0

7) 10 − 8

8) 10 − 8

9) 4 − 4

10) 10 − 3

11) 9 − 4

12) 5 − 5

13) 8 − 8

14) 7 − 5

15) 10 − 9

16) 9 − 3

17) 7 − 5

18) 2 − 2

19) 6 − 5

20) 7 − 7

21) 1 − 1

22) 10 − 0

23) 7 − 6

24) 1 − 0

25) 9 − 2

26) 9 − 2

27) 8 − 6

28) 10 − 2

29) 1 − 1

30) 7 − 7

31) 10 − 1

32) 8 − 6

33) 5 − 2

34) 2 − 2

35) 9 − 1

36) 5 − 4

37) 3 − 3

38) 2 − 1

39) 9 − 1

40) 9 − 0

41) 5 − 5

42) 9 − 8

43) 7 − 7

44) 10 − 2

45) 7 − 6

46) 9 − 7

47) 7 − 3

48) 7 − 5

49) 8 − 3

50) 5 − 3

51) 6 − 5

52) 7 − 4

53) 0 − 0

54) 7 − 0

55) 5 − 2

56) 6 − 5

57) 4 − 2

58) 6 − 6

59) 9 − 9

60) 8 − 0

Name:

Score:

/60

Time   :

1) 5 − 3

2) 7 − 2

3) 6 − 3

4) 3 − 3

5) 9 − 6

6) 9 − 4

7) 8 − 6

8) 0 − 0

9) 9 − 8

10) 1 − 1

11) 7 − 1

12) 5 − 0

13) 7 − 0

14) 4 − 4

15) 9 − 8

16) 3 − 0

17) 10 − 7

18) 10 − 3

19) 9 − 5

20) 10 − 5

21) 8 − 8

22) 1 − 1

23) 9 − 7

24) 9 − 4

25) 9 − 3

26) 10 − 7

27) 6 − 0

28) 10 − 9

29) 10 − 4

30) 5 − 1

31) 10 − 9

32) 9 − 4

33) 2 − 2

34) 6 − 2

35) 4 − 4

36) 10 − 7

37) 10 − 2

38) 6 − 2

39) 8 − 5

40) 9 − 7

41) 5 − 1

42) 5 − 0

43) 8 − 7

44) 5 − 2

45) 4 − 0

46) 7 − 2

47) 6 − 5

48) 2 − 0

49) 1 − 0

50) 8 − 0

51) 8 − 3

52) 8 − 5

53) 3 − 2

54) 8 − 5

55) 3 − 1

56) 8 − 0

57) 2 − 2

58) 10 − 4

59) 8 − 0

60) 9 − 8

Name:

Score:

/60

Time   :

1)
$$9 - 3$$

2)
$$6 - 3$$

3)
$$10 - 4$$

4)
$$7 - 6$$

5)
$$5 - 0$$

6)
$$10 - 6$$

7)
$$4 - 4$$

8)
$$0 - 0$$

9)
$$3 - 1$$

10)
$$4 - 0$$

11)
$$10 - 10$$

12)
$$9 - 5$$

13)
$$4 - 4$$

14)
$$8 - 5$$

15)
$$7 - 7$$

16)
$$5 - 2$$

17)
$$5 - 5$$

18)
$$8 - 5$$

19)
$$2 - 2$$

20)
$$3 - 0$$

21)
$$8 - 2$$

22)
$$9 - 9$$

23)
$$8 - 7$$

24)
$$7 - 1$$

25)
$$8 - 4$$

26)
$$7 - 0$$

27)
$$9 - 5$$

28)
$$7 - 0$$

29)
$$10 - 4$$

30)
$$8 - 1$$

31)
$$8 - 8$$

32)
$$9 - 7$$

33)
$$3 - 0$$

34)
$$6 - 0$$

35)
$$1 - 1$$

36)
$$10 - 1$$

37)
$$7 - 5$$

38)
$$9 - 7$$

39)
$$5 - 3$$

40)
$$10 - 9$$

41)
$$7 - 0$$

42)
$$10 - 0$$

43)
$$9 - 8$$

44)
$$7 - 1$$

45)
$$3 - 1$$

46)
$$10 - 7$$

47)
$$8 - 8$$

48)
$$10 - 4$$

49)
$$5 - 2$$

50)
$$8 - 7$$

51)
$$9 - 9$$

52)
$$7 - 6$$

53)
$$1 - 0$$

54)
$$5 - 2$$

55)
$$10 - 8$$

56)
$$9 - 0$$

57)
$$1 - 0$$

58)
$$5 - 0$$

59)
$$7 - 0$$

60)
$$10 - 10$$

Name:

Score:

/60

time   :

1)
$$10 - 1$$

2)
$$6 - 3$$

3)
$$9 - 0$$

4)
$$3 - 0$$

5)
$$2 - 2$$

6)
$$8 - 6$$

7)
$$10 - 7$$

8)
$$4 - 2$$

9)
$$5 - 2$$

10)
$$1 - 0$$

11)
$$5 - 4$$

12)
$$2 - 1$$

13)
$$7 - 5$$

14)
$$6 - 3$$

15)
$$10 - 0$$

16)
$$9 - 4$$

17)
$$5 - 0$$

18)
$$10 - 1$$

19)
$$9 - 1$$

20)
$$5 - 1$$

21)
$$2 - 0$$

22)
$$8 - 0$$

23)
$$10 - 1$$

24)
$$8 - 2$$

25)
$$9 - 8$$

26)
$$10 - 5$$

27)
$$7 - 2$$

28)
$$7 - 4$$

29)
$$7 - 4$$

30)
$$10 - 9$$

31)
$$9 - 7$$

32)
$$10 - 3$$

33)
$$10 - 3$$

34)
$$5 - 3$$

35)
$$9 - 0$$

36)
$$3 - 1$$

37)
$$10 - 4$$

38)
$$7 - 4$$

39)
$$4 - 1$$

40)
$$10 - 5$$

41)
$$1 - 1$$

42)
$$4 - 4$$

43)
$$5 - 5$$

44)
$$8 - 2$$

45)
$$8 - 3$$

46)
$$5 - 5$$

47)
$$10 - 5$$

48)
$$10 - 8$$

49)
$$10 - 4$$

50)
$$8 - 1$$

51)
$$6 - 5$$

52)
$$10 - 8$$

53)
$$9 - 5$$

54)
$$9 - 4$$

55)
$$9 - 1$$

56)
$$9 - 2$$

57)
$$10 - 9$$

58)
$$9 - 1$$

59)
$$8 - 5$$

60)
$$9 - 2$$

Name:

Score:

/60

time   :

1) 4
  - 4

2) 8
  - 5

3) 4
  - 2

4) 5
  - 3

5) 9
  - 9

6) 6
  - 2

7) 5
  - 4

8) 6
  - 5

9) 9
  - 7

10) 9
   - 9

11) 10
   - 0

12) 8
   - 6

13) 6
   - 4

14) 8
   - 2

15) 8
   - 4

16) 4
   - 3

17) 7
   - 6

18) 9
   - 6

19) 10
   - 3

20) 7
   - 2

21) 1
   - 1

22) 3
   - 2

23) 7
   - 2

24) 7
   - 1

25) 6
   - 3

26) 3
   - 1

27) 5
   - 1

28) 0
   - 0

29) 3
   - 3

30) 6
   - 6

31) 8
   - 0

32) 8
   - 1

33) 3
   - 0

34) 10
   - 1

35) 10
   - 0

36) 1
   - 1

37) 10
   - 5

38) 7
   - 6

39) 9
   - 3

40) 7
   - 7

41) 4
   - 2

42) 9
   - 9

43) 9
   - 5

44) 10
   - 5

45) 4
   - 0

46) 9
   - 5

47) 7
   - 7

48) 7
   - 5

49) 10
   - 7

50) 8
   - 7

51) 2
   - 1

52) 4
   - 0

53) 4
   - 1

54) 3
   - 0

55) 3
   - 1

56) 9
   - 9

57) 3
   - 0

58) 5
   - 2

59) 3
   - 3

60) 4
   - 3

Name:

Score:

/60

time   :

1) 6
  − 3

2) 5
  − 5

3) 10
  − 7

4) 8
  − 1

5) 10
  − 8

6) 9
  − 8

7) 5
  − 4

8) 10
  − 9

9) 4
  − 2

10) 10
  − 3

11) 2
  − 1

12) 6
  − 5

13) 9
  − 8

14) 10
  − 6

15) 10
  − 8

16) 10
  − 9

17) 9
  − 3

18) 5
  − 1

19) 10
  − 4

20) 8
  − 6

21) 6
  − 6

22) 9
  − 2

23) 1
  − 0

24) 10
  − 1

25) 4
  − 0

26) 9
  − 5

27) 9
  − 7

28) 4
  − 2

29) 5
  − 1

30) 9
  − 1

31) 7
  − 1

32) 2
  − 1

33) 1
  − 1

34) 7
  − 1

35) 2
  − 2

36) 7
  − 5

37) 3
  − 1

38) 6
  − 1

39) 5
  − 2

40) 10
  − 0

41) 9
  − 9

42) 2
  − 1

43) 10
  − 0

44) 0
  − 0

45) 2
  − 0

46) 7
  − 0

47) 10
  − 3

48) 4
  − 4

49) 9
  − 2

50) 5
  − 3

51) 7
  − 2

52) 6
  − 5

53) 10
  − 3

54) 6
  − 3

55) 8
  − 3

56) 5
  − 0

57) 4
  − 3

58) 7
  − 3

59) 10
  − 4

60) 6
  − 3

Name:

Score:

/60

Time   :

1)   5
  - 1

2)   4
  - 0

3)   2
  - 0

4)   10
  - 6

5)   9
  - 1

6)   9
  - 9

7)   8
  - 4

8)   10
  - 5

9)   6
  - 2

10)   9
  - 4

11)   3
  - 1

12)   6
  - 1

13)   4
  - 0

14)   3
  - 0

15)   8
  - 1

16)   9
  - 7

17)   6
  - 5

18)   6
  - 3

19)   9
  - 5

20)   8
  - 6

21)   10
  - 10

22)   9
  - 5

23)   7
  - 4

24)   7
  - 1

25)   9
  - 5

26)   10
  - 9

27)   2
  - 2

28)   7
  - 6

29)   9
  - 0

30)   5
  - 3

31)   10
  - 3

32)   7
  - 2

33)   10
  - 1

34)   8
  - 7

35)   0
  - 0

36)   10
  - 6

37)   4
  - 3

38)   10
  - 1

39)   8
  - 1

40)   5
  - 3

41)   10
  - 4

42)   4
  - 1

43)   1
  - 1

44)   5
  - 2

45)   10
  - 4

46)   3
  - 3

47)   8
  - 6

48)   10
  - 4

49)   7
  - 1

50)   6
  - 3

51)   6
  - 1

52)   7
  - 7

53)   10
  - 10

54)   3
  - 2

55)   9
  - 9

56)   5
  - 4

57)   4
  - 2

58)   10
  - 7

59)   9
  - 9

60)   10
  - 3

Score:

/60

time   :

Name:

1)
$$\begin{array}{r} \square \\ - \quad 8 \\ \hline 0 \end{array}$$

2)
$$\begin{array}{r} 10 \\ - \quad \square \\ \hline 10 \end{array}$$

3)
$$\begin{array}{r} \square \\ - \quad 3 \\ \hline 2 \end{array}$$

4)
$$\begin{array}{r} 9 \\ - \quad \square \\ \hline 5 \end{array}$$

5)
$$\begin{array}{r} \square \\ - \quad 7 \\ \hline 2 \end{array}$$

6)
$$\begin{array}{r} 8 \\ - \quad \square \\ \hline 2 \end{array}$$

7)
$$\begin{array}{r} \square \\ - \quad 3 \\ \hline 7 \end{array}$$

8)
$$\begin{array}{r} 7 \\ - \quad \square \\ \hline 4 \end{array}$$

9)
$$\begin{array}{r} \square \\ - \quad 2 \\ \hline 4 \end{array}$$

10)
$$\begin{array}{r} 6 \\ - \quad \square \\ \hline 5 \end{array}$$

11)
$$\begin{array}{r} \square \\ - \quad 5 \\ \hline 2 \end{array}$$

12)
$$\begin{array}{r} 0 \\ - \quad \square \\ \hline 0 \end{array}$$

13)
$$\begin{array}{r} \square \\ - \quad 1 \\ \hline 6 \end{array}$$

14)
$$\begin{array}{r} 10 \\ - \quad \square \\ \hline 2 \end{array}$$

15)
$$\begin{array}{r} \square \\ - \quad 4 \\ \hline 0 \end{array}$$

16)
$$\begin{array}{r} 10 \\ - \quad \square \\ \hline 0 \end{array}$$

17)
$$\begin{array}{r} \square \\ - \quad 0 \\ \hline 2 \end{array}$$

18)
$$\begin{array}{r} 10 \\ - \quad \square \\ \hline 7 \end{array}$$

19)
$$\begin{array}{r} \square \\ - \quad 5 \\ \hline 5 \end{array}$$

20)
$$\begin{array}{r} 10 \\ - \quad \square \\ \hline 7 \end{array}$$

21)
$$\begin{array}{r} \square \\ - \quad 4 \\ \hline 2 \end{array}$$

22)
$$\begin{array}{r} 10 \\ - \quad \square \\ \hline 7 \end{array}$$

23)
$$\begin{array}{r} \square \\ - \quad 3 \\ \hline 5 \end{array}$$

24)
$$\begin{array}{r} 4 \\ - \quad \square \\ \hline 4 \end{array}$$

25)
$$\begin{array}{r} \square \\ - \quad 0 \\ \hline 5 \end{array}$$

26)
$$\begin{array}{r} 3 \\ - \quad \square \\ \hline 2 \end{array}$$

27)
$$\begin{array}{r} \square \\ - \quad 7 \\ \hline 3 \end{array}$$

28)
$$\begin{array}{r} 8 \\ - \quad \square \\ \hline 6 \end{array}$$

29)
$$\begin{array}{r} \square \\ - \quad 2 \\ \hline 4 \end{array}$$

30)
$$\begin{array}{r} 9 \\ - \quad \square \\ \hline 1 \end{array}$$

31)
$$\begin{array}{r} \square \\ - \quad 5 \\ \hline 5 \end{array}$$

32)
$$\begin{array}{r} 4 \\ - \quad \square \\ \hline 1 \end{array}$$

33)
$$\begin{array}{r} \square \\ - \quad 6 \\ \hline 0 \end{array}$$

34)
$$\begin{array}{r} 8 \\ - \quad \square \\ \hline 3 \end{array}$$

35)
$$\begin{array}{r} \square \\ - \quad 4 \\ \hline 5 \end{array}$$

36)
$$\begin{array}{r} 6 \\ - \quad \square \\ \hline 2 \end{array}$$

37)
$$\begin{array}{r} \square \\ - \quad 0 \\ \hline 7 \end{array}$$

38)
$$\begin{array}{r} 2 \\ - \quad \square \\ \hline 0 \end{array}$$

39)
$$\begin{array}{r} \square \\ - \quad 0 \\ \hline 3 \end{array}$$

40)
$$\begin{array}{r} 5 \\ - \quad \square \\ \hline 1 \end{array}$$

41)
$$\begin{array}{r} \square \\ - \quad 4 \\ \hline 1 \end{array}$$

42)
$$\begin{array}{r} 9 \\ - \quad \square \\ \hline 8 \end{array}$$

43)
$$\begin{array}{r} \square \\ - \quad 1 \\ \hline 4 \end{array}$$

44)
$$\begin{array}{r} 5 \\ - \quad \square \\ \hline 4 \end{array}$$

45)
$$\begin{array}{r} \square \\ - \quad 1 \\ \hline 7 \end{array}$$

46)
$$\begin{array}{r} 8 \\ - \quad \square \\ \hline 0 \end{array}$$

47)
$$\begin{array}{r} \square \\ - \quad 0 \\ \hline 10 \end{array}$$

48)
$$\begin{array}{r} 8 \\ - \quad \square \\ \hline 5 \end{array}$$

49)
$$\begin{array}{r} \square \\ - \quad 6 \\ \hline 3 \end{array}$$

50)
$$\begin{array}{r} 2 \\ - \quad \square \\ \hline 1 \end{array}$$

51)
$$\begin{array}{r} \square \\ - \quad 7 \\ \hline 0 \end{array}$$

52)
$$\begin{array}{r} 8 \\ - \quad \square \\ \hline 8 \end{array}$$

53)
$$\begin{array}{r} \square \\ - \quad 9 \\ \hline 1 \end{array}$$

54)
$$\begin{array}{r} 3 \\ - \quad \square \\ \hline 1 \end{array}$$

55)
$$\begin{array}{r} \square \\ - \quad 1 \\ \hline 4 \end{array}$$

56)
$$\begin{array}{r} 3 \\ - \quad \square \\ \hline 3 \end{array}$$

57)
$$\begin{array}{r} \square \\ - \quad 2 \\ \hline 6 \end{array}$$

58)
$$\begin{array}{r} 0 \\ - \quad \square \\ \hline 0 \end{array}$$

59)
$$\begin{array}{r} \square \\ - \quad 4 \\ \hline 4 \end{array}$$

60)
$$\begin{array}{r} 4 \\ - \quad \square \\ \hline 1 \end{array}$$

Score:

/60

Name:

time   :

1)
```
   □
 -  9
 ────
   1
```

2)
```
   7
 - □
 ────
   5
```

3)
```
   □
 -  0
 ────
   1
```

4)
```
   9
 - □
 ────
   4
```

5)
```
   □
 -  3
 ────
   5
```

6)
```
   7
 - □
 ────
   6
```

7)
```
   □
 -  2
 ────
   2
```

8)
```
   8
 - □
 ────
   6
```

9)
```
   □
 -  4
 ────
   5
```

10)
```
   10
 -  □
 ────
   2
```

11)
```
   □
 -  7
 ────
   1
```

12)
```
   8
 - □
 ────
   7
```

13)
```
   □
 -  4
 ────
   1
```

14)
```
   9
 - □
 ────
   6
```

15)
```
   □
 -  3
 ────
   5
```

16)
```
   5
 - □
 ────
   3
```

17)
```
   □
 -  5
 ────
   3
```

18)
```
   1
 - □
 ────
   1
```

19)
```
   □
 -  4
 ────
   1
```

20)
```
   8
 - □
 ────
   0
```

21)
```
   □
 -  4
 ────
   5
```

22)
```
   10
 -  □
 ────
   4
```

23)
```
   □
 -  6
 ────
   4
```

24)
```
   9
 - □
 ────
   7
```

25)
```
   □
 -  0
 ────
   6
```

26)
```
   10
 -  □
 ────
   10
```

27)
```
   □
 -  2
 ────
   4
```

28)
```
   9
 - □
 ────
   9
```

29)
```
   □
 -  3
 ────
   4
```

30)
```
   5
 - □
 ────
   4
```

31)
```
   □
 -  1
 ────
   1
```

32)
```
   3
 - □
 ────
   1
```

33)
```
   □
 -  0
 ────
   10
```

34)
```
   6
 - □
 ────
   2
```

35)
```
   □
 -  5
 ────
   0
```

36)
```
   9
 - □
 ────
   5
```

37)
```
   □
 -  9
 ────
   0
```

38)
```
   6
 - □
 ────
   6
```

39)
```
   □
 -  3
 ────
   6
```

40)
```
   4
 - □
 ────
   4
```

41)
```
   □
 -  0
 ────
   4
```

42)
```
   8
 - □
 ────
   6
```

43)
```
   □
 -  0
 ────
   4
```

44)
```
   4
 - □
 ────
   2
```

45)
```
   □
 -  2
 ────
   4
```

46)
```
   2
 - □
 ────
   0
```

47)
```
   □
 -  1
 ────
   7
```

48)
```
   3
 - □
 ────
   1
```

49)
```
   □
 -  2
 ────
   3
```

50)
```
   6
 - □
 ────
   2
```

51)
```
   □
 -  1
 ────
   9
```

52)
```
   10
 -  □
 ────
   4
```

53)
```
   □
 -  2
 ────
   3
```

54)
```
   8
 - □
 ────
   6
```

55)
```
   □
 -  3
 ────
   1
```

56)
```
   2
 - □
 ────
   0
```

57)
```
   □
 -  5
 ────
   4
```

58)
```
   8
 - □
 ────
   0
```

59)
```
   □
 -  0
 ────
   2
```

60)
```
   4
 - □
 ────
   0
```

Score:

/60

Name:

time   :

1) □
  − 1
  ───
     8

2)   6
  − □
  ───
     1

3) □
  − 2
  ───
     4

4)   10
  − □
  ───
     1

5) □
  − 4
  ───
     6

6)   3
  − □
  ───
     3

7) □
  − 5
  ───
     3

8)   8
  − □
  ───
     4

9) □
  − 2
  ───
     7

10)   10
  − □
  ───
     7

11) □
  − 5
  ───
     2

12)   6
  − □
  ───
     1

13) □
  − 4
  ───
     4

14)   3
  − □
  ───
     3

15) □
  − 3
  ───
     2

16)   5
  − □
  ───
     2

17) □
  − 2
  ───
     0

18)   5
  − □
  ───
     3

19) □
  − 0
  ───
     1

20)   8
  − □
  ───
     3

21) □
  − 2
  ───
     8

22)   6
  − □
  ───
     2

23) □
  − 6
  ───
     0

24)   9
  − □
  ───
     5

25) □
  − 8
  ───
     0

26)   5
  − □
  ───
     2

27) □
  − 9
  ───
     0

28)   10
  − □
  ───
     7

29) □
  − 8
  ───
     2

30)   5
  − □
  ───
     3

31) □
  − 1
  ───
     3

32)   8
  − □
  ───
     8

33) □
  − 3
  ───
     4

34)   8
  − □
  ───
     7

35) □
  − 2
  ───
     2

36)   9
  − □
  ───
     4

37) □
  − 9
  ───
     0

38)   10
  − □
  ───
     4

39) □
  − 7
  ───
     1

40)   4
  − □
  ───
     4

41) □
  − 2
  ───
     3

42)   8
  − □
  ───
     1

43) □
  − 2
  ───
     3

44)   8
  − □
  ───
     4

45) □
  − 1
  ───
     3

46)   10
  − □
  ───
    10

47) □
  − 1
  ───
     7

48)   9
  − □
  ───
     2

49) □
  − 4
  ───
     3

50)   7
  − □
  ───
     0

51) □
  − 1
  ───
     8

52)   5
  − □
  ───
     4

53) □
  − 5
  ───
     5

54)   9
  − □
  ───
     3

55) □
  − 8
  ───
     1

56)   1
  − □
  ───
     0

57) □
  − 5
  ───
     4

58)   8
  − □
  ───
     2

59) □
  − 3
  ───
     4

60)   2
  − □
  ───
     0

Score: /60

Name:

time   :

1)
```
    □
  -  5
  ─────
     0
```

2)
```
    10
  -  □
  ─────
     5
```

3)
```
    □
  -  4
  ─────
     1
```

4)
```
    8
  -  □
  ─────
     3
```

5)
```
    □
  -  7
  ─────
     3
```

6)
```
    6
  -  □
  ─────
     2
```

7)
```
    □
  -  6
  ─────
     0
```

8)
```
    3
  -  □
  ─────
     1
```

9)
```
    □
  -  9
  ─────
     0
```

10)
```
    9
  -  □
  ─────
     7
```

11)
```
    □
  -  9
  ─────
     0
```

12)
```
    7
  -  □
  ─────
     0
```

13)
```
    □
  -  1
  ─────
     3
```

14)
```
    10
  -  □
  ─────
     8
```

15)
```
    □
  -  2
  ─────
     8
```

16)
```
    10
  -  □
  ─────
     7
```

17)
```
    □
  -  5
  ─────
     4
```

18)
```
    4
  -  □
  ─────
     2
```

19)
```
    □
  -  0
  ─────
     2
```

20)
```
    2
  -  □
  ─────
     2
```

21)
```
    □
  -  2
  ─────
     7
```

22)
```
    10
  -  □
  ─────
     2
```

23)
```
    □
  -  3
  ─────
     2
```

24)
```
    4
  -  □
  ─────
     3
```

25)
```
    □
  -  0
  ─────
     7
```

26)
```
    10
  -  □
  ─────
     1
```

27)
```
    □
  -  0
  ─────
     7
```

28)
```
    7
  -  □
  ─────
     7
```

29)
```
    □
  -  7
  ─────
     0
```

30)
```
    7
  -  □
  ─────
     0
```

31)
```
    □
  -  1
  ─────
     4
```

32)
```
    9
  -  □
  ─────
     7
```

33)
```
    □
  -  4
  ─────
     3
```

34)
```
    2
  -  □
  ─────
     0
```

35)
```
    □
  -  3
  ─────
     2
```

36)
```
    10
  -  □
  ─────
    10
```

37)
```
    □
  -  3
  ─────
     6
```

38)
```
    10
  -  □
  ─────
    10
```

39)
```
    □
  -  6
  ─────
     4
```

40)
```
    5
  -  □
  ─────
     3
```

41)
```
    □
  -  9
  ─────
     0
```

42)
```
    8
  -  □
  ─────
     7
```

43)
```
    □
  -  0
  ─────
     3
```

44)
```
    8
  -  □
  ─────
     0
```

45)
```
    □
  -  6
  ─────
     4
```

46)
```
    8
  -  □
  ─────
     1
```

47)
```
    □
  -  0
  ─────
     1
```

48)
```
    9
  -  □
  ─────
     1
```

49)
```
    □
  -  4
  ─────
     6
```

50)
```
    4
  -  □
  ─────
     2
```

51)
```
    □
  -  6
  ─────
     3
```

52)
```
    6
  -  □
  ─────
     3
```

53)
```
    □
  -  0
  ─────
     8
```

54)
```
    10
  -  □
  ─────
     8
```

55)
```
    □
  -  0
  ─────
     0
```

56)
```
    2
  -  □
  ─────
     1
```

57)
```
    □
  -  1
  ─────
     6
```

58)
```
    10
  -  □
  ─────
     6
```

59)
```
    □
  -  0
  ─────
     3
```

60)
```
    8
  -  □
  ─────
     8
```

Score: /60

Name:

time :

1)
```
  □
-  8
  2
```

2)
```
  9
- □
  3
```

3)
```
  □
-  4
  5
```

4)
```
  9
- □
  4
```

5)
```
  □
-  0
  5
```

6)
```
  7
- □
  1
```

7)
```
  □
-  1
  0
```

8)
```
  3
- □
  3
```

9)
```
  □
-  2
  1
```

10)
```
  5
- □
  5
```

11)
```
  □
-  2
  1
```

12)
```
  6
- □
  4
```

13)
```
  □
-  1
  5
```

14)
```
  10
- □
  7
```

15)
```
  □
-  1
  5
```

16)
```
  4
- □
  4
```

17)
```
  □
-  4
  6
```

18)
```
  9
- □
  7
```

19)
```
  □
-  0
  3
```

20)
```
  8
- □
  5
```

21)
```
  □
-  2
  3
```

22)
```
  9
- □
  8
```

23)
```
  □
-  2
  3
```

24)
```
  4
- □
  3
```

25)
```
  □
-  5
  1
```

26)
```
  9
- □
  1
```

27)
```
  □
- 10
  0
```

28)
```
  7
- □
  0
```

29)
```
  □
-  3
  6
```

30)
```
  3
- □
  1
```

31)
```
  □
-  4
  4
```

32)
```
  6
- □
  0
```

33)
```
  □
-  2
  5
```

34)
```
  9
- □
  2
```

35)
```
  □
-  4
  6
```

36)
```
  10
- □
  9
```

37)
```
  □
-  2
  4
```

38)
```
  2
- □
  1
```

39)
```
  □
-  6
  3
```

40)
```
  9
- □
  0
```

41)
```
  □
-  1
  2
```

42)
```
  7
- □
  3
```

43)
```
  □
-  2
  0
```

44)
```
  1
- □
  1
```

45)
```
  □
-  2
  6
```

46)
```
  5
- □
  3
```

47)
```
  □
-  3
  2
```

48)
```
  5
- □
  2
```

49)
```
  □
-  2
  6
```

50)
```
  10
- □
  10
```

51)
```
  □
-  1
  8
```

52)
```
  4
- □
  4
```

53)
```
  □
-  5
  4
```

54)
```
  7
- □
  2
```

55)
```
  □
-  2
  1
```

56)
```
  7
- □
  0
```

57)
```
  □
-  8
  0
```

58)
```
  5
- □
  1
```

59)
```
  □
-  2
  7
```

60)
```
  9
- □
  8
```

Score:

/60

Name:

time   :

1)
```
  □
- 4
───
  0
```

2)
```
  9
- □
───
  4
```

3)
```
  □
- 7
───
  2
```

4)
```
  8
- □
───
  4
```

5)
```
  □
- 0
───
  0
```

6)
```
  3
- □
───
  0
```

7)
```
  □
- 2
───
  5
```

8)
```
  5
- □
───
  3
```

9)
```
  □
- 0
───
  0
```

10)
```
  7
- □
───
  5
```

11)
```
  □
- 1
───
  3
```

12)
```
  9
- □
───
  1
```

13)
```
  □
- 0
───
  4
```

14)
```
  10
- □
───
  9
```

15)
```
  □
- 0
───
  3
```

16)
```
  1
- □
───
  0
```

17)
```
  □
- 2
───
  3
```

18)
```
  7
- □
───
  0
```

19)
```
  □
- 8
───
  0
```

20)
```
  0
- □
───
  0
```

21)
```
  □
- 3
───
  1
```

22)
```
  6
- □
───
  0
```

23)
```
  □
- 2
───
  4
```

24)
```
  9
- □
───
  9
```

25)
```
  □
- 0
───
  3
```

26)
```
  10
- □
───
  3
```

27)
```
  □
- 1
───
  7
```

28)
```
  8
- □
───
  6
```

29)
```
  □
- 1
───
  5
```

30)
```
  1
- □
───
  1
```

31)
```
  □
- 5
───
  2
```

32)
```
  7
- □
───
  4
```

33)
```
  □
- 8
───
  0
```

34)
```
  5
- □
───
  2
```

35)
```
  □
- 1
───
  5
```

36)
```
  8
- □
───
  3
```

37)
```
  □
- 5
───
  5
```

38)
```
  4
- □
───
  4
```

39)
```
  □
- 1
───
  3
```

40)
```
  10
- □
───
  5
```

41)
```
  □
- 0
───
  6
```

42)
```
  10
- □
───
  2
```

43)
```
  □
- 4
───
  0
```

44)
```
  7
- □
───
  2
```

45)
```
  □
- 4
───
  2
```

46)
```
  8
- □
───
  6
```

47)
```
  □
- 3
───
  5
```

48)
```
  10
- □
───
  5
```

49)
```
  □
- 5
───
  4
```

50)
```
  7
- □
───
  6
```

51)
```
  □
- 1
───
  6
```

52)
```
  8
- □
───
  2
```

53)
```
  □
- 6
───
  1
```

54)
```
  10
- □
───
  3
```

55)
```
  □
- 2
───
  6
```

56)
```
  6
- □
───
  2
```

57)
```
  □
- 6
───
  3
```

58)
```
  6
- □
───
  2
```

59)
```
  □
- 3
───
  1
```

60)
```
  9
- □
───
  4
```

Page 136

Score:

/60

Name:

time   :

1)
```
    □
-   2
───
    2
```

2)
```
    7
-   □
───
    1
```

3)
```
    □
-   0
───
    7
```

4)
```
    8
-   □
───
    5
```

5)
```
    □
-   0
───
    1
```

6)
```
    8
-   □
───
    5
```

7)
```
    □
-   2
───
    5
```

8)
```
    6
-   □
───
    0
```

9)
```
    □
-   8
───
    0
```

10)
```
    4
-   □
───
    4
```

11)
```
    □
-   8
───
    0
```

12)
```
    8
-   □
───
    0
```

13)
```
    □
-   2
───
    5
```

14)
```
    8
-   □
───
    0
```

15)
```
    □
-   2
───
    5
```

16)
```
    3
-   □
───
    1
```

17)
```
    □
-   0
───
    0
```

18)
```
    5
-   □
───
    2
```

19)
```
    □
-   0
───
    9
```

20)
```
    7
-   □
───
    3
```

21)
```
    □
-   5
───
    0
```

22)
```
    8
-   □
───
    6
```

23)
```
    □
-   1
───
    7
```

24)
```
   10
-   □
───
    9
```

25)
```
    □
-   5
───
    4
```

26)
```
    5
-   □
───
    5
```

27)
```
    □
-  10
───
    0
```

28)
```
    5
-   □
───
    1
```

29)
```
    □
-   0
───
    2
```

30)
```
    5
-   □
───
    4
```

31)
```
    □
-  10
───
    0
```

32)
```
    9
-   □
───
    8
```

33)
```
    □
-   1
───
    9
```

34)
```
   10
-   □
───
    7
```

35)
```
    □
-   0
───
    0
```

36)
```
    4
-   □
───
    4
```

37)
```
    □
-   3
───
    2
```

38)
```
    7
-   □
───
    5
```

39)
```
    □
-   9
───
    1
```

40)
```
    6
-   □
───
    4
```

41)
```
    □
-   3
───
    0
```

42)
```
    9
-   □
───
    8
```

43)
```
    □
-   2
───
    2
```

44)
```
    4
-   □
───
    1
```

45)
```
    □
-   6
───
    0
```

46)
```
    9
-   □
───
    9
```

47)
```
    □
-   2
───
    1
```

48)
```
   10
-   □
───
    6
```

49)
```
    □
-   7
───
    1
```

50)
```
   10
-   □
───
    8
```

51)
```
    □
-   1
───
    5
```

52)
```
    0
-   □
───
    0
```

53)
```
    □
-   5
───
    1
```

54)
```
    8
-   □
───
    5
```

55)
```
    □
-   8
───
    1
```

56)
```
    5
-   □
───
    0
```

57)
```
    □
-   4
───
    6
```

58)
```
    3
-   □
───
    1
```

59)
```
    □
-   0
───
    7
```

60)
```
    8
-   □
───
    0
```

Score: /60

Name:

Time :

1)
$$\begin{array}{r} \square \\ -\ 1 \\ \hline 7 \end{array}$$

2)
$$\begin{array}{r} 10 \\ -\ \square \\ \hline 0 \end{array}$$

3)
$$\begin{array}{r} \square \\ -\ 1 \\ \hline 5 \end{array}$$

4)
$$\begin{array}{r} 8 \\ -\ \square \\ \hline 8 \end{array}$$

5)
$$\begin{array}{r} \square \\ -\ 1 \\ \hline 3 \end{array}$$

6)
$$\begin{array}{r} 7 \\ -\ \square \\ \hline 7 \end{array}$$

7)
$$\begin{array}{r} \square \\ -\ 4 \\ \hline 2 \end{array}$$

8)
$$\begin{array}{r} 9 \\ -\ \square \\ \hline 7 \end{array}$$

9)
$$\begin{array}{r} \square \\ -\ 8 \\ \hline 1 \end{array}$$

10)
$$\begin{array}{r} 6 \\ -\ \square \\ \hline 3 \end{array}$$

11)
$$\begin{array}{r} \square \\ -\ 1 \\ \hline 7 \end{array}$$

12)
$$\begin{array}{r} 7 \\ -\ \square \\ \hline 6 \end{array}$$

13)
$$\begin{array}{r} \square \\ -\ 1 \\ \hline 3 \end{array}$$

14)
$$\begin{array}{r} 9 \\ -\ \square \\ \hline 5 \end{array}$$

15)
$$\begin{array}{r} \square \\ -\ 6 \\ \hline 1 \end{array}$$

16)
$$\begin{array}{r} 5 \\ -\ \square \\ \hline 3 \end{array}$$

17)
$$\begin{array}{r} \square \\ -\ 0 \\ \hline 0 \end{array}$$

18)
$$\begin{array}{r} 7 \\ -\ \square \\ \hline 3 \end{array}$$

19)
$$\begin{array}{r} \square \\ -\ 8 \\ \hline 1 \end{array}$$

20)
$$\begin{array}{r} 2 \\ -\ \square \\ \hline 0 \end{array}$$

21)
$$\begin{array}{r} \square \\ -\ 3 \\ \hline 1 \end{array}$$

22)
$$\begin{array}{r} 10 \\ -\ \square \\ \hline 7 \end{array}$$

23)
$$\begin{array}{r} \square \\ -\ 6 \\ \hline 2 \end{array}$$

24)
$$\begin{array}{r} 6 \\ -\ \square \\ \hline 0 \end{array}$$

25)
$$\begin{array}{r} \square \\ -\ 1 \\ \hline 1 \end{array}$$

26)
$$\begin{array}{r} 7 \\ -\ \square \\ \hline 0 \end{array}$$

27)
$$\begin{array}{r} \square \\ -\ 0 \\ \hline 1 \end{array}$$

28)
$$\begin{array}{r} 7 \\ -\ \square \\ \hline 5 \end{array}$$

29)
$$\begin{array}{r} \square \\ -\ 8 \\ \hline 1 \end{array}$$

30)
$$\begin{array}{r} 4 \\ -\ \square \\ \hline 2 \end{array}$$

31)
$$\begin{array}{r} \square \\ -\ 4 \\ \hline 5 \end{array}$$

32)
$$\begin{array}{r} 9 \\ -\ \square \\ \hline 8 \end{array}$$

33)
$$\begin{array}{r} \square \\ -\ 4 \\ \hline 0 \end{array}$$

34)
$$\begin{array}{r} 8 \\ -\ \square \\ \hline 4 \end{array}$$

35)
$$\begin{array}{r} \square \\ -\ 9 \\ \hline 0 \end{array}$$

36)
$$\begin{array}{r} 1 \\ -\ \square \\ \hline 0 \end{array}$$

37)
$$\begin{array}{r} \square \\ -\ 3 \\ \hline 1 \end{array}$$

38)
$$\begin{array}{r} 4 \\ -\ \square \\ \hline 3 \end{array}$$

39)
$$\begin{array}{r} \square \\ -\ 6 \\ \hline 0 \end{array}$$

40)
$$\begin{array}{r} 10 \\ -\ \square \\ \hline 10 \end{array}$$

41)
$$\begin{array}{r} \square \\ -\ 5 \\ \hline 5 \end{array}$$

42)
$$\begin{array}{r} 3 \\ -\ \square \\ \hline 0 \end{array}$$

43)
$$\begin{array}{r} \square \\ -\ 2 \\ \hline 3 \end{array}$$

44)
$$\begin{array}{r} 2 \\ -\ \square \\ \hline 0 \end{array}$$

45)
$$\begin{array}{r} \square \\ -\ 0 \\ \hline 5 \end{array}$$

46)
$$\begin{array}{r} 5 \\ -\ \square \\ \hline 4 \end{array}$$

47)
$$\begin{array}{r} \square \\ -\ 5 \\ \hline 5 \end{array}$$

48)
$$\begin{array}{r} 9 \\ -\ \square \\ \hline 5 \end{array}$$

49)
$$\begin{array}{r} \square \\ -\ 4 \\ \hline 1 \end{array}$$

50)
$$\begin{array}{r} 2 \\ -\ \square \\ \hline 2 \end{array}$$

51)
$$\begin{array}{r} \square \\ -\ 0 \\ \hline 8 \end{array}$$

52)
$$\begin{array}{r} 5 \\ -\ \square \\ \hline 2 \end{array}$$

53)
$$\begin{array}{r} \square \\ -\ 6 \\ \hline 0 \end{array}$$

54)
$$\begin{array}{r} 0 \\ -\ \square \\ \hline 0 \end{array}$$

55)
$$\begin{array}{r} \square \\ -\ 7 \\ \hline 1 \end{array}$$

56)
$$\begin{array}{r} 6 \\ -\ \square \\ \hline 5 \end{array}$$

57)
$$\begin{array}{r} \square \\ -\ 9 \\ \hline 1 \end{array}$$

58)
$$\begin{array}{r} 8 \\ -\ \square \\ \hline 0 \end{array}$$

59)
$$\begin{array}{r} \square \\ -\ 6 \\ \hline 4 \end{array}$$

60)
$$\begin{array}{r} 8 \\ -\ \square \\ \hline 2 \end{array}$$

Score:

Name:

/60

Time   :

1) □
  − 0
  ——
   10

2)   4
  − □
  ——
    3

3) □
  − 1
  ——
    8

4)   0
  − □
  ——
    0

5) □
  − 5
  ——
    0

6)   7
  − □
  ——
    3

7) □
  − 0
  ——
    6

8)   6
  − □
  ——
    5

9) □
  − 7
  ——
    0

10) 8
  − □
  ——
    5

11) □
  − 2
  ——
    4

12) 8
  − □
  ——
    8

13) □
  − 1
  ——
    5

14) 5
  − □
  ——
    3

15) □
  − 3
  ——
    3

16) 6
  − □
  ——
    1

17) □
  − 1
  ——
    5

18) 3
  − □
  ——
    1

19) □
  − 8
  ——
    1

20) 7
  − □
  ——
    2

21) □
  − 5
  ——
    2

22) 9
  − □
  ——
    3

23) □
  − 4
  ——
    4

24) 4
  − □
  ——
    2

25) □
  − 2
  ——
    8

26) 7
  − □
  ——
    7

27) □
  − 3
  ——
    3

28) 8
  − □
  ——
    7

29) □
  − 1
  ——
    0

30) 6
  − □
  ——
    3

31) □
  − 2
  ——
    4

32) 7
  − □
  ——
    6

33) □
  − 3
  ——
    1

34) 8
  − □
  ——
    2

35) □
  − 0
  ——
    0

36) 8
  − □
  ——
    2

37) □
  − 5
  ——
    1

38) 6
  − □
  ——
    5

39) □
  − 2
  ——
    5

40) 4
  − □
  ——
    0

41) □
  − 2
  ——
    0

42) 8
  − □
  ——
    4

43) □
  − 4
  ——
    1

44) 3
  − □
  ——
    3

45) □
  − 6
  ——
    2

46) 3
  − □
  ——
    3

47) □
  − 2
  ——
    7

48) 6
  − □
  ——
    2

49) □
  − 0
  ——
    6

50) 10
  − □
  ——
    10

51) □
  − 3
  ——
    2

52) 9
  − □
  ——
    7

53) □
  − 8
  ——
    0

54) 10
  − □
  ——
    5

55) □
  − 1
  ——
    8

56) 5
  − □
  ——
    3

57) □
  − 2
  ——
    8

58) 10
  − □
  ——
    9

59) □
  − 3
  ——
    3

60) 2
  − □
  ——
    1

Score: /60

Name:

Time :

1)
```
  □
- 6
---
  1
```

2)
```
  7
- □
---
  7
```

3)
```
  □
- 5
---
  1
```

4)
```
  6
- □
---
  1
```

5)
```
  □
- 4
---
  0
```

6)
```
  7
- □
---
  5
```

7)
```
  □
- 1
---
  3
```

8)
```
  5
- □
---
  4
```

9)
```
  □
- 5
---
  3
```

10)
```
  7
- □
---
  0
```

11)
```
  □
- 1
---
  3
```

12)
```
  8
- □
---
  2
```

13)
```
  □
- 4
---
  6
```

14)
```
  9
- □
---
  3
```

15)
```
  □
- 3
---
  1
```

16)
```
  9
- □
---
  5
```

17)
```
  □
- 8
---
  1
```

18)
```
  10
- □
---
  9
```

19)
```
  □
- 3
---
  2
```

20)
```
  2
- □
---
  0
```

21)
```
  □
- 9
---
  0
```

22)
```
  3
- □
---
  0
```

23)
```
  □
- 2
---
  5
```

24)
```
  6
- □
---
  4
```

25)
```
  □
- 0
---
  6
```

26)
```
  6
- □
---
  5
```

27)
```
  □
- 4
---
  6
```

28)
```
  8
- □
---
  8
```

29)
```
  □
- 0
---
  10
```

30)
```
  1
- □
---
  0
```

31)
```
  □
- 0
---
  5
```

32)
```
  10
- □
---
  3
```

33)
```
  □
- 3
---
  0
```

34)
```
  9
- □
---
  9
```

35)
```
  □
- 6
---
  4
```

36)
```
  7
- □
---
  5
```

37)
```
  □
- 3
---
  7
```

38)
```
  8
- □
---
  3
```

39)
```
  □
- 5
---
  4
```

40)
```
  5
- □
---
  2
```

41)
```
  □
- 0
---
  4
```

42)
```
  8
- □
---
  6
```

43)
```
  □
- 5
---
  1
```

44)
```
  8
- □
---
  7
```

45)
```
  □
- 2
---
  3
```

46)
```
  10
- □
---
  2
```

47)
```
  □
- 0
---
  0
```

48)
```
  5
- □
---
  4
```

49)
```
  □
- 3
---
  2
```

50)
```
  7
- □
---
  4
```

51)
```
  □
- 2
---
  1
```

52)
```
  10
- □
---
  10
```

53)
```
  □
- 0
---
  2
```

54)
```
  9
- □
---
  0
```

55)
```
  □
- 1
---
  9
```

56)
```
  9
- □
---
  7
```

57)
```
  □
- 1
---
  4
```

58)
```
  10
- □
---
  0
```

59)
```
  □
- 2
---
  4
```

60)
```
  7
- □
---
  2
```

Name:

Score:

/60

time   :

1) 20 − 20

2) 16 − 14

3) 18 − 15

4) 20 − 17

5) 17 − 17

6) 16 − 11

7) 16 − 10

8) 11 − 10

9) 13 − 10

10) 19 − 13

11) 20 − 18

12) 19 − 11

13) 19 − 12

14) 16 − 16

15) 18 − 10

16) 15 − 11

17) 10 − 10

18) 18 − 13

19) 18 − 12

20) 20 − 19

21) 16 − 10

22) 20 − 19

23) 17 − 12

24) 17 − 11

25) 14 − 14

26) 20 − 20

27) 19 − 14

28) 13 − 13

29) 17 − 14

30) 19 − 17

31) 10 − 10

32) 15 − 12

33) 20 − 19

34) 19 − 15

35) 12 − 10

36) 20 − 17

37) 11 − 10

38) 16 − 14

39) 20 − 10

40) 16 − 16

41) 20 − 16

42) 18 − 17

43) 19 − 18

44) 18 − 15

45) 15 − 12

46) 16 − 12

47) 19 − 18

48) 19 − 17

49) 17 − 10

50) 19 − 13

51) 15 − 14

52) 19 − 19

53) 18 − 17

54) 12 − 12

55) 14 − 13

56) 17 − 11

57) 16 − 12

58) 15 − 10

59) 15 − 13

60) 20 − 14

Score:

/60

Name:

Time :

1) 18
   − 17

2) 14
   − 14

3) 17
   − 12

4) 13
   − 12

5) 18
   − 11

6) 12
   − 11

7) 18
   − 14

8) 16
   − 14

9) 10
   − 10

10) 20
    − 14

11) 13
    − 10

12) 15
    − 13

13) 18
    − 13

14) 19
    − 12

15) 17
    − 12

16) 15
    − 15

17) 11
    − 10

18) 15
    − 15

19) 12
    − 11

20) 20
    − 17

21) 20
    − 18

22) 17
    − 17

23) 14
    − 13

24) 20
    − 18

25) 20
    − 12

26) 20
    − 15

27) 19
    − 15

28) 20
    − 13

29) 18
    − 13

30) 20
    − 10

31) 16
    − 16

32) 20
    − 12

33) 19
    − 16

34) 14
    − 13

35) 12
    − 11

36) 18
    − 18

37) 13
    − 13

38) 16
    − 14

39) 18
    − 12

40) 19
    − 12

41) 19
    − 17

42) 20
    − 19

43) 18
    − 11

44) 13
    − 10

45) 15
    − 14

46) 15
    − 13

47) 20
    − 20

48) 13
    − 13

49) 19
    − 17

50) 19
    − 16

51) 19
    − 18

52) 17
    − 11

53) 18
    − 16

54) 15
    − 14

55) 20
    − 20

56) 17
    − 11

57) 20
    − 18

58) 16
    − 16

59) 17
    − 12

60) 18
    − 13

Name: _____

Score:

/60

time   :

1)   11
   - 11

2)   20
   - 13

3)   20
   - 15

4)   14
   - 11

5)   18
   - 18

6)   10
   - 10

7)   20
   - 20

8)   19
   - 18

9)   18
   - 16

10)   19
    - 10

11)   18
    - 17

12)   18
    - 12

13)   18
    - 16

14)   14
    - 13

15)   18
    - 14

16)   13
    - 11

17)   20
    - 11

18)   16
    - 16

19)   19
    - 15

20)   12
    - 11

21)   17
    - 14

22)   18
    - 12

23)   18
    - 15

24)   11
    - 10

25)   15
    - 12

26)   19
    - 12

27)   17
    - 17

28)   12
    - 12

29)   20
    - 11

30)   19
    - 11

31)   20
    - 13

32)   18
    - 15

33)   17
    - 11

34)   20
    - 18

35)   15
    - 10

36)   16
    - 14

37)   18
    - 13

38)   18
    - 13

39)   14
    - 12

40)   18
    - 10

41)   17
    - 14

42)   16
    - 10

43)   15
    - 10

44)   16
    - 10

45)   20
    - 15

46)   17
    - 10

47)   17
    - 17

48)   18
    - 11

49)   15
    - 15

50)   19
    - 14

51)   16
    - 11

52)   13
    - 12

53)   17
    - 13

54)   20
    - 18

55)   20
    - 19

56)   18
    - 15

57)   19
    - 10

58)   16
    - 16

59)   15
    - 10

60)   19
    - 10

Name:

Score:

/60

time   :

1)   16
  − 13

2)   16
  − 15

3)   19
  − 11

4)   20
  − 18

5)   20
  − 13

6)   19
  − 17

7)   12
  − 11

8)   17
  − 16

9)   17
  − 10

10)   19
  − 12

11)   15
  − 12

12)   13
  − 10

13)   14
  − 11

14)   16
  − 11

15)   13
  − 11

16)   17
  − 15

17)   18
  − 14

18)   14
  − 13

19)   14
  − 10

20)   16
  − 16

21)   16
  − 15

22)   19
  − 15

23)   17
  − 13

24)   19
  − 15

25)   17
  − 12

26)   17
  − 14

27)   19
  − 14

28)   13
  − 10

29)   17
  − 14

30)   18
  − 10

31)   19
  − 18

32)   17
  − 15

33)   19
  − 15

34)   15
  − 15

35)   19
  − 13

36)   19
  − 19

37)   10
  − 10

38)   19
  − 14

39)   14
  − 11

40)   17
  − 10

41)   19
  − 11

42)   16
  − 14

43)   18
  − 14

44)   14
  − 14

45)   15
  − 11

46)   15
  − 10

47)   20
  − 13

48)   15
  − 11

49)   15
  − 12

50)   19
  − 18

51)   18
  − 11

52)   13
  − 12

53)   16
  − 16

54)   14
  − 11

55)   17
  − 12

56)   11
  − 10

57)   17
  − 14

58)   17
  − 13

59)   20
  − 17

60)   14
  − 10

Name: _____

Score:

/60

time   :

1)   18
   - 17

2)   14
   - 12

3)   12
   - 10

4)   17
   - 15

5)   15
   - 13

6)   18
   - 13

7)   16
   - 10

8)   17
   - 10

9)   19
   - 10

10) 18
   - 10

11) 20
   - 17

12) 18
   - 10

13) 15
   - 15

14) 18
   - 10

15) 15
   - 15

16) 15
   - 12

17) 13
   - 11

18) 20
   - 10

19) 15
   - 15

20) 19
   - 11

21) 12
   - 10

22) 20
   - 15

23) 20
   - 18

24) 18
   - 18

25) 19
   - 14

26) 19
   - 16

27) 17
   - 17

28) 16
   - 16

29) 19
   - 16

30) 13
   - 12

31) 17
   - 15

32) 17
   - 11

33) 14
   - 11

34) 15
   - 10

35) 18
   - 15

36) 12
   - 12

37) 17
   - 14

38) 17
   - 14

39) 10
   - 10

40) 17
   - 15

41) 19
   - 12

42) 13
   - 12

43) 18
   - 15

44) 10
   - 10

45) 11
   - 11

46) 17
   - 15

47) 10
   - 10

48) 17
   - 12

49) 20
   - 16

50) 16
   - 12

51) 17
   - 17

52) 16
   - 11

53) 17
   - 15

54) 19
   - 12

55) 18
   - 17

56) 18
   - 10

57) 16
   - 16

58) 17
   - 11

59) 18
   - 13

60) 17
   - 11

Name:

Score:

/60

time :

1) 18
  − 16

2) 19
  − 18

3) 14
  − 13

4) 18
  − 13

5) 18
  − 17

6) 18
  − 15

7) 14
  − 11

8) 20
  − 13

9) 20
  − 12

10) 20
  − 10

11) 20
  − 10

12) 13
  − 11

13) 13
  − 11

14) 20
  − 19

15) 15
  − 10

16) 16
  − 15

17) 12
  − 10

18) 18
  − 18

19) 20
  − 11

20) 13
  − 13

21) 17
  − 11

22) 20
  − 16

23) 15
  − 10

24) 14
  − 10

25) 13
  − 13

26) 16
  − 14

27) 19
  − 10

28) 16
  − 13

29) 15
  − 14

30) 13
  − 12

31) 16
  − 12

32) 14
  − 11

33) 15
  − 15

34) 13
  − 11

35) 17
  − 13

36) 18
  − 16

37) 15
  − 13

38) 16
  − 14

39) 16
  − 14

40) 15
  − 10

41) 14
  − 12

42) 15
  − 14

43) 20
  − 17

44) 20
  − 20

45) 17
  − 15

46) 20
  − 17

47) 20
  − 10

48) 18
  − 18

49) 20
  − 13

50) 19
  − 12

51) 18
  − 18

52) 19
  − 15

53) 12
  − 11

54) 20
  − 12

55) 20
  − 18

56) 13
  − 12

57) 18
  − 16

58) 15
  − 14

59) 19
  − 18

60) 13
  − 12

Name:

Score:

/60

time   :

1) 12
  - 11

2) 20
  - 11

3) 17
  - 16

4) 20
  - 11

5) 17
  - 10

6) 11
  - 10

7) 19
  - 12

8) 17
  - 16

9) 19
  - 12

10) 15
   - 10

11) 18
   - 11

12) 17
   - 15

13) 16
   - 14

14) 12
   - 12

15) 19
   - 11

16) 11
   - 10

17) 12
   - 10

18) 18
   - 17

19) 14
   - 13

20) 18
   - 13

21) 15
   - 10

22) 17
   - 10

23) 14
   - 11

24) 20
   - 16

25) 17
   - 13

26) 15
   - 10

27) 19
   - 10

28) 20
   - 11

29) 18
   - 14

30) 19
   - 17

31) 15
   - 13

32) 17
   - 15

33) 18
   - 14

34) 15
   - 11

35) 17
   - 16

36) 13
   - 11

37) 12
   - 11

38) 15
   - 10

39) 14
   - 14

40) 15
   - 11

41) 17
   - 12

42) 15
   - 13

43) 19
   - 19

44) 14
   - 11

45) 19
   - 17

46) 14
   - 12

47) 20
   - 11

48) 20
   - 18

49) 18
   - 10

50) 11
   - 10

51) 16
   - 10

52) 12
   - 11

53) 15
   - 15

54) 17
   - 13

55) 14
   - 11

56) 11
   - 11

57) 18
   - 11

58) 18
   - 10

59) 20
   - 20

60) 18
   - 16

Name:

Score:

/60

time   :

1)   17
  - 17

2)   19
  - 11

3)   17
  - 14

4)   14
  - 12

5)   19
  - 13

6)   20
  - 18

7)   15
  - 12

8)   12
  - 10

9)   17
  - 13

10)   20
  - 11

11)   20
  - 15

12)   14
  - 10

13)   14
  - 11

14)   17
  - 13

15)   15
  - 11

16)   14
  - 13

17)   16
  - 14

18)   15
  - 14

19)   16
  - 14

20)   13
  - 12

21)   20
  - 19

22)   14
  - 10

23)   16
  - 14

24)   18
  - 14

25)   18
  - 16

26)   16
  - 13

27)   18
  - 17

28)   16
  - 12

29)   16
  - 12

30)   14
  - 14

31)   16
  - 10

32)   18
  - 10

33)   16
  - 15

34)   13
  - 13

35)   19
  - 17

36)   20
  - 18

37)   20
  - 16

38)   16
  - 16

39)   19
  - 19

40)   20
  - 10

41)   17
  - 16

42)   20
  - 15

43)   12
  - 11

44)   20
  - 11

45)   18
  - 18

46)   20
  - 13

47)   19
  - 14

48)   19
  - 12

49)   16
  - 14

50)   15
  - 11

51)   20
  - 15

52)   18
  - 11

53)   20
  - 18

54)   18
  - 12

55)   17
  - 14

56)   14
  - 12

57)   13
  - 10

58)   20
  - 16

59)   19
  - 19

60)   16
  - 16

Name:

Score: /60

time :

1) 17 − 15

2) 20 − 15

3) 14 − 11

4) 14 − 12

5) 17 − 17

6) 14 − 13

7) 20 − 20

8) 15 − 11

9) 18 − 17

10) 18 − 12

11) 16 − 14

12) 11 − 10

13) 16 − 16

14) 14 − 10

15) 13 − 11

16) 11 − 11

17) 14 − 12

18) 17 − 11

19) 17 − 12

20) 15 − 13

21) 18 − 15

22) 15 − 14

23) 19 − 18

24) 13 − 11

25) 14 − 13

26) 17 − 17

27) 16 − 10

28) 18 − 12

29) 18 − 18

30) 14 − 14

31) 20 − 15

32) 17 − 10

33) 16 − 14

34) 18 − 13

35) 18 − 17

36) 19 − 11

37) 13 − 10

38) 14 − 12

39) 17 − 10

40) 14 − 11

41) 19 − 12

42) 19 − 10

43) 19 − 18

44) 19 − 10

45) 15 − 15

46) 17 − 12

47) 19 − 16

48) 15 − 11

49) 19 − 14

50) 11 − 11

51) 20 − 19

52) 13 − 13

53) 10 − 10

54) 14 − 12

55) 12 − 11

56) 16 − 13

57) 17 − 14

58) 20 − 11

59) 17 − 14

60) 14 − 13

Name:

Score:

/60

time :

1) 15
  − 14

2) 13
  − 12

3) 17
  − 12

4) 17
  − 15

5) 12
  − 12

6) 18
  − 17

7) 19
  − 11

8) 20
  − 14

9) 13
  − 10

10) 19
  − 19

11) 17
  − 14

12) 20
  − 15

13) 19
  − 17

14) 20
  − 13

15) 19
  − 10

16) 17
  − 12

17) 19
  − 16

18) 20
  − 13

19) 15
  − 14

20) 13
  − 11

21) 14
  − 10

22) 18
  − 15

23) 18
  − 16

24) 19
  − 10

25) 13
  − 13

26) 13
  − 12

27) 11
  − 10

28) 17
  − 11

29) 17
  − 12

30) 15
  − 15

31) 18
  − 15

32) 20
  − 19

33) 19
  − 16

34) 20
  − 19

35) 13
  − 11

36) 13
  − 10

37) 15
  − 10

38) 18
  − 17

39) 13
  − 13

40) 20
  − 17

41) 12
  − 12

42) 17
  − 15

43) 16
  − 16

44) 12
  − 11

45) 16
  − 14

46) 16
  − 13

47) 19
  − 14

48) 13
  − 11

49) 17
  − 15

50) 19
  − 19

51) 14
  − 13

52) 17
  − 17

53) 19
  − 13

54) 16
  − 16

55) 14
  − 13

56) 15
  − 15

57) 20
  − 15

58) 20
  − 19

59) 11
  − 10

60) 20
  − 19

Score:

/60

Name:

time   :

1)
```
   ☐
 - 13
 ───
   3
```

2)
```
   20
 - ☐
 ───
   10
```

3)
```
   ☐
 - 13
 ───
   6
```

4)
```
   17
 - ☐
 ───
   5
```

5)
```
   ☐
 - 12
 ───
   1
```

6)
```
   20
 - ☐
 ───
   1
```

7)
```
   ☐
 - 13
 ───
   6
```

8)
```
   20
 - ☐
 ───
   2
```

9)
```
   ☐
 - 15
 ───
   5
```

10)
```
   19
 - ☐
 ───
   9
```

11)
```
   ☐
 - 10
 ───
   9
```

12)
```
   14
 - ☐
 ───
   2
```

13)
```
   ☐
 - 15
 ───
   4
```

14)
```
   19
 - ☐
 ───
   6
```

15)
```
   ☐
 - 11
 ───
   9
```

16)
```
   18
 - ☐
 ───
   0
```

17)
```
   ☐
 - 18
 ───
   1
```

18)
```
   18
 - ☐
 ───
   6
```

19)
```
   ☐
 - 14
 ───
   6
```

20)
```
   13
 - ☐
 ───
   2
```

21)
```
   ☐
 - 12
 ───
   0
```

22)
```
   16
 - ☐
 ───
   5
```

23)
```
   ☐
 - 18
 ───
   2
```

24)
```
   19
 - ☐
 ───
   8
```

25)
```
   ☐
 - 12
 ───
   6
```

26)
```
   19
 - ☐
 ───
   0
```

27)
```
   ☐
 - 12
 ───
   3
```

28)
```
   17
 - ☐
 ───
   6
```

29)
```
   ☐
 - 15
 ───
   0
```

30)
```
   17
 - ☐
 ───
   6
```

31)
```
   ☐
 - 17
 ───
   2
```

32)
```
   16
 - ☐
 ───
   1
```

33)
```
   ☐
 - 16
 ───
   0
```

34)
```
   20
 - ☐
 ───
   1
```

35)
```
   ☐
 - 14
 ───
   0
```

36)
```
   10
 - ☐
 ───
   0
```

37)
```
   ☐
 - 13
 ───
   7
```

38)
```
   18
 - ☐
 ───
   4
```

39)
```
   ☐
 - 17
 ───
   1
```

40)
```
   15
 - ☐
 ───
   5
```

41)
```
   ☐
 - 10
 ───
   2
```

42)
```
   11
 - ☐
 ───
   1
```

43)
```
   ☐
 - 10
 ───
   1
```

44)
```
   17
 - ☐
 ───
   6
```

45)
```
   ☐
 - 14
 ───
   5
```

46)
```
   12
 - ☐
 ───
   1
```

47)
```
   ☐
 - 11
 ───
   3
```

48)
```
   18
 - ☐
 ───
   0
```

49)
```
   ☐
 - 12
 ───
   3
```

50)
```
   15
 - ☐
 ───
   4
```

51)
```
   ☐
 - 11
 ───
   1
```

52)
```
   16
 - ☐
 ───
   2
```

53)
```
   ☐
 - 11
 ───
   3
```

54)
```
   20
 - ☐
 ───
   6
```

55)
```
   ☐
 - 11
 ───
   2
```

56)
```
   19
 - ☐
 ───
   4
```

57)
```
   ☐
 - 10
 ───
   10
```

58)
```
   20
 - ☐
 ───
   7
```

59)
```
   ☐
 - 11
 ───
   9
```

60)
```
   18
 - ☐
 ───
   3
```

Score:

/60

Name:

Time   :

1) ☐
   − 14
    3

2)   19
   −☐
    8

3) ☐
   − 10
    2

4)   13
   −☐
    2

5) ☐
   − 14
    5

6)   19
   −☐
    7

7) ☐
   − 12
    0

8)   20
   −☐
    5

9) ☐
   − 13
    2

10) 14
   −☐
    4

11) ☐
   − 16
    1

12) 18
   −☐
    8

13) ☐
   − 12
    4

14) 13
   −☐
    1

15) ☐
   − 11
    9

16) 20
   −☐
    9

17) ☐
   − 15
    3

18) 20
   −☐
    8

19) ☐
   − 13
    3

20) 17
   −☐
    2

21) ☐
   − 10
    1

22) 17
   −☐
    4

23) ☐
   − 16
    3

24) 12
   −☐
    2

25) ☐
   − 12
    3

26) 16
   −☐
    4

27) ☐
   − 15
    2

28) 20
   −☐
    10

29) ☐
   − 19
    0

30) 19
   −☐
    5

31) ☐
   − 18
    2

32) 16
   −☐
    0

33) ☐
   − 11
    0

34) 19
   −☐
    0

35) ☐
   − 17
    3

36) 16
   −☐
    1

37) ☐
   − 12
    1

38) 17
   −☐
    2

39) ☐
   − 19
    0

40) 15
   −☐
    1

41) ☐
   − 12
    2

42) 20
   −☐
    9

43) ☐
   − 10
    6

44) 16
   −☐
    6

45) ☐
   − 15
    0

46) 18
   −☐
    5

47) ☐
   − 11
    4

48) 19
   −☐
    8

49) ☐
   − 10
    3

50) 16
   −☐
    1

51) ☐
   − 10
    9

52) 19
   −☐
    9

53) ☐
   − 17
    0

54) 17
   −☐
    6

55) ☐
   − 10
    1

56) 12
   −☐
    0

57) ☐
   − 12
    0

58) 20
   −☐
    1

59) ☐
   − 13
    3

60) 13
   −☐
    0

Page 152

Name: _____

Score: /60

time :

1)
```
  □
- 19
────
   0
```

2)
```
  14
-  □
────
   0
```

3)
```
   □
- 15
────
   0
```

4)
```
  18
-  □
────
   5
```

5)
```
   □
- 19
────
   1
```

6)
```
  20
-  □
────
   6
```

7)
```
   □
- 13
────
   6
```

8)
```
  14
-  □
────
   2
```

9)
```
   □
- 16
────
   4
```

10)
```
  19
-  □
────
   8
```

11)
```
   □
- 10
────
   2
```

12)
```
  19
-  □
────
   0
```

13)
```
   □
- 14
────
   3
```

14)
```
  18
-  □
────
   5
```

15)
```
   □
- 12
────
   8
```

16)
```
  16
-  □
────
   4
```

17)
```
   □
- 10
────
   9
```

18)
```
  17
-  □
────
   7
```

19)
```
   □
- 17
────
   1
```

20)
```
  15
-  □
────
   3
```

21)
```
   □
- 11
────
   6
```

22)
```
  20
-  □
────
   0
```

23)
```
   □
- 11
────
   3
```

24)
```
  20
-  □
────
   5
```

25)
```
   □
- 16
────
   2
```

26)
```
  11
-  □
────
   1
```

27)
```
   □
- 15
────
   3
```

28)
```
  18
-  □
────
   6
```

29)
```
   □
- 10
────
  10
```

30)
```
  20
-  □
────
   8
```

31)
```
   □
- 20
────
   0
```

32)
```
  16
-  □
────
   4
```

33)
```
   □
- 17
────
   1
```

34)
```
  19
-  □
────
   7
```

35)
```
   □
- 10
────
   4
```

36)
```
  20
-  □
────
   4
```

37)
```
   □
- 10
────
   7
```

38)
```
  20
-  □
────
   1
```

39)
```
   □
- 16
────
   2
```

40)
```
  17
-  □
────
   3
```

41)
```
   □
- 19
────
   1
```

42)
```
  13
-  □
────
   0
```

43)
```
   □
- 12
────
   8
```

44)
```
  14
-  □
────
   4
```

45)
```
   □
- 13
────
   4
```

46)
```
  16
-  □
────
   2
```

47)
```
   □
- 12
────
   8
```

48)
```
  19
-  □
────
   5
```

49)
```
   □
- 12
────
   2
```

50)
```
  20
-  □
────
   7
```

51)
```
   □
- 10
────
   9
```

52)
```
  17
-  □
────
   2
```

53)
```
   □
- 11
────
   9
```

54)
```
  12
-  □
────
   2
```

55)
```
   □
- 10
────
   7
```

56)
```
  13
-  □
────
   0
```

57)
```
   □
- 11
────
   5
```

58)
```
  19
-  □
────
   2
```

59)
```
   □
- 11
────
   2
```

60)
```
  14
-  □
────
   4
```

1)
```
    [ ]
  - 16
    4
```

2)
```
   15
  -[ ]
    1
```

3)
```
    [ ]
  - 18
    1
```

4)
```
   19
  -[ ]
    8
```

5)
```
    [ ]
  - 10
    1
```

6)
```
   18
  -[ ]
    8
```

7)
```
    [ ]
  - 12
    1
```

8)
```
   12
  -[ ]
    1
```

9)
```
    [ ]
  - 19
    0
```

10)
```
   18
  -[ ]
    8
```

11)
```
    [ ]
  - 11
    8
```

12)
```
   20
  -[ ]
    7
```

13)
```
    [ ]
  - 14
    2
```

14)
```
   14
  -[ ]
    4
```

15)
```
    [ ]
  - 13
    0
```

16)
```
   18
  -[ ]
    1
```

17)
```
    [ ]
  - 12
    3
```

18)
```
   18
  -[ ]
    1
```

19)
```
    [ ]
  - 16
    2
```

20)
```
   15
  -[ ]
    1
```

21)
```
    [ ]
  - 18
    1
```

22)
```
   15
  -[ ]
    5
```

23)
```
    [ ]
  - 12
    1
```

24)
```
   11
  -[ ]
    0
```

25)
```
    [ ]
  - 14
    2
```

26)
```
   20
  -[ ]
    7
```

27)
```
    [ ]
  - 19
    0
```

28)
```
   18
  -[ ]
    7
```

29)
```
    [ ]
  - 11
    5
```

30)
```
   13
  -[ ]
    2
```

31)
```
    [ ]
  - 14
    2
```

32)
```
   15
  -[ ]
    5
```

33)
```
    [ ]
  - 14
    1
```

34)
```
   15
  -[ ]
    2
```

35)
```
    [ ]
  - 10
    5
```

36)
```
   20
  -[ ]
    4
```

37)
```
    [ ]
  - 10
    6
```

38)
```
   14
  -[ ]
    1
```

39)
```
    [ ]
  - 11
    8
```

40)
```
   16
  -[ ]
    2
```

41)
```
    [ ]
  - 12
    5
```

42)
```
   17
  -[ ]
    6
```

43)
```
    [ ]
  - 11
    2
```

44)
```
   15
  -[ ]
    4
```

45)
```
    [ ]
  - 10
    1
```

46)
```
   16
  -[ ]
    4
```

47)
```
    [ ]
  - 16
    0
```

48)
```
   14
  -[ ]
    1
```

49)
```
    [ ]
  - 11
    2
```

50)
```
   18
  -[ ]
    4
```

51)
```
    [ ]
  - 13
    5
```

52)
```
   12
  -[ ]
    0
```

53)
```
    [ ]
  - 12
    3
```

54)
```
   15
  -[ ]
    5
```

55)
```
    [ ]
  - 10
    7
```

56)
```
   18
  -[ ]
    3
```

57)
```
    [ ]
  - 10
    6
```

58)
```
   19
  -[ ]
    7
```

59)
```
    [ ]
  - 14
    1
```

60)
```
   17
  -[ ]
    6
```

Score:

/60

Name:

time   :

1)
$$\begin{array}{r} \boxed{} \\ -\ 11 \\ \hline 2 \end{array}$$

2)
$$\begin{array}{r} 16 \\ -\ \boxed{} \\ \hline 6 \end{array}$$

3)
$$\begin{array}{r} \boxed{} \\ -\ 12 \\ \hline 1 \end{array}$$

4)
$$\begin{array}{r} 20 \\ -\ \boxed{} \\ \hline 4 \end{array}$$

5)
$$\begin{array}{r} \boxed{} \\ -\ 20 \\ \hline 0 \end{array}$$

6)
$$\begin{array}{r} 19 \\ -\ \boxed{} \\ \hline 5 \end{array}$$

7)
$$\begin{array}{r} \boxed{} \\ -\ 18 \\ \hline 2 \end{array}$$

8)
$$\begin{array}{r} 20 \\ -\ \boxed{} \\ \hline 3 \end{array}$$

9)
$$\begin{array}{r} \boxed{} \\ -\ 12 \\ \hline 0 \end{array}$$

10)
$$\begin{array}{r} 18 \\ -\ \boxed{} \\ \hline 8 \end{array}$$

11)
$$\begin{array}{r} \boxed{} \\ -\ 12 \\ \hline 7 \end{array}$$

12)
$$\begin{array}{r} 14 \\ -\ \boxed{} \\ \hline 1 \end{array}$$

13)
$$\begin{array}{r} \boxed{} \\ -\ 15 \\ \hline 3 \end{array}$$

14)
$$\begin{array}{r} 20 \\ -\ \boxed{} \\ \hline 0 \end{array}$$

15)
$$\begin{array}{r} \boxed{} \\ -\ 20 \\ \hline 0 \end{array}$$

16)
$$\begin{array}{r} 19 \\ -\ \boxed{} \\ \hline 9 \end{array}$$

17)
$$\begin{array}{r} \boxed{} \\ -\ 13 \\ \hline 4 \end{array}$$

18)
$$\begin{array}{r} 16 \\ -\ \boxed{} \\ \hline 2 \end{array}$$

19)
$$\begin{array}{r} \boxed{} \\ -\ 14 \\ \hline 3 \end{array}$$

20)
$$\begin{array}{r} 12 \\ -\ \boxed{} \\ \hline 0 \end{array}$$

21)
$$\begin{array}{r} \boxed{} \\ -\ 11 \\ \hline 2 \end{array}$$

22)
$$\begin{array}{r} 20 \\ -\ \boxed{} \\ \hline 8 \end{array}$$

23)
$$\begin{array}{r} \boxed{} \\ -\ 10 \\ \hline 1 \end{array}$$

24)
$$\begin{array}{r} 17 \\ -\ \boxed{} \\ \hline 4 \end{array}$$

25)
$$\begin{array}{r} \boxed{} \\ -\ 14 \\ \hline 2 \end{array}$$

26)
$$\begin{array}{r} 15 \\ -\ \boxed{} \\ \hline 2 \end{array}$$

27)
$$\begin{array}{r} \boxed{} \\ -\ 14 \\ \hline 6 \end{array}$$

28)
$$\begin{array}{r} 20 \\ -\ \boxed{} \\ \hline 7 \end{array}$$

29)
$$\begin{array}{r} \boxed{} \\ -\ 10 \\ \hline 8 \end{array}$$

30)
$$\begin{array}{r} 13 \\ -\ \boxed{} \\ \hline 3 \end{array}$$

31)
$$\begin{array}{r} \boxed{} \\ -\ 10 \\ \hline 0 \end{array}$$

32)
$$\begin{array}{r} 16 \\ -\ \boxed{} \\ \hline 6 \end{array}$$

33)
$$\begin{array}{r} \boxed{} \\ -\ 11 \\ \hline 1 \end{array}$$

34)
$$\begin{array}{r} 18 \\ -\ \boxed{} \\ \hline 5 \end{array}$$

35)
$$\begin{array}{r} \boxed{} \\ -\ 10 \\ \hline 5 \end{array}$$

36)
$$\begin{array}{r} 14 \\ -\ \boxed{} \\ \hline 2 \end{array}$$

37)
$$\begin{array}{r} \boxed{} \\ -\ 15 \\ \hline 3 \end{array}$$

38)
$$\begin{array}{r} 18 \\ -\ \boxed{} \\ \hline 2 \end{array}$$

39)
$$\begin{array}{r} \boxed{} \\ -\ 11 \\ \hline 3 \end{array}$$

40)
$$\begin{array}{r} 16 \\ -\ \boxed{} \\ \hline 3 \end{array}$$

41)
$$\begin{array}{r} \boxed{} \\ -\ 15 \\ \hline 5 \end{array}$$

42)
$$\begin{array}{r} 13 \\ -\ \boxed{} \\ \hline 3 \end{array}$$

43)
$$\begin{array}{r} \boxed{} \\ -\ 10 \\ \hline 10 \end{array}$$

44)
$$\begin{array}{r} 20 \\ -\ \boxed{} \\ \hline 8 \end{array}$$

45)
$$\begin{array}{r} \boxed{} \\ -\ 10 \\ \hline 3 \end{array}$$

46)
$$\begin{array}{r} 19 \\ -\ \boxed{} \\ \hline 5 \end{array}$$

47)
$$\begin{array}{r} \boxed{} \\ -\ 12 \\ \hline 8 \end{array}$$

48)
$$\begin{array}{r} 14 \\ -\ \boxed{} \\ \hline 2 \end{array}$$

49)
$$\begin{array}{r} \boxed{} \\ -\ 13 \\ \hline 4 \end{array}$$

50)
$$\begin{array}{r} 16 \\ -\ \boxed{} \\ \hline 6 \end{array}$$

51)
$$\begin{array}{r} \boxed{} \\ -\ 14 \\ \hline 2 \end{array}$$

52)
$$\begin{array}{r} 17 \\ -\ \boxed{} \\ \hline 5 \end{array}$$

53)
$$\begin{array}{r} \boxed{} \\ -\ 14 \\ \hline 6 \end{array}$$

54)
$$\begin{array}{r} 17 \\ -\ \boxed{} \\ \hline 5 \end{array}$$

55)
$$\begin{array}{r} \boxed{} \\ -\ 14 \\ \hline 0 \end{array}$$

56)
$$\begin{array}{r} 17 \\ -\ \boxed{} \\ \hline 2 \end{array}$$

57)
$$\begin{array}{r} \boxed{} \\ -\ 10 \\ \hline 4 \end{array}$$

58)
$$\begin{array}{r} 20 \\ -\ \boxed{} \\ \hline 9 \end{array}$$

59)
$$\begin{array}{r} \boxed{} \\ -\ 16 \\ \hline 1 \end{array}$$

60)
$$\begin{array}{r} 14 \\ -\ \boxed{} \\ \hline 4 \end{array}$$

Score: /60

Name:

Time :

1)
$$\begin{array}{r} \boxed{} \\ -\ 13 \\ \hline 1 \end{array}$$

2)
$$\begin{array}{r} 15 \\ -\ \boxed{} \\ \hline 0 \end{array}$$

3)
$$\begin{array}{r} \boxed{} \\ -\ 18 \\ \hline 0 \end{array}$$

4)
$$\begin{array}{r} 20 \\ -\ \boxed{} \\ \hline 8 \end{array}$$

5)
$$\begin{array}{r} \boxed{} \\ -\ 13 \\ \hline 3 \end{array}$$

6)
$$\begin{array}{r} 16 \\ -\ \boxed{} \\ \hline 1 \end{array}$$

7)
$$\begin{array}{r} \boxed{} \\ -\ 16 \\ \hline 1 \end{array}$$

8)
$$\begin{array}{r} 14 \\ -\ \boxed{} \\ \hline 1 \end{array}$$

9)
$$\begin{array}{r} \boxed{} \\ -\ 15 \\ \hline 3 \end{array}$$

10)
$$\begin{array}{r} 15 \\ -\ \boxed{} \\ \hline 3 \end{array}$$

11)
$$\begin{array}{r} \boxed{} \\ -\ 14 \\ \hline 2 \end{array}$$

12)
$$\begin{array}{r} 12 \\ -\ \boxed{} \\ \hline 1 \end{array}$$

13)
$$\begin{array}{r} \boxed{} \\ -\ 10 \\ \hline 10 \end{array}$$

14)
$$\begin{array}{r} 12 \\ -\ \boxed{} \\ \hline 2 \end{array}$$

15)
$$\begin{array}{r} \boxed{} \\ -\ 18 \\ \hline 1 \end{array}$$

16)
$$\begin{array}{r} 16 \\ -\ \boxed{} \\ \hline 2 \end{array}$$

17)
$$\begin{array}{r} \boxed{} \\ -\ 14 \\ \hline 6 \end{array}$$

18)
$$\begin{array}{r} 20 \\ -\ \boxed{} \\ \hline 9 \end{array}$$

19)
$$\begin{array}{r} \boxed{} \\ -\ 19 \\ \hline 0 \end{array}$$

20)
$$\begin{array}{r} 14 \\ -\ \boxed{} \\ \hline 4 \end{array}$$

21)
$$\begin{array}{r} \boxed{} \\ -\ 18 \\ \hline 2 \end{array}$$

22)
$$\begin{array}{r} 20 \\ -\ \boxed{} \\ \hline 3 \end{array}$$

23)
$$\begin{array}{r} \boxed{} \\ -\ 20 \\ \hline 0 \end{array}$$

24)
$$\begin{array}{r} 20 \\ -\ \boxed{} \\ \hline 5 \end{array}$$

25)
$$\begin{array}{r} \boxed{} \\ -\ 10 \\ \hline 9 \end{array}$$

26)
$$\begin{array}{r} 12 \\ -\ \boxed{} \\ \hline 0 \end{array}$$

27)
$$\begin{array}{r} \boxed{} \\ -\ 13 \\ \hline 4 \end{array}$$

28)
$$\begin{array}{r} 17 \\ -\ \boxed{} \\ \hline 0 \end{array}$$

29)
$$\begin{array}{r} \boxed{} \\ -\ 13 \\ \hline 4 \end{array}$$

30)
$$\begin{array}{r} 14 \\ -\ \boxed{} \\ \hline 0 \end{array}$$

31)
$$\begin{array}{r} \boxed{} \\ -\ 13 \\ \hline 2 \end{array}$$

32)
$$\begin{array}{r} 12 \\ -\ \boxed{} \\ \hline 2 \end{array}$$

33)
$$\begin{array}{r} \boxed{} \\ -\ 19 \\ \hline 0 \end{array}$$

34)
$$\begin{array}{r} 15 \\ -\ \boxed{} \\ \hline 3 \end{array}$$

35)
$$\begin{array}{r} \boxed{} \\ -\ 13 \\ \hline 2 \end{array}$$

36)
$$\begin{array}{r} 19 \\ -\ \boxed{} \\ \hline 6 \end{array}$$

37)
$$\begin{array}{r} \boxed{} \\ -\ 11 \\ \hline 7 \end{array}$$

38)
$$\begin{array}{r} 12 \\ -\ \boxed{} \\ \hline 0 \end{array}$$

39)
$$\begin{array}{r} \boxed{} \\ -\ 11 \\ \hline 4 \end{array}$$

40)
$$\begin{array}{r} 17 \\ -\ \boxed{} \\ \hline 0 \end{array}$$

41)
$$\begin{array}{r} \boxed{} \\ -\ 15 \\ \hline 0 \end{array}$$

42)
$$\begin{array}{r} 16 \\ -\ \boxed{} \\ \hline 1 \end{array}$$

43)
$$\begin{array}{r} \boxed{} \\ -\ 10 \\ \hline 5 \end{array}$$

44)
$$\begin{array}{r} 18 \\ -\ \boxed{} \\ \hline 2 \end{array}$$

45)
$$\begin{array}{r} \boxed{} \\ -\ 10 \\ \hline 3 \end{array}$$

46)
$$\begin{array}{r} 19 \\ -\ \boxed{} \\ \hline 4 \end{array}$$

47)
$$\begin{array}{r} \boxed{} \\ -\ 11 \\ \hline 8 \end{array}$$

48)
$$\begin{array}{r} 16 \\ -\ \boxed{} \\ \hline 6 \end{array}$$

49)
$$\begin{array}{r} \boxed{} \\ -\ 15 \\ \hline 1 \end{array}$$

50)
$$\begin{array}{r} 10 \\ -\ \boxed{} \\ \hline 0 \end{array}$$

51)
$$\begin{array}{r} \boxed{} \\ -\ 12 \\ \hline 0 \end{array}$$

52)
$$\begin{array}{r} 17 \\ -\ \boxed{} \\ \hline 2 \end{array}$$

53)
$$\begin{array}{r} \boxed{} \\ -\ 11 \\ \hline 7 \end{array}$$

54)
$$\begin{array}{r} 13 \\ -\ \boxed{} \\ \hline 3 \end{array}$$

55)
$$\begin{array}{r} \boxed{} \\ -\ 11 \\ \hline 0 \end{array}$$

56)
$$\begin{array}{r} 18 \\ -\ \boxed{} \\ \hline 6 \end{array}$$

57)
$$\begin{array}{r} \boxed{} \\ -\ 12 \\ \hline 2 \end{array}$$

58)
$$\begin{array}{r} 18 \\ -\ \boxed{} \\ \hline 3 \end{array}$$

59)
$$\begin{array}{r} \boxed{} \\ -\ 16 \\ \hline 2 \end{array}$$

60)
$$\begin{array}{r} 13 \\ -\ \boxed{} \\ \hline 0 \end{array}$$

Name:

Score:

/60

Time   :

1)
```
    □
-  17
    1
```

2)
```
    16
-  □
    2
```

3)
```
    □
-  19
    1
```

4)
```
    18
-  □
    2
```

5)
```
    □
-  12
    8
```

6)
```
    17
-  □
    1
```

7)
```
    □
-  15
    3
```

8)
```
    20
-  □
    2
```

9)
```
    □
-  10
    4
```

10)
```
    19
-  □
    9
```

11)
```
    □
-  10
    5
```

12)
```
    13
-  □
    1
```

13)
```
    □
-  11
    3
```

14)
```
    17
-  □
    0
```

15)
```
    □
-  15
    4
```

16)
```
    13
-  □
    1
```

17)
```
    □
-  12
    1
```

18)
```
    17
-  □
    0
```

19)
```
    □
-  16
    0
```

20)
```
    18
-  □
    1
```

21)
```
    □
-  14
    3
```

22)
```
    16
-  □
    3
```

23)
```
    □
-  14
    4
```

24)
```
    19
-  □
    1
```

25)
```
    □
-  13
    4
```

26)
```
    17
-  □
    6
```

27)
```
    □
-  11
    8
```

28)
```
    20
-  □
    9
```

29)
```
    □
-  17
    3
```

30)
```
    16
-  □
    3
```

31)
```
    □
-  18
    2
```

32)
```
    20
-  □
    9
```

33)
```
    □
-  10
    0
```

34)
```
    14
-  □
    1
```

35)
```
    □
-  10
    5
```

36)
```
    17
-  □
    2
```

37)
```
    □
-  10
    10
```

38)
```
    14
-  □
    4
```

39)
```
    □
-  11
    1
```

40)
```
    15
-  □
    3
```

41)
```
    □
-  13
    0
```

42)
```
    18
-  □
    0
```

43)
```
    □
-  10
    3
```

44)
```
    20
-  □
    7
```

45)
```
    □
-  12
    8
```

46)
```
    15
-  □
    3
```

47)
```
    □
-  18
    1
```

48)
```
    19
-  □
    6
```

49)
```
    □
-  14
    3
```

50)
```
    15
-  □
    4
```

51)
```
    □
-  11
    8
```

52)
```
    19
-  □
    7
```

53)
```
    □
-  18
    2
```

54)
```
    16
-  □
    6
```

55)
```
    □
-  16
    2
```

56)
```
    16
-  □
    1
```

57)
```
    □
-  12
    0
```

58)
```
    16
-  □
    2
```

59)
```
    □
-  13
    3
```

60)
```
    14
-  □
    2
```

Score: /60

Name:

time :

1) $\boxed{}$ $- 14$ $= 5$

2) 17 $- \boxed{}$ $= 6$

3) $\boxed{}$ $- 14$ $= 2$

4) 19 $- \boxed{}$ $= 4$

5) $\boxed{}$ $- 11$ $= 6$

6) 19 $- \boxed{}$ $= 7$

7) $\boxed{}$ $- 13$ $= 3$

8) 17 $- \boxed{}$ $= 4$

9) $\boxed{}$ $- 10$ $= 1$

10) 16 $- \boxed{}$ $= 0$

11) $\boxed{}$ $- 10$ $= 1$

12) 20 $- \boxed{}$ $= 4$

13) $\boxed{}$ $- 18$ $= 2$

14) 17 $- \boxed{}$ $= 5$

15) $\boxed{}$ $- 18$ $= 0$

16) 17 $- \boxed{}$ $= 1$

17) $\boxed{}$ $- 11$ $= 4$

18) 19 $- \boxed{}$ $= 7$

19) $\boxed{}$ $- 11$ $= 2$

20) 16 $- \boxed{}$ $= 1$

21) $\boxed{}$ $- 10$ $= 4$

22) 18 $- \boxed{}$ $= 7$

23) $\boxed{}$ $- 15$ $= 1$

24) 11 $- \boxed{}$ $= 1$

25) $\boxed{}$ $- 14$ $= 3$

26) 15 $- \boxed{}$ $= 4$

27) $\boxed{}$ $- 11$ $= 6$

28) 15 $- \boxed{}$ $= 0$

29) $\boxed{}$ $- 10$ $= 7$

30) 15 $- \boxed{}$ $= 5$

31) $\boxed{}$ $- 12$ $= 4$

32) 14 $- \boxed{}$ $= 1$

33) $\boxed{}$ $- 10$ $= 8$

34) 16 $- \boxed{}$ $= 0$

35) $\boxed{}$ $- 11$ $= 0$

36) 12 $- \boxed{}$ $= 2$

37) $\boxed{}$ $- 17$ $= 1$

38) 14 $- \boxed{}$ $= 1$

39) $\boxed{}$ $- 11$ $= 4$

40) 15 $- \boxed{}$ $= 1$

41) $\boxed{}$ $- 12$ $= 3$

42) 20 $- \boxed{}$ $= 2$

43) $\boxed{}$ $- 14$ $= 5$

44) 16 $- \boxed{}$ $= 2$

45) $\boxed{}$ $- 15$ $= 1$

46) 19 $- \boxed{}$ $= 6$

47) $\boxed{}$ $- 10$ $= 8$

48) 16 $- \boxed{}$ $= 5$

49) $\boxed{}$ $- 14$ $= 2$

50) 15 $- \boxed{}$ $= 3$

51) $\boxed{}$ $- 11$ $= 5$

52) 18 $- \boxed{}$ $= 8$

53) $\boxed{}$ $- 10$ $= 1$

54) 11 $- \boxed{}$ $= 0$

55) $\boxed{}$ $- 14$ $= 0$

56) 19 $- \boxed{}$ $= 1$

57) $\boxed{}$ $- 12$ $= 3$

58) 15 $- \boxed{}$ $= 4$

59) $\boxed{}$ $- 12$ $= 4$

60) 10 $- \boxed{}$ $= 0$

Score:

/60

Name:

time   :

1)
$$\frac{\boxed{}}{-\ 20}$$
0

2)
$$\frac{20}{-\boxed{}}$$
3

3)
$$\frac{\boxed{}}{-\ 13}$$
6

4)
$$\frac{16}{-\boxed{}}$$
0

5)
$$\frac{\boxed{}}{-\ 10}$$
10

6)
$$\frac{11}{-\boxed{}}$$
1

7)
$$\frac{\boxed{}}{-\ 10}$$
1

8)
$$\frac{17}{-\boxed{}}$$
6

9)
$$\frac{\boxed{}}{-\ 13}$$
4

10)
$$\frac{17}{-\boxed{}}$$
7

11)
$$\frac{\boxed{}}{-\ 11}$$
6

12)
$$\frac{11}{-\boxed{}}$$
0

13)
$$\frac{\boxed{}}{-\ 13}$$
4

14)
$$\frac{19}{-\boxed{}}$$
3

15)
$$\frac{\boxed{}}{-\ 14}$$
2

16)
$$\frac{15}{-\boxed{}}$$
1

17)
$$\frac{\boxed{}}{-\ 11}$$
5

18)
$$\frac{20}{-\boxed{}}$$
2

19)
$$\frac{\boxed{}}{-\ 15}$$
1

20)
$$\frac{15}{-\boxed{}}$$
4

21)
$$\frac{\boxed{}}{-\ 15}$$
1

22)
$$\frac{13}{-\boxed{}}$$
0

23)
$$\frac{\boxed{}}{-\ 10}$$
5

24)
$$\frac{17}{-\boxed{}}$$
6

25)
$$\frac{\boxed{}}{-\ 18}$$
0

26)
$$\frac{18}{-\boxed{}}$$
8

27)
$$\frac{\boxed{}}{-\ 19}$$
0

28)
$$\frac{20}{-\boxed{}}$$
8

29)
$$\frac{\boxed{}}{-\ 20}$$
0

30)
$$\frac{13}{-\boxed{}}$$
2

31)
$$\frac{\boxed{}}{-\ 11}$$
5

32)
$$\frac{17}{-\boxed{}}$$
6

33)
$$\frac{\boxed{}}{-\ 10}$$
10

34)
$$\frac{20}{-\boxed{}}$$
9

35)
$$\frac{\boxed{}}{-\ 12}$$
1

36)
$$\frac{13}{-\boxed{}}$$
3

37)
$$\frac{\boxed{}}{-\ 13}$$
2

38)
$$\frac{18}{-\boxed{}}$$
8

39)
$$\frac{\boxed{}}{-\ 11}$$
9

40)
$$\frac{19}{-\boxed{}}$$
6

41)
$$\frac{\boxed{}}{-\ 13}$$
3

42)
$$\frac{19}{-\boxed{}}$$
4

43)
$$\frac{\boxed{}}{-\ 17}$$
1

44)
$$\frac{19}{-\boxed{}}$$
6

45)
$$\frac{\boxed{}}{-\ 10}$$
9

46)
$$\frac{19}{-\boxed{}}$$
0

47)
$$\frac{\boxed{}}{-\ 10}$$
9

48)
$$\frac{12}{-\boxed{}}$$
2

49)
$$\frac{\boxed{}}{-\ 11}$$
0

50)
$$\frac{14}{-\boxed{}}$$
1

51)
$$\frac{\boxed{}}{-\ 14}$$
1

52)
$$\frac{15}{-\boxed{}}$$
2

53)
$$\frac{\boxed{}}{-\ 12}$$
2

54)
$$\frac{14}{-\boxed{}}$$
0

55)
$$\frac{\boxed{}}{-\ 11}$$
5

56)
$$\frac{14}{-\boxed{}}$$
2

57)
$$\frac{\boxed{}}{-\ 10}$$
6

58)
$$\frac{19}{-\boxed{}}$$
3

59)
$$\frac{\boxed{}}{-\ 14}$$
3

60)
$$\frac{16}{-\boxed{}}$$
2

Page 159

Score: /60

Name:

Time :

1)
```
  □
- 18
───
  2
```

2)
```
  20
-  □
───
  1
```

3)
```
  □
- 10
───
  5
```

4)
```
  15
-  □
───
  2
```

5)
```
  □
- 15
───
  3
```

6)
```
  20
-  □
───
  7
```

7)
```
  □
- 11
───
  7
```

8)
```
  16
-  □
───
  0
```

9)
```
  □
- 10
───
  2
```

10)
```
  15
-  □
───
  4
```

11)
```
  □
- 10
───
  6
```

12)
```
  14
-  □
───
  4
```

13)
```
  □
- 11
───
  2
```

14)
```
  18
-  □
───
  8
```

15)
```
  □
- 17
───
  1
```

16)
```
  18
-  □
───
  8
```

17)
```
  □
- 19
───
  1
```

18)
```
  20
-  □
───
 10
```

19)
```
  □
- 14
───
  3
```

20)
```
  13
-  □
───
  2
```

21)
```
  □
- 17
───
  2
```

22)
```
  14
-  □
───
  4
```

23)
```
  □
- 10
───
  9
```

24)
```
  19
-  □
───
  7
```

25)
```
  □
- 12
───
  7
```

26)
```
  17
-  □
───
  0
```

27)
```
  □
- 13
───
  1
```

28)
```
  15
-  □
───
  4
```

29)
```
  □
- 15
───
  5
```

30)
```
  16
-  □
───
  0
```

31)
```
  □
- 16
───
  3
```

32)
```
  20
-  □
───
  6
```

33)
```
  □
- 13
───
  3
```

34)
```
  14
-  □
───
  2
```

35)
```
  □
- 13
───
  3
```

36)
```
  20
-  □
───
  3
```

37)
```
  □
- 17
───
  0
```

38)
```
  17
-  □
───
  6
```

39)
```
  □
- 11
───
  5
```

40)
```
  20
-  □
───
 10
```

41)
```
  □
- 11
───
  5
```

42)
```
  15
-  □
───
  5
```

43)
```
  □
- 12
───
  4
```

44)
```
  15
-  □
───
  3
```

45)
```
  □
- 19
───
  1
```

46)
```
  17
-  □
───
  6
```

47)
```
  □
- 12
───
  5
```

48)
```
  11
-  □
───
  1
```

49)
```
  □
- 18
───
  1
```

50)
```
  14
-  □
───
  1
```

51)
```
  □
- 11
───
  4
```

52)
```
  12
-  □
───
  0
```

53)
```
  □
- 17
───
  0
```

54)
```
  19
-  □
───
  7
```

55)
```
  □
- 19
───
  0
```

56)
```
  19
-  □
───
  1
```

57)
```
  □
- 11
───
  5
```

58)
```
  19
-  □
───
  1
```

59)
```
  □
- 13
───
  7
```

60)
```
  15
-  □
───
  2
```

Page 1, Item 1:

(1)10 (2)5 (3)9 (4)7 (5)1 (6)6 (7)5 (8)5 (9)0 (10)7 (11)6 (12)6 (13)5 (14)1 (15)4 (16)2 (17)8 (18)2 (19)4 (20)7 (21)5 (22)2 (23)8 (24)4 (25)6 (26)5 (27)6 (28)6 (29)7 (30)7 (31)5 (32)3 (33)6 (34)5 (35)9 (36)5 (37)5 (38)5 (39)6 (40)8 (41)0 (42)3 (43)8 (44)4 (45)7 (46)9 (47)3 (48)7 (49)10 (50)5 (51)3 (52)7 (53)6 (54)5 (55)6 (56)8 (57)5 (58)3 (59)5 (60)3

Page 2, Item 1:

(1)3 (2)6 (3)4 (4)3 (5)4 (6)7 (7)7 (8)1 (9)4 (10)8 (11)5 (12)5 (13)6 (14)5 (15)5 (16)4 (17)5 (18)4 (19)5 (20)3 (21)2 (22)5 (23)5 (24)1 (25)6 (26)8 (27)6 (28)5 (29)8 (30)3 (31)4 (32)7 (33)3 (34)6 (35)7 (36)6 (37)4 (38)5 (39)5 (40)1 (41)1 (42)2 (43)8 (44)7 (45)4 (46)9 (47)9 (48)1 (49)3 (50)9 (51)9 (52)4 (53)1 (54)8 (55)4 (56)1 (57)5 (58)5 (59)6 (60)7

Page 3, Item 1:

(1)7 (2)9 (3)8 (4)8 (5)6 (6)8 (7)8 (8)9 (9)7 (10)6 (11)6 (12)6 (13)5 (14)4 (15)6 (16)6 (17)8 (18)4 (19)8 (20)3 (21)4 (22)8 (23)4 (24)6 (25)5 (26)4 (27)3 (28)7 (29)2 (30)9 (31)5 (32)2 (33)2 (34)6 (35)7 (36)6 (37)5 (38)8 (39)3 (40)1 (41)3 (42)6 (43)2 (44)2 (45)6 (46)8 (47)7 (48)1 (49)5 (50)6 (51)3 (52)6 (53)7 (54)7 (55)7 (56)5 (57)6 (58)4 (59)5 (60)7

Page 4, Item 1:

(1)7 (2)9 (3)7 (4)5 (5)5 (6)5 (7)3 (8)2 (9)3 (10)6 (11)3 (12)10 (13)8 (14)6 (15)3 (16)6 (17)5 (18)10 (19)5 (20)4 (21)9 (22)7 (23)0 (24)5 (25)5 (26)6 (27)4 (28)6 (29)8 (30)8 (31)8 (32)5 (33)6 (34)5 (35)6 (36)3 (37)8 (38)4 (39)6 (40)8 (41)6 (42)4 (43)3 (44)6

(45)1 (46)4 (47)1 (48)9 (49)9 (50)9 (51)10 (52)9 (53)8 (54)1 (55)10 (56)6 (57)3 (58)6 (59)8 (60)7

Page 5, Item 1:

(1)7 (2)5 (3)7 (4)8 (5)4 (6)5 (7)6 (8)4 (9)7 (10)3 (11)2 (12)2 (13)6 (14)8 (15)0 (16)8 (17)1 (18)3 (19)10 (20)8 (21)3 (22)7 (23)5 (24)8 (25)6 (26)0 (27)7 (28)4 (29)5 (30)1 (31)6 (32)5 (33)5 (34)1 (35)8 (36)1 (37)2 (38)5 (39)3 (40)2 (41)1 (42)8 (43)7 (44)3 (45)3 (46)5 (47)7 (48)6 (49)3 (50)4 (51)4 (52)3 (53)4 (54)2 (55)5 (56)5 (57)3 (58)0 (59)9 (60)7

Page 6, Item 1:

(1)4 (2)9 (3)3 (4)7 (5)7 (6)6 (7)4 (8)5 (9)6 (10)1 (11)2 (12)6 (13)7 (14)5 (15)3 (16)6 (17)5 (18)10 (19)6 (20)0 (21)10 (22)5 (23)6 (24)7 (25)2 (26)2 (27)6 (28)7 (29)7 (30)6 (31)2 (32)4 (33)4 (34)5 (35)3 (36)2 (37)5 (38)5 (39)2 (40)6 (41)9 (42)4 (43)2 (44)0 (45)2 (46)6 (47)3 (48)7 (49)8 (50)8 (51)8 (52)5 (53)7 (54)9 (55)10 (56)5 (57)8 (58)2 (59)4 (60)4

Page 7, Item 1:

(1)6 (2)7 (3)3 (4)1 (5)2 (6)5 (7)6 (8)8 (9)1 (10)1 (11)4 (12)2 (13)7 (14)3 (15)5 (16)7 (17)7 (18)7 (19)4 (20)7 (21)7 (22)2 (23)4 (24)6 (25)4 (26)5 (27)7 (28)9 (29)3 (30)9 (31)5 (32)1 (33)6 (34)5 (35)3 (36)7 (37)9 (38)6 (39)3 (40)5 (41)5 (42)5 (43)7 (44)6

(45)6 (46)7 (47)7 (48)7 (49)6 (50)7 (51)4
(52)6 (53)6 (54)4 (55)1 (56)5 (57)5 (58)4
(59)10 (60)5

Page 8, Item 1:

(1)5 (2)3 (3)4 (4)8 (5)9 (6)2 (7)4 (8)4 (9)4
(10)5 (11)10 (12)7 (13)8 (14)4 (15)9 (16)2
(17)6 (18)5 (19)9 (20)5 (21)4 (22)1 (23)8
(24)9 (25)6 (26)6 (27)1 (28)2 (29)3 (30)6
(31)5 (32)6 (33)5 (34)2 (35)4 (36)2 (37)1
(38)9 (39)2 (40)5 (41)0 (42)6 (43)4 (44)6
(45)2 (46)6 (47)3 (48)5 (49)8 (50)1 (51)3
(52)6 (53)5 (54)5 (55)5 (56)3 (57)9 (58)3
(59)2 (60)1

Page 9, Item 1:

(1)6 (2)4 (3)3 (4)6 (5)9 (6)4 (7)3 (8)3 (9)5
(10)6 (11)7 (12)4 (13)6 (14)4 (15)7 (16)5
(17)6 (18)6 (19)4 (20)10 (21)5 (22)3 (23)6
(24)5 (25)4 (26)3 (27)6 (28)5 (29)5 (30)5
(31)6 (32)1 (33)7 (34)5 (35)8 (36)1 (37)7
(38)1 (39)6 (40)7 (41)7 (42)8 (43)5 (44)7
(45)8 (46)8 (47)10 (48)2 (49)2 (50)6 (51)6
(52)10 (53)8 (54)2 (55)10 (56)6 (57)6
(58)4 (59)2 (60)8

Page 10, Item 1:

(1)5 (2)3 (3)3 (4)5 (5)6 (6)8 (7)4 (8)2 (9)5
(10)4 (11)2 (12)1 (13)8 (14)5 (15)5 (16)3
(17)2 (18)8 (19)8 (20)6 (21)3 (22)6 (23)7
(24)10 (25)4 (26)6 (27)6 (28)2 (29)9 (30)5
(31)7 (32)3 (33)1 (34)7 (35)8 (36)0 (37)6
(38)4 (39)7 (40)6 (41)7 (42)3 (43)5 (44)5
(45)4 (46)2 (47)5 (48)5 (49)5 (50)5 (51)0
(52)5 (53)7 (54)1 (55)2 (56)5 (57)9 (58)5
(59)5 (60)5

Page 11, Item 1:

(1)5 (2)4 (3)5 (4)5 (5)3 (6)0 (7)0 (8)0 (9)2
(10)2 (11)2 (12)4 (13)1 (14)3 (15)1 (16)3
(17)2 (18)1 (19)2 (20)2 (21)2 (22)1 (23)2

(24)3 (25)3 (26)2 (27)4 (28)3 (29)2 (30)0
(31)1 (32)4 (33)5 (34)0 (35)0 (36)0 (37)3
(38)5 (39)1 (40)2 (41)2 (42)5 (43)3 (44)3
(45)4 (46)5 (47)0 (48)4 (49)0 (50)3 (51)5
(52)3 (53)1 (54)3 (55)2 (56)4 (57)3 (58)1
(59)3 (60)1

Page 12, Item 1:

(1)3 (2)4 (3)4 (4)5 (5)5 (6)1 (7)2 (8)2 (9)5
(10)4 (11)5 (12)0 (13)1 (14)5 (15)3 (16)3
(17)5 (18)4 (19)0 (20)1 (21)0 (22)1 (23)0
(24)2 (25)3 (26)3 (27)2 (28)2 (29)0 (30)1
(31)1 (32)1 (33)5 (34)0 (35)2 (36)0 (37)5
(38)1 (39)0 (40)3 (41)0 (42)1 (43)4 (44)5
(45)1 (46)1 (47)4 (48)2 (49)3 (50)5 (51)0
(52)4 (53)3 (54)2 (55)1 (56)5 (57)4 (58)5
(59)5 (60)5

Page 13, Item 1:

(1)5 (2)0 (3)2 (4)1 (5)5 (6)2 (7)1 (8)3 (9)1
(10)2 (11)0 (12)0 (13)5 (14)3 (15)2 (16)0
(17)5 (18)3 (19)0 (20)1 (21)3 (22)1 (23)1
(24)2 (25)2 (26)4 (27)1 (28)5 (29)1 (30)4
(31)1 (32)2 (33)0 (34)5 (35)2 (36)5 (37)0
(38)4 (39)1 (40)4 (41)1 (42)4 (43)3 (44)4
(45)4 (46)4 (47)1 (48)0 (49)1 (50)4 (51)3
(52)3 (53)4 (54)1 (55)0 (56)5 (57)1 (58)3
(59)3 (60)2

Page 14, Item 1:

(1)5 (2)4 (3)3 (4)4 (5)2 (6)0 (7)4 (8)3 (9)3
(10)5 (11)3 (12)1 (13)3 (14)0 (15)2 (16)0
(17)1 (18)4 (19)5 (20)1 (21)4 (22)2 (23)0

(24)5 (25)4 (26)1 (27)2 (28)5 (29)0 (30)5
(31)1 (32)1 (33)5 (34)4 (35)2 (36)5 (37)2
(38)1 (39)2 (40)0 (41)2 (42)4 (43)5 (44)3
(45)2 (46)2 (47)5 (48)4 (49)1 (50)1 (51)5
(52)2 (53)5 (54)3 (55)3 (56)3 (57)0 (58)1
(59)0 (60)5
Page 15, Item 1:
(1)5 (2)4 (3)2 (4)1 (5)4 (6)1 (7)3 (8)3 (9)0
(10)4 (11)3 (12)3 (13)0 (14)0 (15)5 (16)4
(17)4 (18)3 (19)1 (20)2 (21)1 (22)5 (23)4
(24)2 (25)4 (26)0 (27)0 (28)0 (29)1 (30)4
(31)4 (32)0 (33)5 (34)0 (35)2 (36)4 (37)5
(38)0 (39)1 (40)3 (41)4 (42)0 (43)2 (44)1
(45)5 (46)1 (47)3 (48)4 (49)0 (50)4 (51)3
(52)5 (53)5 (54)1 (55)1 (56)1 (57)2 (58)1
(59)4 (60)3
Page 16, Item 1:
(1)0 (2)5 (3)0 (4)2 (5)3 (6)3 (7)0 (8)2 (9)5
(10)0 (11)5 (12)2 (13)1 (14)5 (15)0 (16)1
(17)5 (18)5 (19)4 (20)4 (21)0 (22)4 (23)2
(24)3 (25)4 (26)5 (27)4 (28)2 (29)5 (30)4
(31)1 (32)2 (33)1 (34)0 (35)0 (36)0 (37)5
(38)4 (39)5 (40)2 (41)5 (42)1 (43)4 (44)0
(45)3 (46)4 (47)4 (48)1 (49)2 (50)0 (51)4
(52)0 (53)2 (54)5 (55)3 (56)1 (57)2 (58)3
(59)2 (60)4
Page 17, Item 1:
(1)0 (2)4 (3)2 (4)1 (5)5 (6)1 (7)1 (8)3 (9)5
(10)0 (11)3 (12)2 (13)3 (14)2 (15)0 (16)3
(17)5 (18)4 (19)5 (20)4 (21)5 (22)4 (23)1
(24)1 (25)5 (26)1 (27)2 (28)2 (29)4 (30)2
(31)4 (32)3 (33)5 (34)1 (35)4 (36)2 (37)3
(38)5 (39)3 (40)4 (41)5 (42)2 (43)1 (44)3
(45)0 (46)4 (47)1 (48)3 (49)1 (50)3 (51)5
(52)3 (53)0 (54)2 (55)4 (56)0 (57)1 (58)2
(59)3 (60)0
Page 18, Item 1:

(1)5 (2)1 (3)1 (4)2 (5)3 (6)5 (7)5 (8)3 (9)2
(10)4 (11)1 (12)1 (13)1 (14)3 (15)5 (16)0
(17)1 (18)0 (19)5 (20)0 (21)3 (22)3 (23)0
(24)2 (25)1 (26)4 (27)0 (28)5 (29)0 (30)4
(31)3 (32)3 (33)3 (34)2 (35)1 (36)1 (37)0
(38)0 (39)0 (40)3 (41)2 (42)3 (43)3 (44)1
(45)1 (46)2 (47)3 (48)5 (49)3 (50)4 (51)0
(52)1 (53)3 (54)5 (55)3 (56)2 (57)3 (58)1
(59)4 (60)5
Page 19, Item 1:
(1)3 (2)1 (3)5 (4)0 (5)5 (6)2 (7)3 (8)1 (9)0
(10)3 (11)1 (12)3 (13)2 (14)2 (15)0 (16)4
(17)0 (18)1 (19)3 (20)2 (21)2 (22)0 (23)4
(24)3 (25)3 (26)0 (27)0 (28)5 (29)2 (30)2
(31)4 (32)1 (33)5 (34)3 (35)5 (36)0 (37)1
(38)1 (39)4 (40)2 (41)5 (42)5 (43)5 (44)0
(45)0 (46)3 (47)0 (48)5 (49)1 (50)3 (51)0
(52)4 (53)4 (54)4 (55)0 (56)2 (57)2 (58)4
(59)5 (60)5
Page 20, Item 1:
(1)5 (2)5 (3)1 (4)2 (5)5 (6)5 (7)5 (8)0 (9)2
(10)0 (11)5 (12)0 (13)3 (14)3 (15)5 (16)4
(17)1 (18)5 (19)0 (20)5 (21)3 (22)5 (23)4
(24)1 (25)4 (26)0 (27)2 (28)3 (29)2 (30)3
(31)0 (32)3 (33)4 (34)5 (35)2 (36)0 (37)3
(38)3 (39)5 (40)5 (41)0 (42)2 (43)5 (44)3
(45)5 (46)3 (47)1 (48)4 (49)5 (50)4 (51)1
(52)4 (53)5 (54)5 (55)5 (56)5 (57)5 (58)1
(59)2 (60)0
Page 21, Item 1:

(1)8 (2)9 (3)4 (4)5 (5)8 (6)2 (7)3 (8)0 (9)7
(10)6 (11)7 (12)12 (13)4 (14)5 (15)3 (16)4
(17)9 (18)10 (19)7 (20)6 (21)3 (22)12
(23)3 (24)0 (25)5 (26)13 (27)10 (28)12
(29)14 (30)3 (31)10 (32)4 (33)5 (34)4
(35)0 (36)6 (37)9 (38)12 (39)12 (40)3
(41)5 (42)3 (43)5 (44)4 (45)13 (46)3
(47)10 (48)4 (49)7 (50)5 (51)2 (52)6 (53)4
(54)2 (55)10 (56)4 (57)5 (58)10 (59)7
(60)7

Page 22, Item 1:
(1)0 (2)11 (3)6 (4)7 (5)12 (6)6 (7)6 (8)8
(9)10 (10)7 (11)10 (12)8 (13)11 (14)2
(15)9 (16)5 (17)5 (18)9 (19)10 (20)5
(21)14 (22)11 (23)8 (24)11 (25)8 (26)12
(27)6 (28)6 (29)4 (30)6 (31)3 (32)8 (33)8
(34)6 (35)10 (36)7 (37)6 (38)2 (39)6 (40)4
(41)9 (42)2 (43)10 (44)3 (45)7 (46)4 (47)4
(48)6 (49)8 (50)10 (51)8 (52)11 (53)1
(54)8 (55)8 (56)10 (57)7 (58)10 (59)7
(60)5

Page 23, Item 1:
(1)5 (2)6 (3)6 (4)3 (5)11 (6)4 (7)6 (8)13
(9)7 (10)3 (11)13 (12)12 (13)5 (14)5 (15)0
(16)6 (17)9 (18)7 (19)6 (20)0 (21)8 (22)10
(23)11 (24)5 (25)10 (26)7 (27)7 (28)8
(29)1 (30)4 (31)12 (32)7 (33)6 (34)7 (35)8
(36)6 (37)13 (38)7 (39)5 (40)6 (41)8 (42)7
(43)3 (44)7 (45)11 (46)12 (47)5 (48)2
(49)12 (50)7 (51)6 (52)4 (53)8 (54)6 (55)3
(56)5 (57)7 (58)7 (59)9 (60)6

Page 24, Item 1:
(1)6 (2)12 (3)10 (4)5 (5)6 (6)3 (7)9 (8)3
(9)3 (10)1 (11)10 (12)5 (13)5 (14)8 (15)9
(16)9 (17)7 (18)5 (19)5 (20)12 (21)11
(22)3 (23)8 (24)7 (25)9 (26)1 (27)4 (28)8
(29)0 (30)10 (31)9 (32)9 (33)6 (34)1 (35)3

(36)7 (37)5 (38)6 (39)2 (40)3 (41)5 (42)8
(43)9 (44)6 (45)13 (46)8 (47)2 (48)8 (49)4
(50)3 (51)14 (52)12 (53)9 (54)4 (55)4
(56)11 (57)0 (58)10 (59)9 (60)4

Page 25, Item 1:
(1)11 (2)11 (3)9 (4)11 (5)8 (6)9 (7)9 (8)4
(9)4 (10)9 (11)5 (12)9 (13)4 (14)9 (15)7
(16)7 (17)5 (18)14 (19)7 (20)3 (21)6 (22)5
(23)5 (24)7 (25)9 (26)10 (27)5 (28)8 (29)4
(30)10 (31)1 (32)5 (33)2 (34)7 (35)7
(36)12 (37)11 (38)0 (39)7 (40)8 (41)9
(42)8 (43)2 (44)4 (45)5 (46)8 (47)6 (48)3
(49)10 (50)5 (51)9 (52)4 (53)6 (54)10
(55)3 (56)14 (57)9 (58)4 (59)11 (60)5

Page 26, Item 1:
(1)5 (2)8 (3)8 (4)11 (5)6 (6)5 (7)4 (8)6 (9)6
(10)2 (11)6 (12)9 (13)6 (14)13 (15)4 (16)9
(17)10 (18)7 (19)8 (20)8 (21)7 (22)3 (23)5
(24)6 (25)2 (26)11 (27)5 (28)7 (29)2 (30)6
(31)14 (32)7 (33)11 (34)8 (35)11 (36)7
(37)3 (38)6 (39)11 (40)8 (41)11 (42)8
(43)10 (44)9 (45)6 (46)9 (47)9 (48)12
(49)9 (50)3 (51)5 (52)4 (53)6 (54)8 (55)12
(56)6 (57)6 (58)12 (59)7 (60)12

Page 27, Item 1:
(1)7 (2)2 (3)4 (4)8 (5)8 (6)3 (7)4 (8)4 (9)4
(10)8 (11)9 (12)7 (13)7 (14)8 (15)3 (16)4
(17)14 (18)1 (19)3 (20)6 (21)1 (22)10
(23)7 (24)8 (25)6 (26)7 (27)13 (28)7 (29)7
(30)6 (31)14 (32)8 (33)8 (34)7 (35)4 (36)9
(37)3 (38)12 (39)12 (40)7 (41)8 (42)7
(43)1 (44)7 (45)1 (46)6 (47)8 (48)5 (49)9
(50)11 (51)5

(52)8 (53)10 (54)8 (55)8 (56)3 (57)12
(58)8 (59)6 (60)4

Page 28, Item 1:

(1)8 (2)5 (3)9 (4)5 (5)4 (6)10 (7)2 (8)8 (9)8
(10)9 (11)6 (12)6 (13)9 (14)10 (15)4
(16)11 (17)8 (18)6 (19)9 (20)9 (21)10
(22)14 (23)0 (24)8 (25)8 (26)7 (27)8 (28)7
(29)6 (30)10 (31)6 (32)8 (33)4 (34)13
(35)11 (36)9 (37)4 (38)7 (39)1 (40)9
(41)14 (42)5 (43)10 (44)10 (45)6 (46)5
(47)3 (48)7 (49)7 (50)2 (51)8 (52)8 (53)0
(54)10 (55)2 (56)12 (57)9 (58)7 (59)9
(60)6

Page 29, Item 1:

(1)8 (2)10 (3)8 (4)12 (5)8 (6)6 (7)11 (8)7
(9)11 (10)8 (11)8 (12)6 (13)8 (14)9 (15)5
(16)10 (17)8 (18)8 (19)9 (20)6 (21)13
(22)4 (23)4 (24)12 (25)9 (26)5 (27)2 (28)6
(29)9 (30)2 (31)8 (32)14 (33)7 (34)14
(35)8 (36)6 (37)1 (38)9 (39)11 (40)7 (41)7
(42)13 (43)5 (44)9 (45)7 (46)8 (47)7 (48)3
(49)13 (50)5 (51)10 (52)3 (53)6 (54)8
(55)12 (56)5 (57)12 (58)4 (59)8 (60)8

Page 30, Item 1:

(1)11 (2)13 (3)9 (4)5 (5)14 (6)10 (7)2 (8)5
(9)14 (10)8 (11)4 (12)8 (13)10 (14)13
(15)7 (16)4 (17)6 (18)8 (19)1 (20)7 (21)9
(22)11 (23)9 (24)9 (25)4 (26)3 (27)6 (28)0
(29)1 (30)5 (31)5 (32)7 (33)12 (34)8 (35)8
(36)9 (37)11 (38)4 (39)8 (40)12 (41)8
(42)8 (43)5 (44)11 (45)11 (46)11 (47)1
(48)8 (49)8 (50)0 (51)4 (52)11 (53)9 (54)7
(55)4 (56)8 (57)6 (58)10 (59)5 (60)10

Page 31, Item 1:

(1)6 (2)2 (3)0 (4)4 (5)3 (6)1 (7)4 (8)2 (9)4
(10)0 (11)7 (12)4 (13)6 (14)5 (15)4 (16)6
(17)0 (18)0 (19)0 (20)1 (21)1 (22)1 (23)7

(24)1 (25)3 (26)6 (27)1 (28)6 (29)4 (30)5
(31)3 (32)2 (33)3 (34)7 (35)6 (36)2 (37)1
(38)7 (39)0 (40)1 (41)0 (42)6 (43)0 (44)5
(45)5 (46)6 (47)0 (48)5 (49)1 (50)7 (51)7
(52)0 (53)0 (54)5 (55)6 (56)6 (57)7 (58)0
(59)3 (60)4

Page 32, Item 1:

(1)1 (2)2 (3)7 (4)3 (5)0 (6)4 (7)4 (8)6 (9)2
(10)6 (11)0 (12)4 (13)7 (14)6 (15)5 (16)1
(17)6 (18)6 (19)2 (20)1 (21)4 (22)7 (23)2
(24)4 (25)6 (26)4 (27)6 (28)0 (29)5 (30)5
(31)4 (32)0 (33)2 (34)0 (35)4 (36)7 (37)4
(38)1 (39)0 (40)5 (41)3 (42)7 (43)7 (44)5
(45)1 (46)1 (47)3 (48)1 (49)4 (50)1 (51)3
(52)7 (53)4 (54)2 (55)6 (56)4 (57)6 (58)2
(59)0 (60)0

Page 33, Item 1:

(1)5 (2)3 (3)6 (4)5 (5)6 (6)4 (7)3 (8)2 (9)1
(10)3 (11)7 (12)5 (13)1 (14)2 (15)2 (16)0
(17)0 (18)7 (19)0 (20)5 (21)3 (22)2 (23)3
(24)6 (25)1 (26)2 (27)7 (28)0 (29)0 (30)7
(31)4 (32)7 (33)5 (34)0 (35)3 (36)4 (37)0
(38)4 (39)5 (40)5 (41)1 (42)4 (43)0 (44)0
(45)4 (46)5 (47)3 (48)5 (49)3 (50)4 (51)5
(52)6 (53)5 (54)0 (55)4 (56)0 (57)0 (58)5
(59)6 (60)4

Page 34, Item 1:

(1)1 (2)1 (3)4 (4)1 (5)5 (6)0 (7)0 (8)7 (9)0
(10)4 (11)0 (12)5 (13)7 (14)7 (15)5 (16)1
(17)0 (18)6 (19)7 (20)6 (21)6 (22)3 (23)0

(24)6 (25)5 (26)4 (27)7 (28)1 (29)1 (30)5
(31)7 (32)2 (33)6 (34)6 (35)3 (36)0 (37)5
(38)0 (39)4 (40)2 (41)5 (42)7 (43)3 (44)3
(45)6 (46)0 (47)7 (48)6 (49)7 (50)7 (51)4
(52)6 (53)3 (54)1 (55)7 (56)4 (57)6 (58)0
(59)0 (60)4

Page 35, Item 1:

(1)0 (2)6 (3)4 (4)2 (5)7 (6)2 (7)0 (8)2 (9)6
(10)4 (11)1 (12)4 (13)3 (14)3 (15)2 (16)4
(17)3 (18)4 (19)3 (20)3 (21)6 (22)2 (23)3
(24)0 (25)3 (26)7 (27)6 (28)0 (29)3 (30)0
(31)3 (32)3 (33)2 (34)4 (35)3 (36)1 (37)7
(38)7 (39)2 (40)1 (41)0 (42)6 (43)6 (44)6
(45)6 (46)4 (47)2 (48)7 (49)4 (50)6 (51)0
(52)4 (53)5 (54)0 (55)4 (56)1 (57)7 (58)2
(59)1 (60)0

Page 36, Item 1:

(1)7 (2)4 (3)3 (4)0 (5)0 (6)0 (7)7 (8)5 (9)4
(10)2 (11)7 (12)5 (13)3 (14)3 (15)4 (16)5
(17)6 (18)0 (19)5 (20)6 (21)2 (22)4 (23)6
(24)7 (25)5 (26)7 (27)6 (28)3 (29)7 (30)3
(31)3 (32)3 (33)3 (34)2 (35)3 (36)3 (37)4
(38)5 (39)6 (40)2 (41)5 (42)6 (43)1 (44)3
(45)5 (46)5 (47)7 (48)0 (49)7 (50)3 (51)7
(52)1 (53)2 (54)6 (55)2 (56)5 (57)7 (58)2
(59)2 (60)2

Page 37, Item 1:

(1)2 (2)1 (3)6 (4)7 (5)4 (6)6 (7)1 (8)6 (9)4
(10)1 (11)3 (12)7 (13)5 (14)5 (15)2 (16)6
(17)6 (18)3 (19)4 (20)0 (21)5 (22)0 (23)3
(24)1 (25)4 (26)5 (27)6 (28)5 (29)0 (30)7
(31)6 (32)7 (33)1 (34)2 (35)3 (36)1 (37)5
(38)6 (39)1 (40)3 (41)3 (42)4 (43)1 (44)6
(45)2 (46)2 (47)5 (48)5 (49)4 (50)5 (51)6
(52)4 (53)0 (54)5 (55)6 (56)6 (57)7 (58)2
(59)7 (60)3

Page 38, Item 1:

(1)6 (2)1 (3)0 (4)1 (5)6 (6)5 (7)5 (8)7 (9)3
(10)6 (11)6 (12)5 (13)0 (14)2 (15)5 (16)1
(17)4 (18)2 (19)1 (20)4 (21)1 (22)5 (23)6
(24)7 (25)6 (26)5 (27)4 (28)6 (29)0 (30)7
(31)1 (32)3 (33)7 (34)4 (35)3 (36)2 (37)1
(38)0 (39)6 (40)6 (41)7 (42)7 (43)3 (44)1
(45)6 (46)0 (47)6 (48)1 (49)0 (50)4 (51)1
(52)1 (53)0 (54)7 (55)1 (56)4 (57)4 (58)5
(59)7 (60)1

Page 39, Item 1:

(1)7 (2)7 (3)2 (4)3 (5)0 (6)6 (7)6 (8)3 (9)6
(10)1 (11)0 (12)5 (13)1 (14)0 (15)4 (16)2
(17)2 (18)5 (19)3 (20)6 (21)0 (22)5 (23)0
(24)2 (25)4 (26)7 (27)6 (28)5 (29)0 (30)4
(31)6 (32)2 (33)2 (34)5 (35)0 (36)2 (37)3
(38)0 (39)7 (40)5 (41)4 (42)3 (43)1 (44)3
(45)2 (46)5 (47)2 (48)7 (49)6 (50)3 (51)1
(52)0 (53)4 (54)6 (55)7 (56)5 (57)1 (58)2
(59)2 (60)5

Page 40, Item 1:

(1)0 (2)0 (3)7 (4)5 (5)5 (6)6 (7)3 (8)4 (9)0
(10)7 (11)4 (12)7 (13)1 (14)3 (15)1 (16)2
(17)7 (18)3 (19)1 (20)7 (21)2 (22)6 (23)4
(24)1 (25)5 (26)3 (27)1 (28)7 (29)5 (30)4
(31)3 (32)7 (33)7 (34)7 (35)2 (36)3 (37)0
(38)5 (39)6 (40)3 (41)7 (42)4 (43)0 (44)4
(45)4 (46)7 (47)6 (48)0 (49)7 (50)6 (51)3
(52)2 (53)2 (54)5 (55)2 (56)1 (57)4 (58)3
(59)2 (60)5

Page 41, Item 1:

(1)7 (2)4 (3)12 (4)7 (5)11 (6)0 (7)8 (8)14
(9)14 (10)5 (11)8 (12)16 (13)9 (14)9
(15)12 (16)3 (17)6 (18)19 (19)5 (20)14
(21)4 (22)11 (23)8 (24)8 (25)8 (26)10
(27)6 (28)6 (29)13 (30)11 (31)19 (32)9
(33)9 (34)6 (35)17 (36)12 (37)4 (38)9
(39)13 (40)1 (41)6 (42)8 (43)11 (44)13
(45)14 (46)12 (47)4 (48)10 (49)11 (50)8
(51)11 (52)7 (53)6 (54)13 (55)16 (56)2
(57)8 (58)7 (59)10 (60)8

Page 42, Item 1:
(1)14 (2)18 (3)0 (4)9 (5)15 (6)14 (7)6 (8)9
(9)12 (10)9 (11)6 (12)10 (13)11 (14)18
(15)11 (16)2 (17)17 (18)9 (19)7 (20)8
(21)10 (22)9 (23)1 (24)10 (25)2 (26)13
(27)5 (28)8 (29)10 (30)2 (31)15 (32)4
(33)15 (34)1 (35)7 (36)13 (37)3 (38)11
(39)7 (40)10 (41)13 (42)8 (43)12 (44)9
(45)20 (46)16 (47)10 (48)7 (49)16 (50)10
(51)8 (52)9 (53)11 (54)13 (55)19 (56)10
(57)11 (58)6 (59)7 (60)5

Page 43, Item 1:
(1)0 (2)20 (3)5 (4)12 (5)18 (6)10 (7)9 (8)16
(9)10 (10)10 (11)11 (12)6 (13)9 (14)14
(15)18 (16)14 (17)15 (18)17 (19)15 (20)7
(21)8 (22)5 (23)9 (24)7 (25)9 (26)6 (27)19
(28)14 (29)10 (30)10 (31)8 (32)11 (33)12
(34)5 (35)1 (36)7 (37)8 (38)11 (39)7
(40)11 (41)15 (42)10 (43)19 (44)12 (45)3
(46)2 (47)1 (48)15 (49)10 (50)10 (51)18
(52)3 (53)14 (54)10 (55)16 (56)5 (57)8
(58)20 (59)10 (60)5

Page 44, Item 1:
(1)8 (2)5 (3)9 (4)10 (5)11 (6)10 (7)3 (8)12
(9)9 (10)13 (11)8 (12)7 (13)9 (14)5 (15)16
(16)15 (17)4 (18)8 (19)12 (20)5 (21)14
(22)13 (23)11 (24)10 (25)10 (26)12 (27)19

(28)7 (29)12 (30)12 (31)13 (32)10 (33)8
(34)10 (35)14 (36)12 (37)9 (38)9 (39)14
(40)12 (41)6 (42)14 (43)3 (44)12 (45)3
(46)18 (47)7 (48)15 (49)13 (50)3 (51)6
(52)1 (53)12 (54)9 (55)11 (56)4 (57)9
(58)3 (59)4 (60)8

Page 45, Item 1:
(1)10 (2)11 (3)15 (4)7 (5)2 (6)8 (7)8 (8)12
(9)18 (10)15 (11)5 (12)12 (13)11 (14)12
(15)11 (16)9 (17)10 (18)11 (19)1 (20)6
(21)10 (22)12 (23)12 (24)5 (25)17 (26)7
(27)6 (28)12 (29)12 (30)12 (31)14 (32)11
(33)9 (34)11 (35)8 (36)17 (37)9 (38)9
(39)8 (40)1 (41)12 (42)11 (43)7 (44)11
(45)11 (46)2 (47)6 (48)10 (49)13 (50)3
(51)14 (52)9 (53)9 (54)4 (55)15 (56)12
(57)10 (58)8 (59)6 (60)10

Page 46, Item 1:
(1)17 (2)16 (3)8 (4)7 (5)9 (6)7 (7)14 (8)9
(9)3 (10)10 (11)6 (12)10 (13)5 (14)15
(15)9 (16)11 (17)12 (18)10 (19)11 (20)13
(21)9 (22)10 (23)10 (24)9 (25)10 (26)10
(27)12 (28)5 (29)9 (30)15 (31)17 (32)13
(33)9 (34)10 (35)6 (36)10 (37)11 (38)2
(39)20 (40)13 (41)4 (42)3 (43)7 (44)3
(45)9 (46)18 (47)10 (48)14 (49)11 (50)13
(51)4 (52)15 (53)14 (54)12 (55)18 (56)10
(57)11 (58)14 (59)16 (60)10

Page 47, Item 1:

(1)10 (2)13 (3)18 (4)13 (5)13 (6)18 (7)15
(8)8 (9)14 (10)17 (11)15 (12)13 (13)13
(14)13 (15)5 (16)1 (17)18 (18)8 (19)13
(20)11 (21)10 (22)9 (23)6 (24)19 (25)2
(26)6 (27)7 (28)12 (29)5 (30)4 (31)11
(32)7 (33)14 (34)13 (35)6 (36)12 (37)9
(38)10 (39)20 (40)7 (41)9 (42)13 (43)13
(44)9 (45)3 (46)12 (47)15 (48)11 (49)9
(50)15 (51)9 (52)16 (53)5 (54)18 (55)8
(56)8 (57)16 (58)10 (59)14 (60)5

Page 48, Item 1:
(1)2 (2)7 (3)2 (4)12 (5)14 (6)17 (7)1 (8)12
(9)10 (10)17 (11)11 (12)7 (13)2 (14)4
(15)5 (16)16 (17)9 (18)9 (19)9 (20)10
(21)12 (22)5 (23)19 (24)14 (25)9 (26)1
(27)10 (28)10 (29)10 (30)17 (31)7 (32)9
(33)9 (34)9 (35)15 (36)14 (37)11 (38)11
(39)12 (40)7 (41)5 (42)7 (43)10 (44)11
(45)18 (46)3 (47)10 (48)5 (49)6 (50)8
(51)17 (52)10 (53)10 (54)11 (55)13 (56)12
(57)2 (58)10 (59)19 (60)3

Page 49, Item 1:
(1)12 (2)0 (3)9 (4)16 (5)11 (6)7 (7)9 (8)11
(9)13 (10)12 (11)16 (12)10 (13)8 (14)13
(15)8 (16)8 (17)5 (18)12 (19)6 (20)9
(21)19 (22)5 (23)3 (24)9 (25)9 (26)8
(27)12 (28)13 (29)8 (30)14 (31)10 (32)5
(33)17 (34)18 (35)15 (36)17 (37)9 (38)12
(39)12 (40)3 (41)4 (42)3 (43)7 (44)14
(45)7 (46)8 (47)13 (48)8 (49)11 (50)13
(51)4 (52)10 (53)10 (54)3 (55)1 (56)9
(57)12 (58)1 (59)8 (60)11

Page 50, Item 1:
(1)7 (2)15 (3)11 (4)5 (5)6 (6)14 (7)11 (8)10
(9)12 (10)12 (11)9 (12)11 (13)7 (14)8
(15)11 (16)14 (17)15 (18)11 (19)16 (20)8
(21)17 (22)11 (23)9 (24)16 (25)1 (26)9

(27)19 (28)11 (29)9 (30)6 (31)14 (32)16
(33)12 (34)10 (35)8 (36)2 (37)4 (38)4
(39)15 (40)11 (41)14 (42)9 (43)11 (44)8
(45)10 (46)8 (47)13 (48)6 (49)1 (50)18
(51)12 (52)6 (53)15 (54)13 (55)8 (56)7
(57)17 (58)9 (59)9 (60)3

Page 51, Item 1:
(1)8 (2)2 (3)8 (4)0 (5)8 (6)1 (7)0 (8)4 (9)10
(10)1 (11)8 (12)10 (13)9 (14)9 (15)4
(16)10 (17)5 (18)9 (19)1 (20)8 (21)10
(22)1 (23)5 (24)4 (25)4 (26)3 (27)10 (28)8
(29)5 (30)2 (31)1 (32)3 (33)0 (34)7 (35)3
(36)2 (37)6 (38)9 (39)7 (40)3 (41)9 (42)0
(43)1 (44)3 (45)9 (46)9 (47)7 (48)10 (49)3
(50)7 (51)6 (52)4 (53)6 (54)1 (55)2 (56)2
(57)9 (58)3 (59)5 (60)5

Page 52, Item 1:
(1)7 (2)1 (3)6 (4)2 (5)9 (6)6 (7)8 (8)0 (9)2
(10)8 (11)2 (12)4 (13)5 (14)7 (15)3 (16)9
(17)5 (18)0 (19)9 (20)3 (21)6 (22)7 (23)10
(24)10 (25)10 (26)3 (27)8 (28)9 (29)4
(30)6 (31)6 (32)9 (33)9 (34)4 (35)3 (36)2
(37)4 (38)7 (39)1 (40)8 (41)7 (42)7 (43)4
(44)4 (45)5 (46)2 (47)4 (48)3 (49)7 (50)9
(51)0 (52)1 (53)5 (54)2 (55)8 (56)2 (57)6
(58)7 (59)6 (60)10

Page 53, Item 1:
(1)8 (2)1 (3)0 (4)10 (5)10 (6)4 (7)5 (8)7
(9)1 (10)1 (11)5 (12)3 (13)1 (14)2 (15)2
(16)9 (17)2 (18)3 (19)6 (20)5 (21)5 (22)5
(23)0 (24)1 (25)1 (26)8 (27)10 (28)0 (29)8

(30)6 (31)0 (32)8 (33)0 (34)9 (35)7 (36)4
(37)10 (38)10 (39)0 (40)4 (41)10 (42)0
(43)9 (44)1 (45)6 (46)4 (47)2 (48)4 (49)7
(50)8 (51)2 (52)0 (53)7 (54)5 (55)8 (56)2
(57)4 (58)4 (59)2 (60)7
Page 54, Item 1:
(1)4 (2)3 (3)6 (4)8 (5)7 (6)3 (7)3 (8)2 (9)1
(10)4 (11)9 (12)6 (13)1 (14)2 (15)0 (16)2
(17)9 (18)10 (19)2 (20)10 (21)4 (22)6
(23)4 (24)4 (25)8 (26)2 (27)1 (28)2 (29)9
(30)2 (31)1 (32)3 (33)9 (34)5 (35)2 (36)2
(37)5 (38)6 (39)9 (40)5 (41)0 (42)9 (43)4
(44)9 (45)4 (46)1 (47)2 (48)7 (49)1 (50)0
(51)1 (52)7 (53)9 (54)3 (55)4 (56)0 (57)7
(58)2 (59)4 (60)4
Page 55, Item 1:
(1)4 (2)0 (3)4 (4)6 (5)7 (6)9 (7)0 (8)8 (9)3
(10)5 (11)2 (12)1 (13)8 (14)3 (15)7 (16)0
(17)1 (18)8 (19)2 (20)1 (21)3 (22)1 (23)3
(24)5 (25)8 (26)10 (27)10 (28)7 (29)2
(30)2 (31)3 (32)2 (33)6 (34)10 (35)2 (36)1
(37)7 (38)9 (39)0 (40)0 (41)9 (42)5 (43)0
(44)6 (45)2 (46)3 (47)9 (48)2 (49)5 (50)10
(51)7 (52)0 (53)8 (54)1 (55)1 (56)9 (57)0
(58)10 (59)8 (60)8
Page 56, Item 1:
(1)7 (2)0 (3)8 (4)6 (5)7 (6)1 (7)4 (8)0 (9)2
(10)8 (11)8 (12)1 (13)3 (14)5 (15)4 (16)5
(17)6 (18)6 (19)9 (20)9 (21)1 (22)7 (23)1
(24)6 (25)4 (26)8 (27)5 (28)8 (29)10 (30)0
(31)0 (32)7 (33)0 (34)1 (35)2 (36)2 (37)1
(38)4 (39)1 (40)10 (41)4 (42)8 (43)0 (44)0
(45)10 (46)1 (47)0 (48)2 (49)2 (50)0
(51)10 (52)3 (53)4 (54)10 (55)0 (56)4
(57)10 (58)9 (59)2 (60)1
Page 57, Item 1:
(1)8 (2)5 (3)2 (4)4 (5)8 (6)2 (7)6 (8)9 (9)2

(10)5 (11)0 (12)9 (13)7 (14)1 (15)9 (16)6
(17)10 (18)10 (19)3 (20)2 (21)4 (22)5
(23)10 (24)2 (25)4 (26)7 (27)3 (28)10
(29)1 (30)7 (31)5 (32)9 (33)5 (34)2 (35)4
(36)1 (37)5 (38)9 (39)3 (40)3 (41)4 (42)10
(43)9 (44)6 (45)5 (46)0 (47)6 (48)7 (49)0
(50)6 (51)6 (52)6 (53)7 (54)6 (55)2 (56)6
(57)6 (58)4 (59)7 (60)5
Page 58, Item 1:
(1)9 (2)8 (3)7 (4)10 (5)4 (6)3 (7)7 (8)7 (9)7
(10)9 (11)9 (12)9 (13)2 (14)1 (15)7 (16)0
(17)9 (18)10 (19)6 (20)5 (21)9 (22)9 (23)7
(24)1 (25)2 (26)0 (27)8 (28)0 (29)0 (30)8
(31)2 (32)10 (33)4 (34)10 (35)6 (36)6
(37)5 (38)3 (39)2 (40)5 (41)8 (42)3 (43)6
(44)3 (45)1 (46)3 (47)10 (48)3 (49)1 (50)3
(51)1 (52)5 (53)4 (54)9 (55)2 (56)2 (57)5
(58)3 (59)0 (60)9
Page 59, Item 1:
(1)8 (2)1 (3)9 (4)0 (5)1 (6)8 (7)8 (8)3 (9)2
(10)5 (11)6 (12)9 (13)0 (14)7 (15)1 (16)8
(17)10 (18)3 (19)0 (20)6 (21)2 (22)1 (23)5
(24)5 (25)0 (26)4 (27)3 (28)10 (29)1 (30)5
(31)3 (32)7 (33)6 (34)5 (35)4 (36)8 (37)3
(38)0 (39)2 (40)2 (41)10 (42)8 (43)8
(44)10 (45)1 (46)0 (47)3 (48)7 (49)9 (50)9
(51)10 (52)10 (53)0 (54)1 (55)1 (56)5
(57)10 (58)4 (59)9 (60)7
Page 60, Item 1:

(1)1 (2)5 (3)2 (4)9 (5)4 (6)9 (7)4 (8)5 (9)6
(10)2 (11)7 (12)9 (13)6 (14)5 (15)8 (16)8
(17)6 (18)4 (19)8 (20)10 (21)10 (22)3
(23)1 (24)8 (25)1 (26)0 (27)4 (28)3 (29)2
(30)8 (31)7 (32)0 (33)4 (34)5 (35)8 (36)0
(37)7 (38)8 (39)8 (40)4 (41)8 (42)1 (43)1
(44)3 (45)4 (46)9 (47)4 (48)3 (49)2 (50)9
(51)0 (52)9 (53)5 (54)10 (55)8 (56)10
(57)8 (58)7 (59)1 (60)10

Page 61, Item 1:

(1)35 (2)34 (3)33 (4)24 (5)39 (6)23 (7)27
(8)32 (9)28 (10)31 (11)31 (12)37 (13)28
(14)25 (15)30 (16)23 (17)23 (18)21 (19)33
(20)28 (21)29 (22)40 (23)27 (24)37 (25)33
(26)33 (27)24 (28)39 (29)22 (30)29 (31)29
(32)21 (33)27 (34)27 (35)30 (36)29 (37)27
(38)21 (39)24 (40)31 (41)28 (42)37 (43)30
(44)25 (45)27 (46)32 (47)24 (48)26 (49)33
(50)39 (51)32 (52)24 (53)39 (54)28 (55)35
(56)32 (57)28 (58)32 (59)30 (60)32

Page 62, Item 1:

(1)28 (2)37 (3)33 (4)33 (5)32 (6)39 (7)26
(8)34 (9)33 (10)35 (11)24 (12)22 (13)27
(14)36 (15)29 (16)30 (17)37 (18)36 (19)24
(20)24 (21)23 (22)31 (23)35 (24)24 (25)29
(26)29 (27)33 (28)24 (29)37 (30)31 (31)36
(32)27 (33)26 (34)28 (35)27 (36)32 (37)31
(38)36 (39)36 (40)34 (41)35 (42)35 (43)32
(44)28 (45)31 (46)32 (47)30 (48)37 (49)23
(50)35 (51)34 (52)30 (53)24 (54)27 (55)22
(56)28 (57)27 (58)34 (59)25 (60)25

Page 63, Item 1:

(1)34 (2)28 (3)30 (4)33 (5)28 (6)40 (7)31
(8)24 (9)26 (10)25 (11)33 (12)32 (13)20
(14)32 (15)32 (16)33 (17)33 (18)32 (19)37
(20)27 (21)28 (22)33 (23)34 (24)30 (25)33
(26)23 (27)33 (28)27 (29)33 (30)35 (31)30

(32)29 (33)34 (34)27 (35)25 (36)33 (37)40
(38)29 (39)37 (40)25 (41)30 (42)34 (43)34
(44)33 (45)27 (46)31 (47)22 (48)33 (49)29
(50)28 (51)32 (52)26 (53)32 (54)27 (55)26
(56)32 (57)36 (58)31 (59)40 (60)30

Page 64, Item 1:

(1)21 (2)25 (3)28 (4)30 (5)25 (6)24 (7)25
(8)28 (9)26 (10)29 (11)37 (12)27 (13)28
(14)36 (15)29 (16)34 (17)25 (18)27 (19)30
(20)32 (21)25 (22)28 (23)28 (24)36 (25)29
(26)37 (27)31 (28)27 (29)31 (30)28 (31)32
(32)21 (33)31 (34)26 (35)32 (36)26 (37)29
(38)31 (39)23 (40)35 (41)38 (42)32 (43)32
(44)28 (45)28 (46)25 (47)34 (48)35 (49)35
(50)39 (51)32 (52)31 (53)32 (54)26 (55)33
(56)32 (57)24 (58)32 (59)35 (60)33

Page 65, Item 1:

(1)29 (2)26 (3)24 (4)33 (5)25 (6)34 (7)26
(8)25 (9)27 (10)28 (11)29 (12)29 (13)29
(14)24 (15)28 (16)32 (17)27 (18)26 (19)26
(20)23 (21)28 (22)31 (23)35 (24)37 (25)32
(26)38 (27)31 (28)31 (29)32 (30)29 (31)25
(32)30 (33)27 (34)38 (35)35 (36)25 (37)34
(38)27 (39)32 (40)32 (41)30 (42)27 (43)32
(44)36 (45)27 (46)26 (47)30 (48)40 (49)29
(50)34 (51)34 (52)29 (53)30 (54)26 (55)36
(56)26 (57)20 (58)33 (59)35 (60)25

Page 66, Item 1:

(1)31 (2)24 (3)35 (4)29 (5)37 (6)31 (7)33
(8)26 (9)27 (10)33 (11)24 (12)36 (13)30

(14)26 (15)34 (16)33 (17)28 (18)30 (19)30
(20)30 (21)35 (22)34 (23)31 (24)32 (25)31
(26)29 (27)31 (28)26 (29)28 (30)38 (31)26
(32)31 (33)36 (34)28 (35)21 (36)28 (37)30
(38)25 (39)25 (40)34 (41)32 (42)39 (43)32
(44)34 (45)28 (46)25 (47)29 (48)34 (49)35
(50)39 (51)25 (52)28 (53)39 (54)33 (55)33
(56)34 (57)30 (58)32 (59)32 (60)23

Page 67, Item 1:

(1)34 (2)29 (3)29 (4)27 (5)25 (6)29 (7)28
(8)31 (9)24 (10)37 (11)37 (12)29 (13)25
(14)33 (15)34 (16)26 (17)26 (18)30 (19)30
(20)31 (21)28 (22)23 (23)29 (24)25 (25)37
(26)30 (27)27 (28)29 (29)29 (30)27 (31)38
(32)31 (33)27 (34)27 (35)37 (36)32 (37)34
(38)35 (39)33 (40)24 (41)28 (42)38 (43)38
(44)26 (45)26 (46)35 (47)27 (48)37 (49)29
(50)28 (51)23 (52)33 (53)22 (54)30 (55)29
(56)32 (57)21 (58)27 (59)23 (60)24

Page 68, Item 1:

(1)26 (2)37 (3)25 (4)27 (5)27 (6)23 (7)28
(8)33 (9)37 (10)37 (11)30 (12)34 (13)26
(14)27 (15)34 (16)25 (17)29 (18)25 (19)35
(20)34 (21)22 (22)30 (23)32 (24)27 (25)30
(26)27 (27)29 (28)22 (29)32 (30)32 (31)36
(32)31 (33)26 (34)29 (35)27 (36)32 (37)25
(38)38 (39)26 (40)26 (41)29 (42)20 (43)40
(44)37 (45)38 (46)24 (47)26 (48)21 (49)25
(50)30 (51)35 (52)33 (53)32 (54)26 (55)22
(56)32 (57)25 (58)25 (59)26 (60)37

Page 69, Item 1:

(1)26 (2)28 (3)35 (4)25 (5)32 (6)37 (7)22
(8)33 (9)26 (10)30 (11)31 (12)28 (13)24
(14)28 (15)34 (16)29 (17)28 (18)33 (19)33
(20)30 (21)22 (22)30 (23)38 (24)30 (25)36
(26)26 (27)31 (28)26 (29)32 (30)32 (31)25
(32)26 (33)30 (34)24 (35)29 (36)27 (37)29

(38)24 (39)25 (40)32 (41)33 (42)30 (43)39
(44)32 (45)29 (46)29 (47)30 (48)24 (49)36
(50)33 (51)30 (52)30 (53)35 (54)21 (55)34
(56)31 (57)30 (58)35 (59)39 (60)29

Page 70, Item 1:

(1)37 (2)20 (3)36 (4)30 (5)36 (6)30 (7)37
(8)32 (9)23 (10)33 (11)30 (12)31 (13)34
(14)33 (15)32 (16)31 (17)25 (18)30 (19)36
(20)34 (21)31 (22)34 (23)29 (24)31 (25)26
(26)39 (27)27 (28)34 (29)31 (30)36 (31)31
(32)33 (33)27 (34)38 (35)31 (36)24 (37)32
(38)33 (39)29 (40)39 (41)29 (42)34 (43)28
(44)32 (45)30 (46)32 (47)26 (48)29 (49)31
(50)23 (51)24 (52)25 (53)32 (54)32 (55)27
(56)30 (57)35 (58)24 (59)31 (60)38

Page 71, Item 1:

(1)18 (2)11 (3)16 (4)15 (5)20 (6)15 (7)19
(8)11 (9)11 (10)11 (11)14 (12)18 (13)11
(14)19 (15)18 (16)17 (17)13 (18)17 (19)12
(20)16 (21)15 (22)16 (23)18 (24)14 (25)15
(26)10 (27)11 (28)17 (29)14 (30)20 (31)13
(32)12 (33)18 (34)10 (35)17 (36)11 (37)19
(38)12 (39)10 (40)16 (41)11 (42)16 (43)20
(44)11 (45)18 (46)20 (47)12 (48)11 (49)18
(50)14 (51)19 (52)10 (53)13 (54)20 (55)14
(56)15 (57)19 (58)12 (59)14 (60)16

Page 72, Item 1:

(1)13 (2)19 (3)11 (4)16 (5)15 (6)20 (7)14
(8)11 (9)19 (10)17 (11)12 (12)19 (13)18
(14)20 (15)16 (16)20 (17)19 (18)15 (19)19

(20)13 (21)17 (22)16 (23)11 (24)19 (25)12
(26)16 (27)20 (28)10 (29)12 (30)19 (31)10
(32)11 (33)20 (34)14 (35)11 (36)11 (37)10
(38)18 (39)16 (40)18 (41)10 (42)17 (43)17
(44)18 (45)11 (46)17 (47)11 (48)17 (49)15
(50)17 (51)19 (52)17 (53)17 (54)20 (55)12
(56)19 (57)14 (58)12 (59)13 (60)10

Page 73, Item 1:
(1)17 (2)17 (3)20 (4)10 (5)12 (6)13 (7)19
(8)14 (9)16 (10)14 (11)17 (12)12 (13)16
(14)14 (15)17 (16)16 (17)12 (18)18 (19)14
(20)18 (21)13 (22)19 (23)16 (24)11 (25)20
(26)19 (27)11 (28)10 (29)11 (30)14 (31)17
(32)20 (33)17 (34)19 (35)20 (36)17 (37)11
(38)13 (39)16 (40)12 (41)14 (42)15 (43)11
(44)11 (45)10 (46)20 (47)17 (48)12 (49)15
(50)18 (51)10 (52)20 (53)11 (54)14 (55)12
(56)19 (57)13 (58)20 (59)20 (60)10

Page 74, Item 1:
(1)18 (2)12 (3)19 (4)17 (5)12 (6)10 (7)19
(8)14 (9)18 (10)12 (11)16 (12)12 (13)15
(14)17 (15)15 (16)13 (17)14 (18)11 (19)11
(20)14 (21)17 (22)18 (23)15 (24)13 (25)12
(26)15 (27)12 (28)14 (29)13 (30)11 (31)10
(32)13 (33)18 (34)18 (35)19 (36)20 (37)13
(38)11 (39)15 (40)14 (41)10 (42)13 (43)14
(44)11 (45)14 (46)14 (47)10 (48)15 (49)11
(50)16 (51)20 (52)20 (53)19 (54)20 (55)20
(56)13 (57)18 (58)13 (59)20 (60)18

Page 75, Item 1:
(1)20 (2)12 (3)14 (4)17 (5)13 (6)15 (7)19
(8)18 (9)14 (10)11 (11)10 (12)12 (13)18
(14)11 (15)16 (16)20 (17)10 (18)11 (19)12
(20)13 (21)16 (22)14 (23)10 (24)12 (25)10
(26)18 (27)10 (28)11 (29)14 (30)20 (31)20
(32)17 (33)18 (34)18 (35)13 (36)16 (37)19
(38)17 (39)17 (40)20 (41)11 (42)20 (43)20

(44)18 (45)14 (46)10 (47)15 (48)18 (49)19
(50)20 (51)16 (52)20 (53)12 (54)18 (55)13
(56)12 (57)16 (58)11 (59)17 (60)16

Page 76, Item 1:
(1)19 (2)10 (3)20 (4)12 (5)10 (6)17 (7)10
(8)12 (9)10 (10)10 (11)11 (12)14 (13)16
(14)16 (15)17 (16)13 (17)15 (18)17 (19)12
(20)18 (21)19 (22)12 (23)10 (24)11 (25)20
(26)14 (27)13 (28)11 (29)15 (30)12 (31)17
(32)10 (33)10 (34)10 (35)12 (36)11 (37)16
(38)14 (39)11 (40)13 (41)11 (42)15 (43)13
(44)19 (45)14 (46)11 (47)14 (48)10 (49)19
(50)20 (51)12 (52)10 (53)20 (54)19 (55)15
(56)17 (57)15 (58)15 (59)18 (60)10

Page 77, Item 1:
(1)13 (2)15 (3)13 (4)13 (5)15 (6)12 (7)11
(8)11 (9)14 (10)10 (11)15 (12)19 (13)15
(14)19 (15)11 (16)13 (17)14 (18)11 (19)10
(20)14 (21)14 (22)15 (23)19 (24)11 (25)18
(26)14 (27)18 (28)12 (29)11 (30)12 (31)17
(32)13 (33)19 (34)16 (35)11 (36)14 (37)16
(38)16 (39)13 (40)12 (41)14 (42)18 (43)16
(44)10 (45)18 (46)20 (47)13 (48)16 (49)19
(50)15 (51)13 (52)13 (53)16 (54)11 (55)20
(56)20 (57)15 (58)20 (59)11 (60)13

Page 78, Item 1:
(1)12 (2)13 (3)15 (4)16 (5)20 (6)10 (7)11
(8)20 (9)15 (10)12 (11)18 (12)10 (13)13
(14)14 (15)12 (16)11 (17)18 (18)17 (19)14
(20)11 (21)15 (22)16 (23)19 (24)11 (25)13

(26)17 (27)18 (28)10 (29)20 (30)12 (31)15
(32)16 (33)10 (34)11 (35)12 (36)19 (37)14
(38)17 (39)20 (40)20 (41)18 (42)18 (43)19
(44)10 (45)18 (46)14 (47)14 (48)18 (49)12
(50)10 (51)14 (52)17 (53)18 (54)20 (55)13
(56)16 (57)12 (58)14 (59)15 (60)20

Page 79, Item 1:

(1)20 (2)15 (3)16 (4)10 (5)14 (6)13 (7)17
(8)19 (9)17 (10)16 (11)18 (12)20 (13)13
(14)17 (15)18 (16)18 (17)18 (18)11 (19)10
(20)19 (21)19 (22)18 (23)13 (24)13 (25)16
(26)10 (27)19 (28)16 (29)19 (30)10 (31)13
(32)19 (33)16 (34)18 (35)13 (36)11 (37)14
(38)13 (39)12 (40)15 (41)17 (42)11 (43)13
(44)14 (45)16 (46)20 (47)19 (48)14 (49)19
(50)13 (51)20 (52)13 (53)14 (54)19 (55)11
(56)15 (57)12 (58)12 (59)14 (60)17

Page 80, Item 1:

(1)19 (2)18 (3)16 (4)16 (5)11 (6)20 (7)16
(8)14 (9)18 (10)11 (11)20 (12)14 (13)11
(14)14 (15)20 (16)15 (17)11 (18)15 (19)11
(20)19 (21)17 (22)14 (23)16 (24)11 (25)11
(26)15 (27)11 (28)11 (29)11 (30)14 (31)11
(32)13 (33)20 (34)16 (35)20 (36)20 (37)12
(38)13 (39)20 (40)18 (41)10 (42)13 (43)13
(44)10 (45)16 (46)20 (47)19 (48)13 (49)17
(50)19 (51)16 (52)16 (53)18 (54)16 (55)18
(56)10 (57)11 (58)17 (59)10 (60)13

Page 81, Item 1:

(1)2 (2)4 (3)3 (4)0 (5)1 (6)1 (7)1 (8)0 (9)2
(10)3 (11)5 (12)3 (13)0 (14)0 (15)1 (16)2
(17)0 (18)4 (19)2 (20)0 (21)1 (22)3 (23)4
(24)0 (25)3 (26)3 (27)1 (28)0 (29)2 (30)5
(31)3 (32)0 (33)4 (34)1 (35)4 (36)1 (37)2
(38)2 (39)5 (40)0 (41)3 (42)0 (43)4 (44)4
(45)2 (46)4 (47)2 (48)4 (49)0 (50)4 (51)2
(52)1 (53)0 (54)5 (55)4 (56)3 (57)0 (58)1

(59)1 (60)3

Page 82, Item 1:

(1)0 (2)2 (3)0 (4)0 (5)2 (6)3 (7)0 (8)0 (9)1
(10)2 (11)0 (12)5 (13)2 (14)1 (15)0 (16)2
(17)2 (18)2 (19)1 (20)1 (21)0 (22)0 (23)1
(24)3 (25)3 (26)0 (27)0 (28)1 (29)3 (30)2
(31)0 (32)3 (33)1 (34)4 (35)1 (36)1 (37)0
(38)3 (39)0 (40)4 (41)0 (42)0 (43)2 (44)1
(45)1 (46)0 (47)1 (48)2 (49)0 (50)5 (51)2
(52)0 (53)1 (54)4 (55)0 (56)3 (57)1 (58)1
(59)1 (60)2

Page 83, Item 1:

(1)3 (2)3 (3)4 (4)3 (5)2 (6)4 (7)1 (8)4 (9)0
(10)0 (11)1 (12)1 (13)0 (14)3 (15)0 (16)2
(17)1 (18)4 (19)0 (20)2 (21)1 (22)3 (23)4
(24)3 (25)1 (26)3 (27)1 (28)3 (29)0 (30)0
(31)2 (32)1 (33)2 (34)0 (35)5 (36)5 (37)2
(38)1 (39)4 (40)1 (41)3 (42)1 (43)2 (44)5
(45)0 (46)1 (47)2 (48)3 (49)5 (50)1 (51)0
(52)5 (53)0 (54)1 (55)3 (56)3 (57)0 (58)1
(59)4 (60)0

Page 84, Item 1:

(1)0 (2)5 (3)3 (4)0 (5)1 (6)3 (7)0 (8)2 (9)0
(10)1 (11)0 (12)0 (13)1 (14)4 (15)4 (16)0
(17)1 (18)0 (19)4 (20)0 (21)0 (22)1 (23)4
(24)0 (25)0 (26)2 (27)1 (28)2 (29)0 (30)0
(31)4 (32)3 (33)2 (34)1 (35)1 (36)1 (37)0
(38)0 (39)3 (40)1 (41)1 (42)2 (43)2 (44)1
(45)0 (46)0 (47)0 (48)4 (49)3 (50)0 (51)0
(52)1 (53)2 (54)1 (55)1 (56)3 (57)4 (58)3
(59)0 (60)0

Page 85, Item 1:
(1)4 (2)3 (3)4 (4)5 (5)0 (6)0 (7)4 (8)1 (9)2
(10)4 (11)2 (12)0 (13)0 (14)2 (15)2 (16)4
(17)1 (18)2 (19)1 (20)0 (21)0 (22)3 (23)5
(24)3 (25)3 (26)4 (27)1 (28)1 (29)5 (30)2
(31)3 (32)1 (33)1 (34)3 (35)2 (36)5 (37)1
(38)1 (39)3 (40)3 (41)2 (42)2 (43)0 (44)1
(45)0 (46)0 (47)1 (48)3 (49)2 (50)3 (51)0
(52)0 (53)0 (54)0 (55)2 (56)2 (57)1 (58)3
(59)0 (60)2

Page 86, Item 1:
(1)0 (2)1 (3)0 (4)0 (5)1 (6)4 (7)2 (8)3 (9)0
(10)1 (11)1 (12)1 (13)4 (14)0 (15)1 (16)5
(17)2 (18)2 (19)0 (20)0 (21)0 (22)1 (23)1
(24)0 (25)2 (26)0 (27)3 (28)3 (29)0 (30)1
(31)0 (32)4 (33)3 (34)2 (35)2 (36)4 (37)2
(38)5 (39)1 (40)1 (41)4 (42)0 (43)1 (44)0
(45)5 (46)0 (47)0 (48)0 (49)3 (50)1 (51)3
(52)3 (53)1 (54)4 (55)4 (56)2 (57)1 (58)3
(59)4 (60)0

Page 87, Item 1:
(1)1 (2)1 (3)3 (4)0 (5)3 (6)2 (7)5 (8)1 (9)1
(10)1 (11)1 (12)2 (13)2 (14)0 (15)3 (16)4
(17)2 (18)3 (19)3 (20)0 (21)3 (22)0 (23)0
(24)1 (25)2 (26)2 (27)0 (28)0 (29)2 (30)2
(31)1 (32)2 (33)5 (34)3 (35)0 (36)2 (37)0
(38)0 (39)1 (40)1 (41)0 (42)1 (43)3 (44)0
(45)0 (46)1 (47)3 (48)0 (49)0 (50)0 (51)2
(52)1 (53)1 (54)3 (55)1 (56)4 (57)0 (58)1
(59)2 (60)5

Page 88, Item 1:
(1)1 (2)1 (3)0 (4)4 (5)1 (6)3 (7)3 (8)1 (9)4
(10)1 (11)2 (12)0 (13)3 (14)5 (15)0 (16)0
(17)2 (18)0 (19)3 (20)0 (21)0 (22)1 (23)5
(24)0 (25)0 (26)1 (27)1 (28)0 (29)0 (30)3
(31)2 (32)4 (33)2 (34)1 (35)0 (36)3 (37)2
(38)1 (39)1 (40)0 (41)0 (42)0 (43)3 (44)2

(45)1 (46)1 (47)3 (48)2 (49)0 (50)3 (51)0
(52)2 (53)3 (54)5 (55)3 (56)1 (57)0 (58)4
(59)0 (60)1

Page 89, Item 1:
(1)0 (2)1 (3)4 (4)3 (5)0 (6)4 (7)0 (8)3 (9)5
(10)1 (11)4 (12)4 (13)4 (14)5 (15)0 (16)1
(17)2 (18)2 (19)0 (20)2 (21)0 (22)1 (23)0
(24)1 (25)3 (26)0 (27)1 (28)1 (29)0 (30)2
(31)0 (32)3 (33)0 (34)0 (35)0 (36)3 (37)1
(38)3 (39)4 (40)1 (41)1 (42)1 (43)3 (44)0
(45)5 (46)2 (47)3 (48)0 (49)2 (50)2 (51)3
(52)1 (53)0 (54)5 (55)2 (56)4 (57)1 (58)0
(59)0 (60)3

Page 90, Item 1:
(1)2 (2)1 (3)2 (4)3 (5)3 (6)3 (7)3 (8)1 (9)0
(10)3 (11)3 (12)2 (13)0 (14)5 (15)2 (16)1
(17)1 (18)2 (19)3 (20)5 (21)0 (22)3 (23)1
(24)2 (25)2 (26)0 (27)1 (28)4 (29)1 (30)1
(31)1 (32)1 (33)0 (34)1 (35)0 (36)1 (37)0
(38)4 (39)2 (40)1 (41)0 (42)3 (43)2 (44)3
(45)0 (46)4 (47)1 (48)0 (49)3 (50)1 (51)0
(52)4 (53)0 (54)0 (55)1 (56)3 (57)0 (58)1
(59)4 (60)5

Page 91, Item 1:
(1)5 (2)3 (3)5 (4)1 (5)5 (6)0 (7)0 (8)4 (9)5
(10)0 (11)5 (12)2 (13)3 (14)1 (15)2 (16)0
(17)3 (18)1 (19)4 (20)3 (21)5 (22)0 (23)5
(24)1 (25)2 (26)2 (27)2 (28)0 (29)4 (30)3
(31)5 (32)1 (33)5 (34)1 (35)5 (36)4 (37)4
(38)1 (39)4 (40)0 (41)0 (42)3 (43)5 (44)1

(45)3 (46)2 (47)3 (48)0 (49)3 (50)0 (51)5
(52)3 (53)5 (54)5 (55)4 (56)0 (57)4 (58)1
(59)2 (60)0

Page 92, Item 1:

(1)3 (2)0 (3)4 (4)1 (5)3 (6)4 (7)1 (8)1 (9)5
(10)2 (11)3 (12)0 (13)4 (14)0 (15)5 (16)1
(17)5 (18)5 (19)5 (20)1 (21)4 (22)2 (23)4
(24)1 (25)3 (26)2 (27)4 (28)2 (29)2 (30)2
(31)4 (32)0 (33)2 (34)0 (35)3 (36)0 (37)5
(38)3 (39)4 (40)2 (41)5 (42)0 (43)4 (44)1
(45)4 (46)0 (47)5 (48)0 (49)4 (50)1 (51)2
(52)1 (53)5 (54)0 (55)5 (56)0 (57)5 (58)1
(59)1 (60)4

Page 93, Item 1:

(1)5 (2)5 (3)4 (4)0 (5)5 (6)1 (7)5 (8)5 (9)4
(10)2 (11)4 (12)1 (13)4 (14)0 (15)5 (16)1
(17)4 (18)3 (19)5 (20)0 (21)5 (22)0 (23)2
(24)0 (25)4 (26)3 (27)1 (28)2 (29)4 (30)0
(31)5 (32)0 (33)2 (34)2 (35)3 (36)2 (37)4
(38)0 (39)5 (40)1 (41)5 (42)1 (43)4 (44)2
(45)4 (46)4 (47)5 (48)1 (49)3 (50)1 (51)4
(52)4 (53)1 (54)4 (55)2 (56)1 (57)3 (58)0
(59)4 (60)0

Page 94, Item 1:

(1)3 (2)4 (3)3 (4)2 (5)5 (6)0 (7)2 (8)1 (9)4
(10)0 (11)3 (12)1 (13)0 (14)5 (15)5 (16)0
(17)5 (18)2 (19)3 (20)0 (21)1 (22)4 (23)4
(24)1 (25)3 (26)1 (27)4 (28)1 (29)1 (30)1
(31)4 (32)0 (33)4 (34)1 (35)4 (36)0 (37)4
(38)3 (39)3 (40)2 (41)5 (42)2 (43)2 (44)3
(45)4 (46)1 (47)3 (48)1 (49)5 (50)0 (51)5
(52)2 (53)1 (54)0 (55)3 (56)0 (57)5 (58)1
(59)5 (60)0

Page 95, Item 1:

(1)5 (2)1 (3)4 (4)0 (5)3 (6)0 (7)5 (8)0 (9)5
(10)4 (11)1 (12)1 (13)3 (14)1 (15)5 (16)0
(17)5 (18)5 (19)2 (20)3 (21)3 (22)0 (23)5

(24)0 (25)5 (26)4 (27)4 (28)0 (29)2 (30)0
(31)3 (32)2 (33)3 (34)1 (35)4 (36)4 (37)4
(38)0 (39)4 (40)3 (41)4 (42)0 (43)5 (44)2
(45)5 (46)3 (47)3 (48)3 (49)2 (50)4 (51)3
(52)2 (53)5 (54)4 (55)4 (56)1 (57)4 (58)4
(59)4 (60)3

Page 96, Item 1:

(1)4 (2)1 (3)5 (4)1 (5)5 (6)3 (7)5 (8)1 (9)2
(10)1 (11)4 (12)1 (13)5 (14)3 (15)1 (16)4
(17)2 (18)1 (19)4 (20)2 (21)4 (22)1 (23)3
(24)2 (25)2 (26)3 (27)5 (28)3 (29)5 (30)4
(31)3 (32)1 (33)5 (34)1 (35)4 (36)1 (37)5
(38)5 (39)2 (40)0 (41)2 (42)1 (43)4 (44)0
(45)5 (46)1 (47)4 (48)3 (49)5 (50)0 (51)5
(52)4 (53)2 (54)2 (55)3 (56)4 (57)0 (58)3
(59)4 (60)0

Page 97, Item 1:

(1)4 (2)4 (3)2 (4)5 (5)1 (6)4 (7)4 (8)1 (9)4
(10)1 (11)1 (12)2 (13)2 (14)0 (15)3 (16)1
(17)5 (18)0 (19)3 (20)5 (21)5 (22)2 (23)4
(24)0 (25)3 (26)1 (27)4 (28)4 (29)4 (30)3
(31)2 (32)5 (33)4 (34)0 (35)5 (36)2 (37)5
(38)2 (39)1 (40)2 (41)1 (42)0 (43)0 (44)3
(45)5 (46)1 (47)4 (48)3 (49)1 (50)0 (51)2
(52)4 (53)4 (54)5 (55)4 (56)2 (57)4 (58)2
(59)3 (60)3

Page 98, Item 1:

(1)5 (2)1 (3)2 (4)4 (5)0 (6)5 (7)4 (8)0 (9)0
(10)1 (11)3 (12)2 (13)3 (14)0 (15)3 (16)1
(17)5 (18)1 (19)5 (20)0 (21)4 (22)0 (23)4

(24)0 (25)5 (26)1 (27)5 (28)2 (29)5 (30)1
(31)1 (32)1 (33)2 (34)1 (35)4 (36)2 (37)3
(38)5 (39)3 (40)0 (41)0 (42)1 (43)3 (44)5
(45)5 (46)0 (47)5 (48)1 (49)3 (50)0 (51)5
(52)0 (53)5 (54)0 (55)3 (56)1 (57)4 (58)0
(59)4 (60)2

Page 99, Item 1:

(1)5 (2)0 (3)4 (4)3 (5)1 (6)0 (7)5 (8)3 (9)3
(10)1 (11)4 (12)4 (13)4 (14)3 (15)5 (16)2
(17)5 (18)0 (19)4 (20)2 (21)1 (22)0 (23)5
(24)0 (25)2 (26)0 (27)5 (28)2 (29)2 (30)2
(31)1 (32)2 (33)4 (34)2 (35)4 (36)1 (37)4
(38)2 (39)4 (40)4 (41)4 (42)0 (43)0 (44)1
(45)3 (46)2 (47)0 (48)0 (49)3 (50)1 (51)5
(52)4 (53)2 (54)5 (55)4 (56)0 (57)2 (58)4
(59)4 (60)1

Page 100, Item 1:

(1)5 (2)3 (3)3 (4)0 (5)2 (6)0 (7)3 (8)2 (9)5
(10)0 (11)0 (12)0 (13)3 (14)2 (15)5 (16)5
(17)3 (18)5 (19)5 (20)1 (21)5 (22)1 (23)5
(24)4 (25)2 (26)1 (27)0 (28)0 (29)5 (30)5
(31)2 (32)3 (33)4 (34)2 (35)5 (36)1 (37)5
(38)2 (39)5 (40)2 (41)3 (42)0 (43)5 (44)0
(45)4 (46)1 (47)0 (48)4 (49)5 (50)1 (51)5
(52)2 (53)4 (54)1 (55)2 (56)2 (57)3 (58)2
(59)1 (60)0

Page 101, Item 1:

(1)1 (2)5 (3)6 (4)7 (5)1 (6)6 (7)3 (8)0 (9)1
(10)0 (11)7 (12)4 (13)6 (14)1 (15)2 (16)2
(17)7 (18)4 (19)1 (20)0 (21)5 (22)5 (23)0
(24)3 (25)0 (26)0 (27)1 (28)5 (29)1 (30)0
(31)4 (32)2 (33)0 (34)0 (35)5 (36)4 (37)1
(38)4 (39)2 (40)3 (41)3 (42)6 (43)5 (44)5
(45)5 (46)6 (47)5 (48)1 (49)2 (50)0 (51)6
(52)0 (53)1 (54)0 (55)0 (56)6 (57)3 (58)4
(59)1 (60)6

Page 102, Item 1:

(1)1 (2)1 (3)3 (4)6 (5)2 (6)0 (7)0 (8)0 (9)4
(10)6 (11)6 (12)5 (13)6 (14)1 (15)2 (16)0
(17)0 (18)1 (19)5 (20)2 (21)4 (22)2 (23)6
(24)0 (25)5 (26)0 (27)3 (28)3 (29)1 (30)3
(31)2 (32)5 (33)2 (34)0 (35)4 (36)4 (37)5
(38)1 (39)5 (40)1 (41)0 (42)6 (43)0 (44)1
(45)0 (46)6 (47)0 (48)3 (49)0 (50)3 (51)3
(52)4 (53)0 (54)5 (55)2 (56)1 (57)4 (58)2
(59)2 (60)3

Page 103, Item 1:

(1)0 (2)2 (3)4 (4)1 (5)4 (6)0 (7)3 (8)0 (9)1
(10)5 (11)1 (12)0 (13)1 (14)0 (15)3 (16)2
(17)3 (18)0 (19)1 (20)0 (21)1 (22)4 (23)0
(24)1 (25)6 (26)3 (27)4 (28)5 (29)2 (30)5
(31)2 (32)1 (33)3 (34)2 (35)5 (36)1 (37)1
(38)4 (39)1 (40)3 (41)6 (42)2 (43)6 (44)1
(45)1 (46)0 (47)0 (48)1 (49)4 (50)0 (51)1
(52)5 (53)3 (54)3 (55)5 (56)2 (57)4 (58)2
(59)1 (60)1

Page 104, Item 1:

(1)3 (2)5 (3)5 (4)0 (5)4 (6)0 (7)3 (8)1 (9)5
(10)1 (11)0 (12)0 (13)0 (14)3 (15)2 (16)1
(17)3 (18)0 (19)0 (20)1 (21)1 (22)0 (23)3
(24)3 (25)2 (26)2 (27)3 (28)2 (29)1 (30)3
(31)2 (32)0 (33)0 (34)0 (35)1 (36)0 (37)1
(38)0 (39)5 (40)0 (41)1 (42)2 (43)3 (44)2
(45)2 (46)1 (47)4 (48)0 (49)5 (50)4 (51)3
(52)4 (53)4 (54)2 (55)6 (56)3 (57)3 (58)0
(59)3 (60)3

Page 105, Item 1:

(1)0 (2)1 (3)2 (4)7 (5)3 (6)2 (7)2 (8)3 (9)2
(10)0 (11)1 (12)4 (13)2 (14)0 (15)4 (16)1
(17)5 (18)3 (19)2 (20)6 (21)3 (22)5 (23)0
(24)4 (25)3 (26)0 (27)0 (28)3 (29)2 (30)0
(31)3 (32)6 (33)0 (34)3 (35)7 (36)1 (37)4
(38)2 (39)1 (40)2 (41)0 (42)2 (43)5 (44)0
(45)1 (46)0 (47)1 (48)0 (49)4 (50)0 (51)7
(52)2 (53)1 (54)6 (55)7 (56)2 (57)5 (58)0
(59)2 (60)2

Page 106, Item 1:

(1)2 (2)2 (3)0 (4)3 (5)0 (6)0 (7)2 (8)3 (9)1
(10)2 (11)4 (12)6 (13)4 (14)3 (15)4 (16)1
(17)1 (18)4 (19)2 (20)3 (21)4 (22)0 (23)1
(24)0 (25)0 (26)5 (27)3 (28)5 (29)0 (30)2
(31)6 (32)3 (33)6 (34)0 (35)7 (36)0 (37)3
(38)2 (39)1 (40)2 (41)1 (42)6 (43)1 (44)0
(45)2 (46)6 (47)4 (48)1 (49)2 (50)0 (51)0
(52)4 (53)4 (54)3 (55)5 (56)1 (57)4 (58)1
(59)0 (60)4

Page 107, Item 1:

(1)5 (2)0 (3)1 (4)2 (5)4 (6)1 (7)0 (8)0 (9)1
(10)5 (11)1 (12)1 (13)1 (14)3 (15)1 (16)0
(17)1 (18)0 (19)4 (20)6 (21)7 (22)1 (23)0
(24)0 (25)3 (26)0 (27)0 (28)4 (29)3 (30)3
(31)1 (32)1 (33)5 (34)6 (35)0 (36)0 (37)6
(38)4 (39)1 (40)1 (41)4 (42)0 (43)1 (44)0
(45)5 (46)1 (47)2 (48)0 (49)3 (50)3 (51)0
(52)6 (53)1 (54)3 (55)4 (56)6 (57)1 (58)1
(59)7 (60)0

Page 108, Item 1:

(1)3 (2)0 (3)7 (4)3 (5)6 (6)1 (7)3 (8)1 (9)2
(10)6 (11)6 (12)0 (13)3 (14)0 (15)3 (16)2
(17)3 (18)1 (19)4 (20)4 (21)5 (22)3 (23)1
(24)1 (25)1 (26)6 (27)1 (28)0 (29)6 (30)3
(31)0 (32)2 (33)5 (34)0 (35)3 (36)2 (37)4
(38)0 (39)4 (40)0 (41)5 (42)0 (43)4 (44)2
(45)0 (46)0 (47)0 (48)0 (49)3 (50)6 (51)5

(52)1 (53)7 (54)6 (55)0 (56)0 (57)1 (58)4
(59)3 (60)0

Page 109, Item 1:

(1)5 (2)4 (3)1 (4)6 (5)5 (6)0 (7)0 (8)4 (9)1
(10)0 (11)0 (12)2 (13)0 (14)2 (15)5 (16)0
(17)0 (18)4 (19)2 (20)1 (21)1 (22)5 (23)1
(24)2 (25)5 (26)5 (27)1 (28)0 (29)2 (30)0
(31)1 (32)1 (33)0 (34)2 (35)0 (36)5 (37)0
(38)0 (39)4 (40)2 (41)0 (42)0 (43)2 (44)1
(45)5 (46)3 (47)0 (48)0 (49)0 (50)3 (51)6
(52)0 (53)0 (54)1 (55)1 (56)4 (57)7 (58)4
(59)0 (60)6

Page 110, Item 1:

(1)0 (2)0 (3)1 (4)0 (5)6 (6)5 (7)5 (8)0 (9)3
(10)0 (11)1 (12)0 (13)1 (14)2 (15)0 (16)7
(17)1 (18)0 (19)2 (20)3 (21)4 (22)0 (23)4
(24)3 (25)1 (26)2 (27)2 (28)5 (29)0 (30)5
(31)3 (32)5 (33)1 (34)0 (35)5 (36)0 (37)4
(38)2 (39)3 (40)2 (41)7 (42)5 (43)0 (44)0
(45)0 (46)3 (47)6 (48)1 (49)3 (50)3 (51)3
(52)1 (53)0 (54)4 (55)0 (56)1 (57)6 (58)2
(59)3 (60)4

Page 111, Item 1:

(1)5 (2)4 (3)4 (4)2 (5)3 (6)0 (7)4 (8)4 (9)1
(10)2 (11)2 (12)2 (13)7 (14)2 (15)2 (16)1
(17)4 (18)1 (19)7 (20)3 (21)5 (22)6 (23)2
(24)1 (25)5 (26)5 (27)2 (28)6 (29)3 (30)2
(31)6 (32)4 (33)3 (34)3 (35)3 (36)3 (37)1
(38)2 (39)6 (40)4 (41)5 (42)5 (43)1 (44)0
(45)7 (46)2 (47)4 (48)0 (49)5 (50)3 (51)1

(52)0 (53)6 (54)6 (55)6 (56)6 (57)6 (58)3
(59)5 (60)4

Page 112, Item 1:

(1)7 (2)0 (3)4 (4)7 (5)6 (6)1 (7)5 (8)0 (9)6
(10)0 (11)5 (12)4 (13)6 (14)0 (15)2 (16)1
(17)7 (18)2 (19)7 (20)3 (21)5 (22)0 (23)5
(24)1 (25)4 (26)1 (27)4 (28)1 (29)6 (30)0
(31)5 (32)2 (33)7 (34)1 (35)5 (36)6 (37)6
(38)2 (39)2 (40)5 (41)5 (42)2 (43)1 (44)1
(45)3 (46)0 (47)7 (48)5 (49)7 (50)2 (51)1
(52)5 (53)2 (54)0 (55)6 (56)1 (57)6 (58)2
(59)2 (60)4

Page 113, Item 1:

(1)3 (2)2 (3)4 (4)2 (5)5 (6)2 (7)7 (8)5 (9)6
(10)6 (11)5 (12)3 (13)3 (14)1 (15)2 (16)0
(17)3 (18)0 (19)0 (20)4 (21)0 (22)2 (23)6
(24)0 (25)7 (26)2 (27)6 (28)3 (29)6 (30)1
(31)0 (32)5 (33)6 (34)1 (35)4 (36)3 (37)5
(38)6 (39)4 (40)3 (41)6 (42)2 (43)2 (44)2
(45)5 (46)5 (47)6 (48)0 (49)5 (50)0 (51)5
(52)1 (53)7 (54)1 (55)4 (56)4 (57)5 (58)4
(59)7 (60)1

Page 114, Item 1:

(1)3 (2)2 (3)3 (4)3 (5)5 (6)0 (7)7 (8)0 (9)7
(10)2 (11)5 (12)0 (13)6 (14)2 (15)5 (16)0
(17)4 (18)1 (19)6 (20)4 (21)6 (22)3 (23)5
(24)2 (25)3 (26)2 (27)4 (28)4 (29)6 (30)0
(31)0 (32)7 (33)7 (34)4 (35)6 (36)1 (37)1
(38)6 (39)7 (40)3 (41)3 (42)2 (43)6 (44)0
(45)6 (46)0 (47)7 (48)0 (49)7 (50)1 (51)2
(52)2 (53)3 (54)1 (55)7 (56)1 (57)6 (58)2
(59)4 (60)0

Page 115, Item 1:

(1)7 (2)5 (3)6 (4)0 (5)5 (6)1 (7)7 (8)1 (9)7
(10)1 (11)7 (12)0 (13)2 (14)1 (15)4 (16)0
(17)3 (18)1 (19)3 (20)1 (21)7 (22)1 (23)6
(24)4 (25)6 (26)3 (27)7 (28)3 (29)7 (30)1

(31)5 (32)2 (33)7 (34)2 (35)3 (36)6 (37)0
(38)2 (39)5 (40)0 (41)3 (42)5 (43)6 (44)0
(45)4 (46)3 (47)6 (48)4 (49)7 (50)3 (51)5
(52)2 (53)4 (54)2 (55)7 (56)0 (57)3 (58)2
(59)6 (60)1

Page 116, Item 1:

(1)6 (2)1 (3)4 (4)3 (5)4 (6)0 (7)6 (8)0 (9)4
(10)2 (11)3 (12)6 (13)4 (14)5 (15)2 (16)2
(17)3 (18)7 (19)6 (20)5 (21)6 (22)4 (23)5
(24)0 (25)4 (26)0 (27)6 (28)2 (29)7 (30)1
(31)6 (32)0 (33)6 (34)0 (35)6 (36)3 (37)6
(38)5 (39)7 (40)1 (41)4 (42)5 (43)1 (44)0
(45)3 (46)7 (47)5 (48)3 (49)5 (50)5 (51)7
(52)3 (53)7 (54)6 (55)6 (56)2 (57)7 (58)2
(59)3 (60)1

Page 117, Item 1:

(1)5 (2)6 (3)6 (4)0 (5)5 (6)2 (7)6 (8)0 (9)6
(10)0 (11)6 (12)1 (13)2 (14)1 (15)7 (16)2
(17)4 (18)1 (19)5 (20)0 (21)7 (22)2 (23)1
(24)4 (25)1 (26)7 (27)1 (28)1 (29)5 (30)2
(31)2 (32)1 (33)7 (34)1 (35)2 (36)1 (37)6
(38)1 (39)6 (40)0 (41)6 (42)3 (43)4 (44)6
(45)6 (46)3 (47)7 (48)5 (49)7 (50)3 (51)7
(52)1 (53)3 (54)0 (55)6 (56)4 (57)7 (58)0
(59)6 (60)2

Page 118, Item 1:

(1)7 (2)4 (3)2 (4)0 (5)2 (6)4 (7)5 (8)2 (9)6
(10)5 (11)7 (12)4 (13)2 (14)2 (15)4 (16)4
(17)6 (18)6 (19)5 (20)6 (21)6 (22)4 (23)1

(24)3 (25)5 (26)0 (27)7 (28)5 (29)5 (30)0
(31)6 (32)4 (33)5 (34)0 (35)3 (36)2 (37)7
(38)5 (39)3 (40)3 (41)7 (42)4 (43)3 (44)0
(45)1 (46)0 (47)7 (48)1 (49)2 (50)4 (51)6
(52)3 (53)0 (54)0 (55)3 (56)4 (57)6 (58)3
(59)7 (60)4
Page 119, Item 1:
(1)1 (2)6 (3)1 (4)2 (5)5 (6)2 (7)6 (8)3 (9)4
(10)5 (11)0 (12)2 (13)4 (14)0 (15)7 (16)0
(17)6 (18)1 (19)3 (20)1 (21)4 (22)1 (23)1
(24)0 (25)5 (26)1 (27)7 (28)1 (29)4 (30)2
(31)7 (32)4 (33)0 (34)0 (35)6 (36)7 (37)5
(38)0 (39)6 (40)0 (41)4 (42)0 (43)3 (44)4
(45)7 (46)1 (47)1 (48)5 (49)5 (50)1 (51)3
(52)0 (53)4 (54)4 (55)7 (56)3 (57)4 (58)2
(59)3 (60)2
Page 120, Item 1:
(1)5 (2)3 (3)7 (4)0 (5)4 (6)4 (7)4 (8)5 (9)3
(10)4 (11)3 (12)4 (13)6 (14)5 (15)1 (16)4
(17)6 (18)7 (19)7 (20)4 (21)5 (22)4 (23)6
(24)0 (25)1 (26)1 (27)5 (28)6 (29)2 (30)6
(31)7 (32)6 (33)1 (34)1 (35)5 (36)1 (37)6
(38)0 (39)6 (40)4 (41)6 (42)0 (43)6 (44)1
(45)5 (46)4 (47)6 (48)1 (49)4 (50)2 (51)6
(52)3 (53)0 (54)2 (55)3 (56)3 (57)7 (58)4
(59)7 (60)3
Page 121, Item 1:
(1)2 (2)7 (3)1 (4)2 (5)3 (6)0 (7)2 (8)3 (9)7
(10)8 (11)3 (12)6 (13)1 (14)8 (15)0 (16)2
(17)2 (18)4 (19)4 (20)1 (21)2 (22)1 (23)6
(24)2 (25)1 (26)6 (27)5 (28)1 (29)5 (30)2
(31)2 (32)0 (33)4 (34)0 (35)0 (36)2 (37)5
(38)3 (39)3 (40)1 (41)8 (42)0 (43)4 (44)6
(45)6 (46)7 (47)1 (48)2 (49)3 (50)0 (51)6
(52)2 (53)7 (54)8 (55)3 (56)1 (57)0 (58)9
(59)8 (60)2
Page 122, Item 1:

(1)0 (2)10 (3)3 (4)0 (5)1 (6)6 (7)3 (8)4 (9)5
(10)2 (11)5 (12)0 (13)2 (14)8 (15)0 (16)10
(17)1 (18)3 (19)8 (20)4 (21)4 (22)0 (23)0
(24)6 (25)6 (26)5 (27)4 (28)4 (29)5 (30)0
(31)4 (32)2 (33)6 (34)3 (35)0 (36)0 (37)9
(38)0 (39)2 (40)1 (41)8 (42)0 (43)0 (44)5
(45)2 (46)4 (47)2 (48)3 (49)3 (50)7 (51)6
(52)7 (53)2 (54)5 (55)6 (56)0 (57)2 (58)2
(59)3 (60)0
Page 123, Item 1:
(1)3 (2)7 (3)1 (4)5 (5)9 (6)8 (7)5 (8)8 (9)5
(10)7 (11)0 (12)7 (13)5 (14)1 (15)1 (16)7
(17)2 (18)2 (19)2 (20)1 (21)5 (22)3 (23)8
(24)1 (25)5 (26)6 (27)0 (28)1 (29)1 (30)4
(31)5 (32)2 (33)4 (34)2 (35)0 (36)5 (37)6
(38)10 (39)4 (40)0 (41)0 (42)5 (43)7 (44)0
(45)0 (46)1 (47)1 (48)9 (49)2 (50)4 (51)3
(52)6 (53)3 (54)6 (55)0 (56)0 (57)9 (58)6
(59)0 (60)3
Page 124, Item 1:
(1)1 (2)0 (3)7 (4)5 (5)1 (6)8 (7)2 (8)2 (9)0
(10)7 (11)5 (12)0 (13)0 (14)2 (15)1 (16)6
(17)2 (18)0 (19)1 (20)0 (21)0 (22)10 (23)1
(24)1 (25)7 (26)7 (27)2 (28)8 (29)0 (30)0
(31)9 (32)2 (33)3 (34)0 (35)8 (36)1 (37)0
(38)1 (39)8 (40)9 (41)0 (42)1 (43)0 (44)8
(45)1 (46)2 (47)4 (48)2 (49)5 (50)2 (51)1
(52)3 (53)0 (54)7 (55)3 (56)1 (57)2 (58)0
(59)0 (60)8
Page 125, Item 1:

(1)2 (2)5 (3)3 (4)0 (5)3 (6)5 (7)2 (8)0 (9)1
(10)0 (11)6 (12)5 (13)7 (14)0 (15)1 (16)3
(17)3 (18)7 (19)4 (20)5 (21)0 (22)0 (23)2
(24)5 (25)6 (26)3 (27)6 (28)1 (29)6 (30)4
(31)1 (32)5 (33)0 (34)4 (35)0 (36)3 (37)8
(38)4 (39)3 (40)2 (41)4 (42)5 (43)1 (44)3
(45)4 (46)5 (47)1 (48)2 (49)1 (50)8 (51)5
(52)3 (53)1 (54)3 (55)2 (56)8 (57)0 (58)6
(59)8 (60)1

Page 126, Item 1:
(1)6 (2)3 (3)6 (4)1 (5)5 (6)4 (7)0 (8)0 (9)2
(10)4 (11)0 (12)4 (13)0 (14)3 (15)0 (16)3
(17)0 (18)3 (19)0 (20)3 (21)6 (22)0 (23)1
(24)6 (25)4 (26)7 (27)4 (28)7 (29)6 (30)7
(31)0 (32)2 (33)3 (34)6 (35)0 (36)9 (37)2
(38)2 (39)2 (40)1 (41)7 (42)10 (43)1 (44)6
(45)2 (46)3 (47)0 (48)6 (49)3 (50)1 (51)0
(52)1 (53)1 (54)3 (55)2 (56)9 (57)1 (58)5
(59)7 (60)0

Page 127, Item 1:
(1)9 (2)3 (3)9 (4)3 (5)0 (6)2 (7)3 (8)2 (9)3
(10)1 (11)1 (12)1 (13)2 (14)3 (15)10 (16)5
(17)5 (18)9 (19)8 (20)4 (21)2 (22)8 (23)9
(24)6 (25)1 (26)5 (27)5 (28)3 (29)3 (30)1
(31)2 (32)7 (33)7 (34)2 (35)9 (36)2 (37)6
(38)3 (39)3 (40)5 (41)0 (42)0 (43)0 (44)6
(45)5 (46)0 (47)5 (48)2 (49)6 (50)7 (51)1
(52)2 (53)4 (54)5 (55)8 (56)7 (57)1 (58)8
(59)3 (60)7

Page 128, Item 1:
(1)0 (2)3 (3)2 (4)2 (5)0 (6)4 (7)1 (8)1 (9)2
(10)0 (11)10 (12)2 (13)2 (14)6 (15)4 (16)1
(17)1 (18)3 (19)7 (20)5 (21)0 (22)1 (23)5
(24)6 (25)3 (26)2 (27)4 (28)0 (29)0 (30)0
(31)8 (32)7 (33)3 (34)9 (35)10 (36)0 (37)5
(38)1 (39)6 (40)0 (41)2 (42)0 (43)4 (44)5
(45)4 (46)4 (47)0 (48)2 (49)3 (50)1 (51)1

(52)4 (53)3 (54)3 (55)2 (56)0 (57)3 (58)3
(59)0 (60)1

Page 129, Item 1:
(1)3 (2)0 (3)3 (4)7 (5)2 (6)1 (7)1 (8)1 (9)2
(10)7 (11)1 (12)1 (13)1 (14)4 (15)2 (16)1
(17)6 (18)4 (19)6 (20)2 (21)0 (22)7 (23)1
(24)9 (25)4 (26)4 (27)2 (28)2 (29)4 (30)8
(31)6 (32)1 (33)0 (34)6 (35)0 (36)2 (37)2
(38)5 (39)3 (40)10 (41)0 (42)1 (43)10
(44)0 (45)2 (46)7 (47)7 (48)0 (49)7 (50)2
(51)5 (52)1 (53)7 (54)3 (55)5 (56)5 (57)1
(58)4 (59)6 (60)3

Page 130, Item 1:
(1)4 (2)4 (3)2 (4)4 (5)8 (6)0 (7)4 (8)5 (9)4
(10)5 (11)2 (12)5 (13)4 (14)3 (15)7 (16)2
(17)1 (18)3 (19)4 (20)2 (21)0 (22)4 (23)3
(24)6 (25)4 (26)1 (27)0 (28)1 (29)9 (30)2
(31)7 (32)5 (33)9 (34)1 (35)0 (36)4 (37)1
(38)9 (39)7 (40)2 (41)6 (42)3 (43)0 (44)3
(45)6 (46)0 (47)2 (48)6 (49)6 (50)3 (51)5
(52)0 (53)0 (54)1 (55)0 (56)1 (57)2 (58)3
(59)0 (60)7

Page 131, Item 1:
(1)8 (2)0 (3)5 (4)4 (5)9 (6)6 (7)10 (8)3 (9)6
(10)1 (11)7 (12)0 (13)7 (14)8 (15)4 (16)10
(17)2 (18)3 (19)10 (20)3 (21)6 (22)3 (23)8
(24)0 (25)5 (26)1 (27)10 (28)2 (29)6 (30)8
(31)10 (32)3 (33)6 (34)5 (35)9 (36)4 (37)7
(38)2 (39)3 (40)4 (41)5 (42)1 (43)5 (44)1
(45)8 (46)8 (47)10 (48)3 (49)9 (50)1 (51)7

(52)0 (53)10 (54)2 (55)5 (56)0 (57)8 (58)0 (59)8 (60)3

Page 132, Item 1:

(1)10 (2)2 (3)1 (4)5 (5)8 (6)1 (7)4 (8)2 (9)9 (10)8 (11)8 (12)1 (13)5 (14)3 (15)8 (16)2 (17)8 (18)0 (19)5 (20)8 (21)9 (22)6 (23)10 (24)2 (25)6 (26)0 (27)6 (28)0 (29)7 (30)1 (31)2 (32)2 (33)10 (34)4 (35)5 (36)4 (37)9 (38)0 (39)9 (40)0 (41)4 (42)2 (43)4 (44)2 (45)6 (46)2 (47)8 (48)2 (49)5 (50)4 (51)10 (52)6 (53)5 (54)2 (55)4 (56)2 (57)9 (58)8 (59)2 (60)4

Page 133, Item 1:

(1)9 (2)5 (3)6 (4)9 (5)10 (6)0 (7)8 (8)4 (9)9 (10)3 (11)7 (12)5 (13)8 (14)0 (15)5 (16)3 (17)2 (18)2 (19)1 (20)5 (21)10 (22)4 (23)6 (24)4 (25)8 (26)3 (27)9 (28)3 (29)10 (30)2 (31)4 (32)0 (33)7 (34)1 (35)4 (36)5 (37)9 (38)6 (39)8 (40)0 (41)5 (42)7 (43)5 (44)4 (45)4 (46)0 (47)8 (48)7 (49)7 (50)7 (51)9 (52)1 (53)10 (54)6 (55)9 (56)1 (57)9 (58)6 (59)7 (60)2

Page 134, Item 1:

(1)5 (2)5 (3)5 (4)5 (5)10 (6)4 (7)6 (8)2 (9)9 (10)2 (11)9 (12)7 (13)4 (14)2 (15)10 (16)3 (17)9 (18)2 (19)2 (20)0 (21)9 (22)8 (23)5 (24)1 (25)7 (26)9 (27)7 (28)0 (29)7 (30)7 (31)5 (32)2 (33)7 (34)2 (35)5 (36)0 (37)9 (38)0 (39)10 (40)2 (41)9 (42)1 (43)3 (44)8 (45)10 (46)7 (47)1 (48)8 (49)10 (50)2 (51)9 (52)3 (53)8 (54)2 (55)0 (56)1 (57)7 (58)4 (59)3 (60)0

Page 135, Item 1:

(1)10 (2)6 (3)9 (4)5 (5)5 (6)6 (7)1 (8)0 (9)3 (10)0 (11)3 (12)2 (13)6 (14)3 (15)6 (16)0 (17)10 (18)2 (19)3 (20)3 (21)5 (22)1 (23)5 (24)1 (25)6 (26)8 (27)10 (28)7 (29)9 (30)2

(31)8 (32)6 (33)7 (34)7 (35)10 (36)1 (37)6 (38)1 (39)9 (40)9 (41)3 (42)4 (43)2 (44)0 (45)8 (46)2 (47)5 (48)3 (49)8 (50)0 (51)9 (52)0 (53)9 (54)5 (55)3 (56)7 (57)8 (58)4 (59)9 (60)1

Page 136, Item 1:

(1)4 (2)5 (3)9 (4)4 (5)0 (6)3 (7)7 (8)2 (9)0 (10)2 (11)4 (12)8 (13)4 (14)1 (15)3 (16)1 (17)5 (18)7 (19)8 (20)0 (21)4 (22)6 (23)6 (24)0 (25)3 (26)7 (27)8 (28)2 (29)6 (30)0 (31)7 (32)3 (33)8 (34)3 (35)6 (36)5 (37)10 (38)0 (39)4 (40)5 (41)6 (42)8 (43)4 (44)5 (45)6 (46)2 (47)8 (48)5 (49)9 (50)1 (51)7 (52)6 (53)7 (54)7 (55)8 (56)4 (57)9 (58)4 (59)4 (60)5

Page 137, Item 1:

(1)4 (2)6 (3)7 (4)3 (5)1 (6)3 (7)7 (8)6 (9)8 (10)0 (11)8 (12)8 (13)7 (14)8 (15)7 (16)2 (17)0 (18)3 (19)9 (20)4 (21)5 (22)2 (23)8 (24)1 (25)9 (26)0 (27)10 (28)4 (29)2 (30)1 (31)10 (32)1 (33)10 (34)3 (35)0 (36)0 (37)5 (38)2 (39)10 (40)2 (41)3 (42)1 (43)4 (44)3 (45)6 (46)0 (47)3 (48)4 (49)8 (50)2 (51)6 (52)0 (53)6 (54)3 (55)9 (56)5 (57)10 (58)2 (59)7 (60)8

Page 138, Item 1:

(1)8 (2)10 (3)6 (4)0 (5)4 (6)0 (7)6 (8)2 (9)9 (10)3 (11)8 (12)1 (13)4 (14)4 (15)7 (16)2 (17)0 (18)4 (19)9 (20)2 (21)4 (22)3 (23)8

(24)6 (25)2 (26)7 (27)1 (28)2 (29)9 (30)2
(31)9 (32)1 (33)4 (34)4 (35)9 (36)1 (37)4
(38)1 (39)6 (40)0 (41)10 (42)3 (43)5 (44)2
(45)5 (46)1 (47)10 (48)4 (49)5 (50)0 (51)8
(52)3 (53)6 (54)0 (55)8 (56)1 (57)10 (58)8
(59)10 (60)6

Page 139, Item 1:
(1)10 (2)1 (3)9 (4)0 (5)5 (6)4 (7)6 (8)1 (9)7
(10)3 (11)6 (12)0 (13)6 (14)2 (15)6 (16)5
(17)6 (18)2 (19)9 (20)5 (21)7 (22)6 (23)8
(24)2 (25)10 (26)0 (27)6 (28)1 (29)1 (30)3
(31)6 (32)1 (33)4 (34)6 (35)0 (36)6 (37)6
(38)1 (39)7 (40)4 (41)2 (42)4 (43)5 (44)0
(45)8 (46)0 (47)9 (48)4 (49)6 (50)0 (51)5
(52)2 (53)8 (54)5 (55)9 (56)2 (57)10 (58)1
(59)6 (60)1

Page 140, Item 1:
(1)7 (2)0 (3)6 (4)5 (5)4 (6)2 (7)4 (8)1 (9)8
(10)7 (11)4 (12)6 (13)10 (14)6 (15)4 (16)4
(17)9 (18)1 (19)5 (20)2 (21)9 (22)3 (23)7
(24)2 (25)6 (26)1 (27)10 (28)0 (29)10
(30)1 (31)5 (32)7 (33)3 (34)0 (35)10 (36)2
(37)10 (38)5 (39)9 (40)3 (41)4 (42)2 (43)6
(44)1 (45)5 (46)8 (47)0 (48)1 (49)5 (50)3
(51)3 (52)0 (53)2 (54)9 (55)10 (56)2 (57)5
(58)10 (59)6 (60)5

Page 141, Item 1:
(1)0 (2)2 (3)3 (4)3 (5)0 (6)5 (7)6 (8)1 (9)3
(10)6 (11)2 (12)8 (13)7 (14)0 (15)8 (16)4
(17)0 (18)5 (19)6 (20)1 (21)6 (22)1 (23)5
(24)6 (25)0 (26)0 (27)5 (28)0 (29)3 (30)2
(31)0 (32)3 (33)1 (34)4 (35)2 (36)3 (37)1
(38)2 (39)10 (40)0 (41)4 (42)1 (43)1 (44)3
(45)3 (46)4 (47)1 (48)2 (49)7 (50)6 (51)1
(52)0 (53)1 (54)0 (55)1 (56)6 (57)4 (58)5
(59)2 (60)6

Page 142, Item 1:

(1)1 (2)0 (3)5 (4)1 (5)7 (6)1 (7)4 (8)2 (9)0
(10)6 (11)3 (12)2 (13)5 (14)7 (15)5 (16)0
(17)1 (18)0 (19)1 (20)3 (21)2 (22)0 (23)1
(24)2 (25)8 (26)5 (27)4 (28)7 (29)5 (30)10
(31)0 (32)8 (33)3 (34)1 (35)1 (36)0 (37)0
(38)2 (39)6 (40)7 (41)2 (42)1 (43)7 (44)3
(45)1 (46)2 (47)0 (48)0 (49)2 (50)3 (51)1
(52)6 (53)2 (54)1 (55)0 (56)6 (57)2 (58)0
(59)5 (60)5

Page 143, Item 1:
(1)0 (2)7 (3)5 (4)3 (5)0 (6)0 (7)0 (8)1 (9)2
(10)9 (11)1 (12)6 (13)2 (14)1 (15)4 (16)2
(17)9 (18)0 (19)4 (20)1 (21)3 (22)6 (23)3
(24)1 (25)3 (26)7 (27)0 (28)0 (29)9 (30)8
(31)7 (32)3 (33)6 (34)2 (35)5 (36)2 (37)5
(38)5 (39)2 (40)8 (41)3 (42)6 (43)5 (44)6
(45)5 (46)7 (47)0 (48)7 (49)0 (50)5 (51)5
(52)1 (53)4 (54)2 (55)1 (56)3 (57)9 (58)0
(59)5 (60)9

Page 144, Item 1:
(1)3 (2)1 (3)8 (4)2 (5)7 (6)2 (7)1 (8)1 (9)7
(10)7 (11)3 (12)3 (13)3 (14)5 (15)2 (16)2
(17)4 (18)1 (19)4 (20)0 (21)1 (22)4 (23)4
(24)4 (25)5 (26)3 (27)5 (28)3 (29)3 (30)8
(31)1 (32)2 (33)4 (34)0 (35)6 (36)0 (37)0
(38)5 (39)3 (40)7 (41)8 (42)2 (43)4 (44)0
(45)4 (46)5 (47)7 (48)4 (49)3 (50)1 (51)7
(52)1 (53)0 (54)3 (55)5 (56)1 (57)3 (58)4
(59)3 (60)4

Page 145, Item 1:

(1)1 (2)2 (3)2 (4)2 (5)2 (6)5 (7)6 (8)7 (9)9 (10)8 (11)3 (12)8 (13)0 (14)8 (15)0 (16)3 (17)2 (18)10 (19)0 (20)8 (21)2 (22)5 (23)2 (24)0 (25)5 (26)3 (27)0 (28)0 (29)3 (30)1 (31)2 (32)6 (33)3 (34)5 (35)3 (36)0 (37)3 (38)3 (39)0 (40)2 (41)7 (42)1 (43)3 (44)0 (45)0 (46)2 (47)0 (48)5 (49)4 (50)4 (51)0 (52)5 (53)2 (54)7 (55)1 (56)8 (57)0 (58)6 (59)5 (60)6

Page 146, Item 1:

(1)2 (2)1 (3)1 (4)5 (5)1 (6)3 (7)3 (8)7 (9)8 (10)10 (11)10 (12)2 (13)2 (14)1 (15)5 (16)1 (17)2 (18)0 (19)9 (20)0 (21)6 (22)4 (23)5 (24)4 (25)0 (26)2 (27)9 (28)3 (29)1 (30)1 (31)4 (32)3 (33)0 (34)2 (35)4 (36)2 (37)2 (38)2 (39)2 (40)5 (41)2 (42)1 (43)3 (44)0 (45)2 (46)3 (47)10 (48)0 (49)7 (50)7 (51)0 (52)4 (53)1 (54)8 (55)2 (56)1 (57)2 (58)1 (59)1 (60)1

Page 147, Item 1:

(1)1 (2)9 (3)1 (4)9 (5)7 (6)1 (7)7 (8)1 (9)7 (10)5 (11)7 (12)2 (13)2 (14)0 (15)8 (16)1 (17)2 (18)1 (19)1 (20)5 (21)5 (22)7 (23)3 (24)4 (25)4 (26)5 (27)9 (28)9 (29)4 (30)2 (31)2 (32)2 (33)4 (34)4 (35)1 (36)2 (37)1 (38)5 (39)0 (40)4 (41)5 (42)2 (43)0 (44)3 (45)2 (46)2 (47)9 (48)2 (49)8 (50)1 (51)6 (52)1 (53)0 (54)4 (55)3 (56)0 (57)7 (58)8 (59)0 (60)2

Page 148, Item 1:

(1)0 (2)8 (3)3 (4)2 (5)6 (6)2 (7)3 (8)2 (9)4 (10)9 (11)5 (12)4 (13)3 (14)4 (15)4 (16)1 (17)2 (18)1 (19)2 (20)1 (21)1 (22)4 (23)2 (24)4 (25)2 (26)3 (27)1 (28)4 (29)4 (30)0 (31)6 (32)8 (33)1 (34)0 (35)2 (36)2 (37)4 (38)0 (39)0 (40)10 (41)1 (42)5 (43)1 (44)9 (45)0 (46)7 (47)5 (48)7 (49)2 (50)4 (51)5

(52)7 (53)2 (54)6 (55)3 (56)2 (57)3 (58)4 (59)0 (60)0

Page 149, Item 1:

(1)2 (2)5 (3)3 (4)2 (5)0 (6)1 (7)0 (8)4 (9)1 (10)6 (11)2 (12)1 (13)0 (14)4 (15)2 (16)0 (17)2 (18)6 (19)5 (20)2 (21)3 (22)1 (23)1 (24)2 (25)1 (26)0 (27)6 (28)6 (29)0 (30)0 (31)5 (32)7 (33)2 (34)5 (35)1 (36)8 (37)3 (38)2 (39)7 (40)3 (41)7 (42)9 (43)1 (44)9 (45)0 (46)5 (47)3 (48)4 (49)5 (50)0 (51)1 (52)0 (53)0 (54)2 (55)1 (56)3 (57)3 (58)9 (59)3 (60)1

Page 150, Item 1:

(1)1 (2)1 (3)5 (4)2 (5)0 (6)1 (7)8 (8)6 (9)3 (10)0 (11)3 (12)5 (13)2 (14)7 (15)9 (16)5 (17)3 (18)7 (19)1 (20)2 (21)4 (22)3 (23)2 (24)9 (25)0 (26)1 (27)1 (28)6 (29)5 (30)0 (31)3 (32)1 (33)3 (34)1 (35)2 (36)3 (37)5 (38)1 (39)0 (40)3 (41)0 (42)2 (43)0 (44)1 (45)2 (46)3 (47)5 (48)2 (49)2 (50)0 (51)1 (52)0 (53)6 (54)0 (55)1 (56)0 (57)5 (58)1 (59)1 (60)1

Page 151, Item 1:

(1)16 (2)10 (3)19 (4)12 (5)13 (6)19 (7)19 (8)18 (9)20 (10)10 (11)19 (12)12 (13)19 (14)13 (15)20 (16)18 (17)19 (18)12 (19)20 (20)11 (21)12 (22)11 (23)20 (24)11 (25)18 (26)19 (27)15 (28)11 (29)15 (30)11 (31)19 (32)15 (33)16 (34)19 (35)14 (36)10 (37)20 (38)14 (39)18 (40)10 (41)12 (42)10 (43)11

(44)11 (45)19 (46)11 (47)14 (48)18 (49)15 (50)11 (51)12 (52)14 (53)14 (54)14 (55)13 (56)15 (57)20 (58)13 (59)20 (60)15

Page 152, Item 1:

(1)17 (2)11 (3)12 (4)11 (5)19 (6)12 (7)12 (8)15 (9)15 (10)10 (11)17 (12)10 (13)16 (14)12 (15)20 (16)11 (17)18 (18)12 (19)16 (20)15 (21)11 (22)13 (23)19 (24)10 (25)15 (26)12 (27)17 (28)10 (29)19 (30)14 (31)20 (32)16 (33)11 (34)19 (35)20 (36)15 (37)13 (38)15 (39)19 (40)14 (41)14 (42)11 (43)16 (44)10 (45)15 (46)13 (47)15 (48)11 (49)13 (50)15 (51)19 (52)10 (53)17 (54)11 (55)11 (56)12 (57)12 (58)19 (59)16 (60)13

Page 153, Item 1:

(1)19 (2)14 (3)15 (4)13 (5)20 (6)14 (7)19 (8)12 (9)20 (10)11 (11)12 (12)19 (13)17 (14)13 (15)20 (16)12 (17)19 (18)10 (19)18 (20)12 (21)17 (22)20 (23)14 (24)15 (25)18 (26)10 (27)18 (28)12 (29)20 (30)12 (31)20 (32)12 (33)18 (34)12 (35)14 (36)16 (37)17 (38)19 (39)18 (40)14 (41)20 (42)13 (43)20 (44)10 (45)17 (46)14 (47)20 (48)14 (49)14 (50)13 (51)19 (52)15 (53)20 (54)10 (55)17 (56)13 (57)16 (58)17 (59)13 (60)10

Page 154, Item 1:

(1)20 (2)14 (3)19 (4)11 (5)11 (6)10 (7)13 (8)11 (9)19 (10)10 (11)19 (12)13 (13)16 (14)10 (15)13 (16)17 (17)15 (18)17 (19)18 (20)14 (21)19 (22)10 (23)13 (24)11 (25)16 (26)13 (27)19 (28)11 (29)16 (30)11 (31)16 (32)10 (33)15 (34)13 (35)15 (36)16 (37)16 (38)13 (39)19 (40)14 (41)17 (42)11 (43)13 (44)11 (45)11 (46)12 (47)16 (48)13 (49)13 (50)14 (51)18 (52)12 (53)15 (54)10 (55)17 (56)15 (57)16 (58)12 (59)15 (60)11

Page 155, Item 1:

(1)13 (2)10 (3)13 (4)16 (5)20 (6)14 (7)20 (8)17 (9)12 (10)10 (11)19 (12)13 (13)18 (14)20 (15)20 (16)10 (17)17 (18)14 (19)17 (20)12 (21)13 (22)12 (23)11 (24)13 (25)16 (26)13 (27)20 (28)13 (29)18 (30)10 (31)10 (32)10 (33)12 (34)13 (35)15 (36)12 (37)18 (38)16 (39)14 (40)13 (41)20 (42)10 (43)20 (44)12 (45)13 (46)14 (47)20 (48)12 (49)17 (50)10 (51)16 (52)12 (53)20 (54)12 (55)14 (56)15 (57)14 (58)11 (59)17 (60)10

Page 156, Item 1:

(1)14 (2)15 (3)18 (4)12 (5)16 (6)15 (7)17 (8)13 (9)18 (10)12 (11)16 (12)11 (13)20 (14)10 (15)19 (16)14 (17)20 (18)11 (19)19 (20)10 (21)20 (22)17 (23)20 (24)15 (25)19 (26)12 (27)17 (28)17 (29)17 (30)14 (31)15 (32)10 (33)19 (34)12 (35)15 (36)13 (37)18 (38)12 (39)15 (40)17 (41)15 (42)15 (43)15 (44)16 (45)13 (46)15 (47)19 (48)10 (49)16 (50)10 (51)12 (52)15 (53)18 (54)10 (55)11 (56)12 (57)14 (58)15 (59)18 (60)13

Page 157, Item 1:

(1)18 (2)14 (3)20 (4)16 (5)20 (6)16 (7)18 (8)18 (9)14 (10)10 (11)15 (12)12 (13)14 (14)17 (15)19 (16)12 (17)13 (18)17 (19)16 (20)17 (21)17 (22)13 (23)18 (24)18 (25)17 (26)11 (27)19 (28)11 (29)20 (30)13 (31)20 (32)11 (33)10 (34)13 (35)15 (36)15 (37)20 (38)10 (39)12 (40)12 (41)13 (42)18 (43)13 (44)13 (45)20 (46)12 (47)19 (48)13 (49)17

(50)11 (51)19 (52)12 (53)20 (54)10 (55)18
(56)15 (57)12 (58)14 (59)16 (60)12
Page 158, Item 1:
(1)19 (2)11 (3)16 (4)15 (5)17 (6)12 (7)16
(8)13 (9)11 (10)16 (11)11 (12)16 (13)20
(14)12 (15)18 (16)16 (17)15 (18)12 (19)13
(20)15 (21)14 (22)11 (23)16 (24)10 (25)17
(26)11 (27)17 (28)15 (29)17 (30)10 (31)16
(32)13 (33)18 (34)16 (35)11 (36)10 (37)18
(38)13 (39)15 (40)14 (41)15 (42)18 (43)19
(44)14 (45)16 (46)13 (47)18 (48)11 (49)16
(50)12 (51)16 (52)10 (53)11 (54)11 (55)14
(56)18 (57)15 (58)11 (59)16 (60)10
Page 159, Item 1:
(1)20 (2)17 (3)19 (4)16 (5)20 (6)10 (7)11
(8)11 (9)17 (10)10 (11)17 (12)11 (13)17
(14)16 (15)16 (16)14 (17)16 (18)18 (19)16
(20)11 (21)16 (22)13 (23)15 (24)11 (25)18
(26)10 (27)19 (28)12 (29)20 (30)11 (31)16
(32)11 (33)20 (34)11 (35)13 (36)10 (37)15
(38)10 (39)20 (40)13 (41)16 (42)15 (43)18
(44)13 (45)19 (46)19 (47)19 (48)10 (49)11
(50)13 (51)15 (52)13 (53)14 (54)14 (55)16
(56)12 (57)16 (58)16 (59)17 (60)14
Page 160, Item 1:
(1)20 (2)19 (3)15 (4)13 (5)18 (6)13 (7)18
(8)16 (9)12 (10)11 (11)16 (12)10 (13)13
(14)10 (15)18 (16)10 (17)20 (18)10 (19)17
(20)11 (21)19 (22)10 (23)19 (24)12 (25)19
(26)17 (27)14 (28)11 (29)20 (30)16 (31)19
(32)14 (33)16 (34)12 (35)16 (36)17 (37)17
(38)11 (39)16 (40)10 (41)16 (42)10 (43)16
(44)12 (45)20 (46)11 (47)17 (48)10 (49)19
(50)13 (51)15 (52)12 (53)17 (54)12 (55)19
(56)18 (57)16 (58)18 (59)20 (60)13

76843146R00105